Schildt's
Expert C++

About the Author ...

Herbert Schildt is the world's leading programming author. He is an expert on the C and C++ languages and Windows programming. His programming books have sold nearly two million copies worldwide and have been translated into all major foreign languages. He is the author of numerous best-sellers, including *C: The Complete Reference, 3rd Ed.*; *C++: The Complete Reference, 2nd Ed.*; *C++ From the Ground Up*; *Teach Yourself C, 2nd Ed.*; *Teach Yourself C++, 2nd Ed.*; *The Annotated ANSI C Standard*; and *Schildt's Windows 95 Programming in C and C++*. He also wrote *Schildt's Advanced Windows 95 Programming in C and C++* and coauthored the three-volume *Osborne Windows Programming Series*. He is president of Universal Computing Laboratories, Inc., and holds a master's degree in computer science from the University of Illinois at Urbana-Champaign.

Schildt's
Expert C++

Herbert Schildt

Osborne **McGraw-Hill**

Berkeley New York St. Louis San Francisco Auckland Bogotá Hamburg
London Madrid Mexico City Milan Montreal New Delhi Panama City
Paris São Paulo Singapore Sydney Tokyo Toronto

Osborne **McGraw-Hill**
2600 Tenth Street
Berkeley, California 94710
U.S.A.

For information on translations or book distributors outside the U.S.A., or to arrange bulk purchase discounts for sales promotions, premiums, or fundraisers, please contact Osborne **McGraw-Hill** at the above address.

Schildt's Expert C++

1234567890 DOC 99876

ISBN 0-07-882209-2

Acquisitions Editor
Wendy Rinaldi

Project Editor
Mark Karmendy

Technical Editor
Jim Turley

Copy Editor
Jan Jue

Proofreader
Mick Arellano

Computer Designer
Roberta Steele

Illustrator
Lance Ravella

Series Design
Peter Hancik

Quality Control Specialist
Joe Scuderi

Contents at a Glance

Table of Contents

Introduction

If you're like me, then you want a computer language that gives you control over your programming environment and mastery over the machine. C++ is such a language. It combines form with function, it tempers compexity with clarity, and in return for power it requires responsibility. C++ was created by and for real, working programmers. It was expressly designed to allow the next generation of software to be written. In C++ there are no boundaries that can't be expanded, no limits that can't be exceeded, and no rules that can't (at least once in a while) be broken. It has been some years now since I wrote my first program. Programming languages have come and gone, operating systems have changed, and methodologies have advanced. But the power of C++ has endured. If you want to harness that power, then this book is for you.

In this book you will learn to take charge of C++ and see how it can be applied to several interesting programming tasks. Along the way, you will learn some of the tricks and techniques used by master programmers to create world-class programs.

What's Inside

In this book you will learn several C++ techniques that will help you supercharge your applications. For example, you will learn how to get the most from templates (which are used to create generic functions and classes), build container classes, implement sparse arrays, build expression parsers, use run-time type information (RTTI), use the new **string** class, interface your program to assembly code, and integrate new data types into your C++

programming environment. You will also learn how to design your own computer language and then write an interpreter for it. The final chapter is an overview of Java, the Internet language that is based on C++.

As you may know, an ANSI standard for C++ is in the process of being created. As such, C++ has been undergoing rapid change and development. Many new features have been added. Several of the techniques described in this book make use of these new features. As you will see, they have expanded the power of C++ significantly.

This is first and foremost a practical book. Each chapter contains real, working code which you can either use as-is or adapt to meet your own specific needs. For example, you can easily adapt the BASIC interpreter shown in Chapter 10 so that it interprets nearly any type of language. You could modify it to accept a database query language or file transfer script language, for instance. The expression parser described in Chapter 3 could form the basis for a pop-up calculator. The container classes developed in Chapter 2 could be the starting point for your own container class library. If you like experimenting with encryption, then the simple ciphers in Chapter 7 can serve as a starting point. No matter how you use C++, you will find the information and techniques contained in this book helpful.

Who Is This Book For?

This book is designed specifically for readers who have already mastered the basics of C++ programming. This means that you should be able to write simple programs that include such things as classes, overloaded functions, and overloaded operators. You should be familiar with C++-style I/O and be able to easily handle constructors, destructors, and the like. If you have read and worked through any introductory book on C++ programming, then you have the necessary background. For example, any of my introductory books on C++ (*Teach Yourself C++*, *C++ From the Ground Up*, or *C++ Nuts & Bolts*) provide an excellent foundation for this book.

What Programming Tools You Will Need

The code in this book was written, compiled, and tested using Microsoft's Visual C++ and Borland C++. You will need one of these compilers or another contemporary C/C++ compiler. Be sure that the compiler you choose can compile modern C++ code, including templates and exception handling.

—HS

Mahomet, Illinois

For Further Study

Schildt's Expert C++ is just one of the many programming books written by Herbert Schildt. Here are some others that you will find of interest. To learn more about C++, you will find these books especially helpful:

- ◆ *C++: The Complete Reference, Second Edition*
- ◆ *Teach Yourself C++, Second Edition*
- ◆ *C++ From the Ground Up*
- ◆ *C++ Nuts and Bolts*

If you want to learn more about the C language (the foundation of C++), the following titles will be of interest:

- ◆ *C: The Complete Reference, Third Edition*
- ◆ *The Annotated ANSI C Standard*
- ◆ *Teach Yourself C, Second Edition*

To learn Windows 95 programming, we recommend the following:

- ◆ *Schildt's Windows 95 Programming in C and C++*
- ◆ *Schildt's Advanced Windows 95 Programming in C and C++*
- ◆ *Windows 95 Programming Nuts & Bolts*

These books provide an in-depth look at the basics of Windows 95 programming. You will also want to examine the *Osborne Windows Programming Series*, co-authored by Herbert Schildt. You will find it to be invaluable when trying to understand the complexities of Windows. The series titles are

♦ *Volume 1: Programming Fundamentals*

♦ *Volume 2: General Purpose API Functions*

♦ *Volume 3: Special Purpose API Functions*

Finally, here are some other books about C and C++ written by Herbert Schildt:

♦ *The Art of C*

♦ *The Craft of C*

♦ *Turbo C/C++: The Complete Reference*

When you need solid answers, fast, turn to Herbert Schildt, the recognized authority on programming.

Diskette Offer

There are many useful and interesting programs contained in this book. If you're like me, you probably would like to try them, but hate typing them into the computer. When I key in routines from a book it always seems that I type something wrong and spend hours trying to get the program to work. You may also find this to be true, especially for many of the programs in this book, which tend to be long. For this reason, I am offering the source code on diskette for all the programs contained in this book for $24.95. Just fill in the order blank on the next page and mail it, along with your payment, to the address shown. Or, if you're in a hurry, just call (217) 586-4021 (the number of my consulting office) and place your order by telephone. You can FAX your order to (217) 586-4997. (Visa and Mastercard accepted.) Site licenses are also available. Call for information.

Please send me _____ copies, at $24.95 each, of the programs in *Schildt's Expert C++* on an IBM compatible diskette.

Foreign orders: Checks must be drawn on a U.S. bank, and please add $5 shipping and handling.

_____
Name

_____
Address

_____ _____ _____
City   State   ZIP

_____
Telephone

Diskette size (check one): 5 1/4" _____   3 1/2"_____

Method of payment: Check_____   Visa_____   MC_____

Credit card number: _____

Expiration date: _____

Signature: _____

Send to:

  Herbert Schildt
  398 County Rd 2500 N
  Mahomet, IL 61853

  or phone: (217) 586-4021
  FAX: (217) 586-4997

This offer subject to change or cancellation at any time.

Chapter

1

Unlocking the Power of Template Functions

Perhaps the single most important advanced feature of C++ is the *template*. The reason for this is that templates are fundamentally changing the face of programming. By using a template, you can create generalized specifications for functions and for classes, often called *generic functions* and *generic classes,* respectively. A generic function defines a general procedure that can be applied to various types of data. A generic class defines a general class that can be applied to varying types of data. In both cases, the specific type of data operated upon is passed as a parameter. As you can imagine, this makes templates a valuable tool, indeed. In C++, a function or class template is declared using the keyword **template**. You probably already know the basics of using **template**. In this chapter, you will learn how to unleash its power.

As just mentioned, **template** is used to create both generic functions and generic classes. This chapter explores generic functions. (In the next chapter, generic classes are examined.) This chapter examines the reason behind the creation of templates, explains why they are more efficient than other means used to create generalized functions, and then illustrates their application to real-world functions.

The vehicles that will be used to demonstrate template functions are *sorting* and *searching,* two of the computer world's most common operations. Sorting and searching algorithms are chosen for three reasons. First, they are easily converted into template forms and, as you will see, their power is greatly enhanced by that conversion. Second, sorting and searching are used in all types of programs, and most programmers will benefit from having a number of generic sorts and searches at their disposal. Third, the sorting algorithms constitute one of the most interesting—and intriguing—areas of computer programming. It is also one topic that is often taken for granted. For example, most programmers simply rely upon the sort function provided in the C++ standard library when sorting is required. However, as you will soon see, because of templates, it's now time to revisit this important topic.

Why Generic Functions?

Since the earliest days of programming, programmers have recognized the need for generalized, reusable subroutines. As you know, many algorithms are independent of the type of data being manipulated. For example, consider the following sequence that exchanges the values of two variables:

```
DataType temp, x, y;

// ...

temp = x;

x = y;

y = temp;
```

Aside from intentionally malicious cases, this algorithm works no matter what type of data DataType actually is. For example, the sequence is the same when exchanging integers as it is when exchanging **double**s or **long**s. Thus, the logic of the algorithm is the same for all types of data. However, for most programming languages, a new version of this algorithm would need to be written for each type of data being exchanged, even though the underlying algorithm remains the same. This situation can be generalized. For many algorithms, the method is separate from the data. For these algorithms, it would be advantageous to be able to define and debug the logic of an algorithm once, and then apply that algorithm to a variety of data types without rewriting. Not only would this save much tedious programming, but it also would help prevent errors, because the same, debugged code could be applied to any situation.

Early Methods of Generalization

1

Given the obvious benefits that can be derived from generalized routines, it makes sense that programmers would try to create them. However, prior to the invention of templates, such attempts met with only partial success. The reason for this is easy to understand: there was no good way to create a generic function. Since programmers tend to be resourceful and the desire for generic functions was so great, two less-than-perfect methods were devised. The first way that generic "functions" were created was through the use of function-like macros. For example, the following macro creates a "generic function" that performs negation:

```
#define neg(a) (((a)<0) ? -(a) : (a))
```

Since a compiler simply performs a text substitution when this (or any other macro) is encountered, the **neg( )** function-like macro can be used with any of the built-in data types. That is, these calls to **neg( )** are both valid:

```
char x;
float f;

x = neg(-10);
f = neg(123.23);
```

However, there is no easy way to make **neg( )** work with user-defined types. And because it cannot perform any type checking, **neg( )** could be accidentally used for data types (strings, for example) for which negation is undefined. Although somewhat practical for very small functions, function-like macros are not a good general solution.

The second method used to create a generalized function was to add one or more parameters that defined the type of data upon which the function would operate. For example, one common approach was to pass a pointer to the data as one parameter and to pass the size of the data, in bytes, in another parameter. Inside the function, the size parameter was used to allow different types of data to be handled. Of course, the use of an extra parameter means that extra overhead is generated when the function is called. As you probably know, function parameters are passed on the stack. For each parameter, several machine instructions are generated to accomplish this. Thus, each additional parameter increases the time it takes to call a function. If the function is called repeatedly, this overhead can quickly become a problem. Therefore, in the past, to generalize a function meant that you were also going to slow it down. Thus, the benefits of generalization carried a heavy price.

To put the foregoing discussion into concrete terms, let's look at one of the best-known examples of an old-style generalized function—**qsort( )**. As you probably know, **qsort( )** is the C++ standard library sorting function. It sorts any type of data using a quicksort algorithm. (You will see how to implement your own version of a quicksort later in this chapter.) However, since **qsort( )** is a holdover from the C library, it uses the old-style, parameter-based approach to generalization. Its prototype is shown here:

```
void qsort(void *buf, size_t num, size_t size,
           int (*comp) (const void *, const void *));
```

Here, *buf* is a pointer to the array that holds the data to be sorted. The number of elements to be sorted is passed in *num*. These are the only two parameters that are technically necessary to support the sorting algorithm. However, to generalize the function, the size of an array element must be passed in *size,* and a pointer to a function that compares two elements must be passed in *comp*. This means that generalization adds the overhead of two parameters. If the function were only called occasionally, this would not be of too much concern. However, as you will see later in this chapter, **qsort( )** is usually implemented as a *recursive* function. This means that the added overhead of the two additional parameters greatly affects its performance.

For many years, the trade-off between the benefits of generalization and the detriments of the added overhead hindered the large-scale development of generic functions. However, the invention of templates changed this situation for the better.

The Invention of Templates

Although template functions and the keyword **template** are some of the language's most important features, they were not part of C++ from the start. In fact, for several years, the specification for C++ did not include **template**. However, some method of defining generic functions and classes had always been deemed necessary. At the core of generic functions and classes is the concept of the *parameterized type*. The problem was how best to implement such a feature. According to Stroustrup in his book *The Design and Evolution of C++* (Addison-Wesley, 1994): "In the original design of C++, parameterized types were considered but postponed because there wasn't time to do a thorough job of exploring the design and implementation issues." However, parameterized types (which allow the creation of generic functions and classes) were considered to be essential for C++'s long-term acceptance.

(Specifically, they are needed to support generalized *container classes,* which are discussed in Chapter 2.) Toward this end, Stroustrup began defining **template** in 1986. By 1990, he presented his experimental design for the feature in his book *The Annotated C++ Reference Manual* (Addison-Wesley, 1990). It is this version of **template** that was added to the evolving ANSI C++ standard in 1990. It is now supported by all mainstream C++ compilers.

The development of templates turned on three points: efficiency, type safety, and ease of use. Stroustrup wanted template functions to be as efficient as their nontemplate versions. As you have seen, an inefficient means of generalizing a function already existed. What was desired was an efficient approach. He also wanted to maintain the type checking between function arguments and parameters. As mentioned, the lack of type checking is a fundamental problem when using function-like macros. Finally, Stroustrup believed that templates should be easy for the programmer to use. As you probably already know from your own programming experience, when a language feature is difficult to use, few programmers use it. Thus, ease-of-use is an important concern any time a new element is added to a language. Fortunately, with one masterful stroke Stroustrup was able to achieve these goals. The implementation of **template** is an impressive addition to C++ which is both functionally and esthetically pleasing—no small task!

A Review of Template Functions

Before applying templates, a short review of their syntax and features is in order. A generic function is created by use of the keyword **template**. The normal meaning of the word "template" accurately reflects its use in C++. It is used to create a template (or framework) which describes what a function will do, leaving it to the compiler to fill in the details as needed.

A template function defines a general set of operations that will be applied to various types of data. A template function has the type of data that it will operate upon passed to it as a parameter *during compilation.* Using this mechanism, the same general procedure can be applied to a wide range of data. By creating a template function, you define—independent of any data—the nature of the algorithm. Once this is done, the compiler automatically generates the correct code for the type of data that is actually used when you call the function. In essence, when you create a generic function, you are creating a function that can automatically overload itself.

The general form of a **template** function definition is shown here:

```
template <class Ttype> ret-type func-name(parameter list)
{
  // body of function
}
```

Here, *Ttype* is a placeholder name for a data type used by the function. This name may be used within the function definition. However, it is only a placeholder which the compiler will automatically replace with an actual data type when it creates a specific version of the function. You may define more than one generic data type in the **template** statement, using a comma-separated list.

Here is one way to create a generic function that exchanges the values of its two parameters:

```
template <class SwapType> void swap(SwapType &x, SwapType &y)
{
  SwapType temp;

  temp = x;
  x = y;
  y = temp;
}
```

This function can be called with any type of variable. The compiler will automatically create the appropriate specific instance of the function.

Other terms are sometimes used when discussing templates, and you may encounter them in other C++ literature. When the compiler creates a specific version of the function, it is said to have created a *generated function*. The act of generating a function is referred to as *instantiating* it. Put differently, a generated function is a specific instance of a template function.

Even though a template function overloads itself as needed, you can explicitly overload one, too. If you overload a generic function, then that overloaded function overrides (or "hides") the generic function relative to that specific version. Manual overloading of a template allows you to specially tailor a version of a generic function to accommodate a special situation. However, in general, if you need to have different versions of a function for different data types, you should use overloaded functions rather than templates.

Template Functions Are Efficient

Unlike the old-style method used to create generalized functions, templates are very efficient. As you know, prior to the inclusion of the keyword **template**, the only way that a generic function could be written was to pass type-related information into the function (as described earlier). Inside the function, this extra information would be used to allow the function to operate on various types of data. As explained, this approach is inherently inefficient because of the extra overhead of the additional parameters and because of the additional size computations that would need to occur inside the function. However, template functions avoid this problem. Here is why.

Each time that you instantiate a template function, the compiler automatically creates a specific version of the function. That is, the compiler automatically creates an overloaded version of the generic function in which the placeholder data types are filled in with the actual types being operated upon. This means that the instantiated version has no extra overhead associated with it. Instead, it is as efficient as if you had written a specific version of the function. It is just that the process has been automated. As you will see later in this chapter, the efficiency differences between the old-style generalized functions and template functions are dramatic.

Now that the stage has been set, let's see how templates can be applied to one of programming's most common tasks: sorting.

Creating Generic Sorts

Sorting is the process of arranging a set of similar information into an increasing or decreasing order. Sorting is one of the most intellectually pleasing categories of algorithms because the process is so well defined. Sorting algorithms have also been extensively analyzed and are well understood. Unfortunately, therefore, sorting is sometimes taken for granted. In fact, when data needs to be sorted, most programmers simply use a sorting function provided by the library that comes with their C++ compiler without giving it any thought. However, as you will see, different approaches to sorting have different characteristics. While some sorts may be better than others on average, no sort is perfect for all situations. Therefore, having several types of sorts is a useful addition to any programmer's toolbox. The fact that these sorts can now be made into template functions increases their value even more.

As you probably know, most C++ compilers supply the standard function **qsort( )** as part of their standard library. While **qsort( )** is generally implemented efficiently, after reading this chapter you will not want to use it for two reasons. First, **qsort( )** is a holdover from the C library. As you have seen, even though it is capable of sorting most types of data, it achieves its generic nature through a rather clumsy, manual means. By using a template sorting function, you can create a generalized template which will be used to create specific versions of a sort for any type of data without the extra overhead that is incurred by the approach used by **qsort( )**. Second, although the quicksort algorithm (used by **qsort( )**) is very effective in the general case, it is not always the best for specialized situations. Therefore, to ensure the fastest run times in all situations, you must have a number of different sorting algorithms at your disposal.

There are two general categories of sorting algorithms: algorithms that sort arrays and algorithms that sort sequential disk or tape files. This chapter is concerned only with the first category, because it is most relevant to the average programmer.

Most often, when information is sorted, only a portion of that information is used as the *sort key*. The key is that part of the data that determines which item comes before another. Thus, the key is used in comparisons, but when an exchange is made, the entire data structure is swapped. For example, in a mailing list the ZIP code field might be used as the key, but the entire address is sorted. For the sake of simplicity, the next few examples will sort only arrays of built-in types, in which the key and the data are one and the same. Later, you will see how they can be used to sort any user-defined type.

Classes of Sorting Algorithms

Although there are many methods by which data may be sorted, they all fall into one of the following categories:

♦ Exchange

♦ Selection

♦ Insertion

To understand these three methods, imagine a deck of cards. To sort the cards by using *exchange*, spread them on a table, face up, and then exchange out-of-order cards until the deck is ordered. Using *selection*, spread the cards on the table, select the card of lowest value, take it out of the deck, and hold it in your hand. Then, from the remaining cards on the table, select the lowest card and place it behind the one already in your hand. This process continues until all the cards are in your hand. The cards in your hand will be sorted when you finish the process. To sort the cards by using *insertion*, hold all the cards in your hand. Place one card at a time on the table, always inserting it in the correct position. The deck will be sorted when you have no cards in your hand.

To best see the differences between these three approaches, a representative sort from each category is developed.

Judging Sorting Algorithms

Since there are many different sorting algorithms, how can you judge the relative merits of one approach over another? Certainly the speed at which a sort executes is important, but many sorts have unique characteristics that affect their applicability to special cases. Thus, you will sometimes have to weigh average speed of execution with other factors. Here are four criteria to be used for judging a sorting algorithm.

♦　How fast can it sort information in an average case?

♦　How fast are its best and worst cases?

♦　Does it exhibit natural or unnatural behavior?

♦　Does it rearrange elements with equal keys?

Look closely at these criteria now. Clearly, how fast a particular algorithm sorts is of great concern. The speed with which an array can be sorted is directly related to the number of comparisons and the number of exchanges that take place, with exchanges taking more time. A *comparison* occurs when one array element is compared with another; an *exchange* happens when two elements are swapped. As you will soon see, the run times of some sorts increase exponentially, and run times of others increase logarithmically, relative to the number of items being sorted.

The best- and worst-case run times are important if you expect to encounter one of these situations frequently. Often a sort has a good average case but a terrible worst case.

A sort is said to exhibit *natural* behavior if it works least when the list is already in order, works harder as the list becomes less ordered, and works hardest when a list is in inverse order. How hard a sort works is based on the number of comparisons and exchanges that it executes.

To understand why rearranging elements with equal keys may be important, imagine a database such as a mailing list, which is sorted on a main key and a subkey. The main key is the ZIP code, and within ZIP codes the last name is the subkey. When a new address is added to the list and the list is re-sorted, you do not want the subkeys (that is, the last names within ZIP codes) to be rearranged. To guarantee that this doesn't happen, a sort must not exchange main keys of equal value.

The Bubble Sort—The Demon of Exchange

The most well-known (and infamous) sort is the *bubble sort*. Its popularity is derived from its catchy name and its simplicity. However, for the average case, it is one of the worst sorts ever conceived.

The bubble sort is an exchange sort. It involves the repeated comparison and, if necessary, the exchange of adjacent elements. The elements are like bubbles in a tank of water—each seeks its own level. To begin, let's first implement a nongeneric form of the bubble sort so that you can clearly see its operation. The following program shows a nontemplate version of the bubble sort which may be used to sort character arrays.

```
// A simple bubble sort for characters.
#include <iostream.h>
#include <string.h>

void bubble(char *item, int count);

main()
{
  char str[] = "dcab";

  bubble(str, (int) strlen(str));
  cout << "The sorted string is: " << str << endl;

  return 0;
}

// A simple version of the bubble sort.
void bubble(char *item, int count)
{
  register int a, b;
  char t;

  for(a=1; a<count; ++a)
    for(b=count-1; b>=a; --b) {
      if(item[b-1] > item[b]) {
        // exchange elements
        t = item[b-1];
        item[b-1] = item[b];
        item[b] = t;
      }
    }
}
```

In **bubble( )**, **item** is a pointer to the character array to be sorted, and **count** is the number of elements in the array. The bubble sort is driven by two loops. Given that there are **count** elements in the array, the outer loop causes the array to be scanned **count**-1 times. This ensures that, in the worst case, every element is in its proper position when the function terminates. The inner loop actually performs the comparisons and exchanges. (A slightly improved version of the bubble sort terminates if no exchanges occur, but this adds another comparison in each pass through the inner loop.) You can use this version of the bubble sort to sort a character array into ascending order.

To see how the bubble sort works, each pass through the loop is shown here:

initial	d c a b
pass 1	a d c b
pass 2	a b d c
pass 3	a b c d

In analyzing any sort, you should determine how many comparisons and exchanges will be performed for the best, average, and worst case. With the bubble sort, the number of comparisons is always the same, because the two **for** loops repeat the specified number of times whether the list is ordered or not. This means that the bubble sort always performs

$$1/2(n^2-n)$$

comparisons, where n is the number of elements to be sorted. This formula is derived from the fact that the outer loop executes $n-1$ times and the inner loop $n/2$ times. Multiplied together, these numbers result in the preceding formula.

The number of exchanges is zero for the best case, an already sorted list. The number of exchanges for the average- and worst-case exchanges are

average $3/4(n^2-n)$

worst $3/2(n^2-n)$

It is beyond the scope of this book to explain the derivation of the preceding formulas, but you can guess that as the list becomes less ordered, the number of elements out of order approaches the number of comparisons.

The bubble sort is said to be an *n-squared algorithm,* because its execution time is a multiple of the square of the number of elements. This type of algorithm is very ineffective when applied to a large number of elements, because execution time is directly related to the number of comparisons and exchanges. For example, ignoring the time that it takes to exchange any out-of-position element, assume that each comparison takes 0.001 second. Sorting ten elements takes about 0.05 second, sorting 100 elements takes about 5 seconds, and sorting 1,000 elements takes about 500 seconds. A sort of 100,000 elements, the number in a small phone book, takes about 5,000,000 seconds, or about 1,400 hours—that is, two months of continuous sorting! Figure 1-1 shows how execution time increases relative to the size of the array.

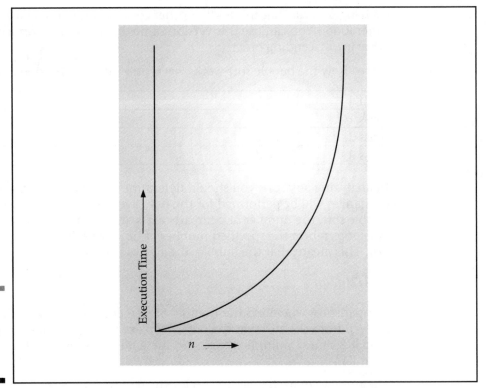

Execution
time of an n^2
sort in relation
to array size
Figure 1-1.

It is a simple matter to transform the specific version of the bubble sort just shown into a template function. To do so, the type of data being sorted must be parameterized. The template version of **bubble( )** is shown here:

```cpp
// A generic bubble sort.
#include <iostream.h>
#include <string.h>

template <class Stype> void bubble(Stype *item, int count);

main()
{
  // sort a character array
  char str[] = "dcab";

  bubble(str, (int) strlen(str));
  cout << "The sorted string is " << str << endl;

  // sort some integers
  int nums[] = { 5, 7, 3, 9, 5, 1, 8 };
```

1

```
   int i;

   bubble(nums, 7);
   cout << "The sorted numbers are : ";
   for(i=0; i<7; i++) cout << nums[i] << " ";

   return 0;
}

// A generic bubble sort.
template <class Stype> void bubble(Stype *item, int count)
{
   register int a, b;
   Stype t;

   for(a=1; a<count; ++a)
     for(b=count-1; b>=a; --b) {
       if(item[b-1] > item[b]) {
         // exchange elements
         t = item[b-1];
         item[b-1] = item[b];
         item[b] = t;
       }
     }
}
```

As you can see, the type of data being sorted is now specified using the generic type **Stype**. Also, inside **bubble( )** the temporary variable **t** is declared to be of type **Stype**. Inside **main( )**, each time the generic function **bubble( )** is called, a specific instance of it is generated by the compiler. In the first case, a sort for an array of characters is created. In the second case, a sort of integers is generated. What is important to understand is that in both cases, the compiler substitutes the actual data type for the **Stype** placeholder. Thus, each generated function is specific to its own type of data. Therefore, this generic version of the bubble sort can be applied to any type of data. Before continuing, you might want to confirm this fact by sorting an array of **double**s, for example.

Sorting by Selection

A selection sort selects the element with the lowest value and exchanges it with the first element. Then from the remaining $n-1$ elements, the element with the smallest key is found and exchanged with the second element, and so forth. The exchanges continue to the last two elements. For example, if the selection method were used on the array "dcab", each pass would look like this:

initial	d c a b
pass 1	a c d b
pass 2	a b d c
pass 3	a b c d

The following program contains a generic version of a selection sort.

```cpp
// A generic selection sort.
#include <iostream.h>
#include <string.h>

template <class Stype> void select(Stype *item, int count);

main()
{
  // sort a character array
  char str[] = "dcab";

  select(str, (int) strlen(str));
  cout << "The sorted string is " << str << endl;

  // sort some integers
  int nums[] = { 5, 7, 3, 9, 5, 1, 8 };
  int i;

  select(nums, 7);
  cout << "The sorted numbers are : ";
  for(i=0; i<7; i++) cout << nums[i] << " ";

  return 0;
}

// The generic selection sort.
template <class Stype> void select(Stype *item, int count)
{
  register int a, b, c;
  int exchange;
  Stype t;

  for(a=0; a<count-1; ++a) {
    exchange = 0;
    c = a;
    t = item[a];
    for(b=a+1; b<count; ++b) {
      if(item[b]<t) {
        c = b;
        t = item[b];
```

```
         exchange = 1;
      }
    }
    if(exchange) {
      item[c] = item[a];
      item[a] = t;
    }
  }
}
```

Unfortunately, the selection sort is also an n-squared algorithm. Its outer loop executes $n-1$ times and the inner loop $1/2n$ times. As a result, the selection sort requires

$1/2(n^2-n)$

comparisons, making it too slow for a large number of items. The number of exchanges for the best and worst cases are

best $3(n-1)$

worst $n^2/4+3 (n-1)$

For the best case, only $n-1$ elements need to be moved if the list is ordered, and each move requires three exchanges. The worst case approximates the number of comparisons. The average case is difficult to determine, and its derivation is beyond the scope of this book. However, it is

$n(\log n+y)$

where y is Euler's constant, about 0.577216.

Although the number of comparisons for both the bubble sort and the selection sort are the same, the number of exchanges in the average case is far fewer for the selection sort. However, better sorts exist.

Sorting by Insertion

The insertion sort is the third and last of the basic sorting algorithms. It initially sorts the first two members of the array. Next, the algorithm inserts the third member into its sorted position in relation to the first two members. Then it inserts the fourth element into the list of three elements. The process continues until all elements have been sorted. For example, given the array "dcab", each pass of the insertion sort is shown here:

initial	d c a b
pass 1	c d a b
pass 2	a c d b
pass 3	a b c d

The following program contains a simple version of the insertion sort.

```cpp
// A generic insertion sort.
#include <iostream.h>
#include <string.h>

template <class Stype> void insert(Stype *item, int count);

main()
{
  // sort a character array
  char str[] = "dcab";

  insert(str, (int) strlen(str));
  cout << "The sorted string is " << str << endl;

  // sort some integers
  int nums[] = { 5, 7, 3, 9, 5, 1, 8 };
  int i;

  insert(nums, 7);
  cout << "The sorted numbers are : ";
  for(i=0; i<7; i++) cout << nums[i] << " ";

  return 0;
}

// The generic insertion sort.
template <class Stype> void insert(Stype *item, int count)
{
  register int a, b;
  Stype t;

  for(a=1; a<count; ++a) {
    t = item[a];
    for(b=a-1; b>=0 && t<item[b]; b--)
      item[b+1] = item[b];
    item[b+1] = t;
  }
}
```

Unlike the bubble and selection sorts, the number of comparisons that occur during an insertion sort depends upon how the list is initially ordered. If the list is in order, the number of comparisons is $n-1$. If it is out of order, it is

$$1/2(n^2+n)$$

1

The average case is

$$1/4(n^2+n)$$

The number of exchanges are

best	$2(n-1)$
average	$1/4(n^2+n)$
worst	$1/2(n^2+n)$

Therefore, for worst cases, the insertion sort is as bad as the bubble sort and selection sort; for average cases, it is only slightly better. However, the insertion sort does have two advantages. First, it behaves naturally. That is, it works the least when the array is already sorted and the hardest when the array is sorted in inverse order. This makes the insertion sort excellent for arrays that are almost in order. The second advantage is that it leaves the order of equal keys the same. This means that if a list is sorted by two keys, it remains sorted for both keys after an insertion sort.

Even though the number of comparisons may be fairly low for certain sets of data, the array must always be shifted each time an element is placed in its proper location. As a result, the number of moves can be significant. However, still better sorts exist.

Improved Sorts

All of the algorithms in the preceding section had the fatal flaw of executing in n-squared time. For large amounts of data, this makes the sorts very slow. In fact, at some point, the sorts would be too slow to use. Unfortunately, horror stories of "the sort that took three days" are often real. When a sort takes too long, it is usually the fault of the underlying algorithm. However, the first response is often "let's hand-optimize" using assembly language. While manual optimization does sometimes speed up a routine by a constant factor, if the underlying algorithm is inefficient, the sort will be slow no matter how optimal the coding. Remember: When a routine is running relative to n^2, increasing the speed of the code or the computer only causes a small improvement, because the rate at which the run time is increasing is exponential. (In essence, the n^2 curve in Figure 1-1 is shifted to the right slightly, but is otherwise unchanged.) The rule of thumb is that if the routine is exponentially too slow, no amount of hand optimization will make it fast enough. The solution is to use a better sorting algorithm.

This section describes two excellent sorts. The first is the Shell sort. The second, the quicksort, is usually considered the best sorting routine. Both of these improved sorts are substantially better than any of the simple sorts in their general performance.

The Shell Sort

The Shell sort is named after its inventor, D.L. Shell. However, the name probably stuck because its method of operation is often described in terms of seashells piled upon one another.

The general sorting method is derived from the insertion sort and is based on diminishing increments. Consider the diagram in Figure 1-2. First, all elements that are three positions apart are sorted. Then, all elements that are two positions apart are sorted. Finally, all elements adjacent to each other are sorted.

It is not easy to see that this method yields good results, or in fact that it even sorts the array. But it does. Each sorting pass involves relatively few elements, or elements that are already in reasonable order, so the Shell sort is efficient, and each pass increases order.

The exact sequence for the increments can be changed. The only rule is that the last increment must be 1. For example, the sequence

9, 5, 3, 2, 1

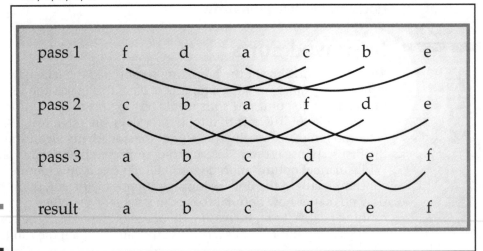

The Shell sort
Figure 1-2.

works well and is used in the Shell sort shown here. Avoid sequences that are powers of 2—for mathematically complex reasons, they reduce the efficiency of the sorting algorithm (but the sort still works).

1

```cpp
// A generic shell sort.
#include <iostream.h>
#include <string.h>

template <class Stype> void shell(Stype *item, int count);

main()
{
  // sort a character array
  char str[] = "dcab";

  shell(str, (int) strlen(str));
  cout << "The sorted string is " << str << endl;

  // sort some integers
  int nums[] = { 5, 7, 3, 9, 5, 1, 8 };
  int i;

  shell(nums, 7);
  cout << "The sorted numbers are : ";
  for(i=0; i<7; i++) cout << nums[i] << " ";

  return 0;
}

// The generic shell sort.
template <class Stype> void shell(Stype *item, int count)
{
  register int i, j, gap, k;
  Stype x;
  char a[5];

  a[0]=9; a[1]=5; a[2]=3; a[3]=2; a[4]=1;

  for(k=0; k<5; k++) {
    gap = a[k];
    for(i=gap; i<count; ++i) {
      x = item[i];
      for(j=i-gap; x<item[j] && j>=0; j=j-gap)
        item[j+gap] = item[j];
      item[j+gap] = x;
    }
  }
}
```

You may have noticed that the inner **for** loop has two test conditions. The comparison **x<item[j]** is obviously necessary for the sorting process. The test **j>=0** keeps the sort from overrunning the boundary of the array **item**. These extra checks will degrade the performance of the Shell sort to some extent. Slightly different versions of the sort employ special array elements called *sentinels,* which are not actually part of the array to be sorted. Sentinels hold special termination values that indicate the least and greatest possible element. In this way, the bounds checks are unnecessary. However, using sentinels requires a specific knowledge of the data, which limits the generality of the sort function.

The Shell sort presents some difficult mathematical problems that are far beyond the scope of this discussion. Take it on faith that execution time is proportional to

$$n^{1.2}$$

for sorting *n* elements. This is a significant improvement over the *n*-squared

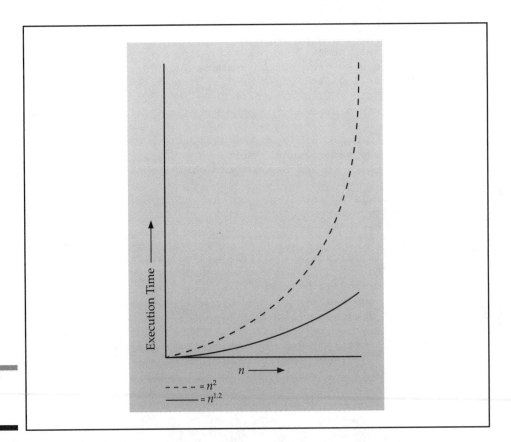

The n^2 and $n^{1.2}$ curves

Figure 1-3.

sorts. To understand how great the improvement is, see Figure 1-3, which graphs both an n^2 and an $n^{1.2}$ sort. However, before getting too excited about the Shell sort, you should know that the quicksort is even better.

The Quicksort

The quicksort, invented and named by C.A.R. Hoare, is superior to all others in this book, and it is considered the best general-purpose sorting algorithm currently available. It is based on the exchange sort—surprising, in light of the terrible performance of the bubble sort!

The quicksort is built on the idea of partitions. The general procedure is to select a value, called the *comparand,* and then to partition the array into two sections. All elements greater than or equal to the partition value are put on one side, and those less than the value are put on the other. This process is then repeated for each remaining section until the array is sorted. For example, given the array "fedacb" and using the value 'd' as the comparand, the first pass of the quicksort would rearrange the array as follows:

initial	f e d a c b
pass1	b c a d e f

This process is then repeated for each section—that is, "bca" and "def". As you can see, the process is essentially recursive in nature and, indeed, the cleanest implementations of quicksort are recursive algorithms.

You can select the middle comparand value in two ways. You can either choose it at random, or you can select it by averaging a small set of values taken from the partition. For optimal sorting, you should select a value that is precisely in the middle of the range of values. However, this is not easy to do for most sets of data. In the worst case, the value chosen is at one extremity. Even in this case, however, quicksort still works. The following version of quicksort selects the middle element of each partition as the comparand.

```
// A generic quick sort.
#include <iostream.h>
#include <string.h>

template <class Stype> void quick(Stype *item, int count);
template <class Stype> void qs(Stype *item, int left, int right);

main()
{
  // sort a character array
  char str[] = "dcab";
```

```
  quick(str, (int) strlen(str));
  cout << "The sorted string is " << str << endl;

  // sort some integers
  int nums[] = { 5, 7, 3, 9, 5, 1, 8 };
  int i;

  quick(nums, 7);
  cout << "The sorted numbers are : ";
  for(i=0; i<7; i++) cout << nums[i] << " ";

  return 0;
}

// Quicksort entry function.
template <class Stype> void quick(Stype *item, int count)
{
  qs(item, 0, count-1);
}

// The generic quicksort.
template <class Stype> void qs(Stype *item, int left, int right)
{
  register int i, j;
  Stype x, y;

  i = left; j = right;
  x = item[(left+right)/2];

  do {
    while(item[i]<x && i<right) i++;
    while(x<item[j] && j>left) j--;

    if(i<=j) {
      y = item[i];
      item[i] = item[j];
      item[j] = y;
      i++; j--;
    }
  } while(i<=j);

  if(left<j) qs(item, left, j);
  if(i<right) qs(item, i, right);
}
```

In this version, the function **quick( )** sets up a call to the main sorting function **qs( )**. This enables the same common interface of **item** and **count** to be maintained, but it is not essential because **qs( )** could have been called directly using three arguments.

Deriving the number of comparisons and exchanges that quicksort performs requires mathematics beyond the scope of this book. However, the average number of comparisons is

$n \log n$

and the average number of exchanges is approximately

$n/6 \log n$

These numbers are significantly lower than those provided by any of the previous sorts.

You should be aware of one particularly problematic aspect to quicksort. If the comparand value for each partition is the largest value, quicksort degenerates into "slowsort" with an *n*-squared run time. Generally, however, this does not happen.

You must carefully choose a method of defining the value of the comparand. The method is frequently determined by the data that you are sorting. In very large mailing lists, where the sorting is often by ZIP code, the selection is simple because the ZIP codes are fairly evenly distributed—and a simple algebraic function can determine a suitable comparand. However, in certain databases, the keys may be the same or so close in value that a random selection is often the best one. A common and fairly effective method is to sample three elements from a partition and take the middle value.

Comparing the Generic Quicksort to qsort( )

To fully appreciate why template functions are a better approach to creating a general-purpose function than is the old-style method, run the following program. It sorts 10,000 randomly generated integers, first using the standard (and old-style) **qsort( )** function and then using the template version of quicksort just shown. As you will see, the template version runs approximately *twice as fast!*

```
// A comparison of qsort() with its template counterpart.
#include <iostream.h>
#include <stdlib.h>
#include <time.h>

template <class Stype> void quick(Stype *item, int count);
template <class Stype> void qs(Stype *item, int left, int right);
```

```cpp
int comp(const void *a, const void *b);

main()
{
  int nums1[10000], nums2[10000];
  int i;
  time_t start, end;

  for(i=0; i<10000; i++) nums1[i] = nums2[i] = rand();

  start = clock();
  quick(nums1, 10000);
  end = clock();

  cout << "Sorting time using template quicksort: ";
  cout << end - start << endl;

  start = clock();
  qsort(nums2, (unsigned) 10000, sizeof(int), comp);
  end = clock();

  cout << "Sorting time using qsort() library function: ";
  cout << end - start << endl;

  return 0;
}

// Quicksort entry function.
template <class Stype> void quick(Stype *item, int count)
{
  qs(item, 0, count-1);
}

// The generic quicksort.
template <class Stype> void qs(Stype *item, int left, int right)
{
  register int i, j;
  Stype x, y;

  i = left; j = right;
  x = item[(left+right)/2];

  do {
    while(item[i]<x && i<right) i++;
    while(x<item[j] && j>left) j--;

    if(i<=j) {
      y = item[i];
```

```
        item[i] = item[j];
        item[j] = y;
        i++; j--;
      }
    } while(i<=j);

    if(left<j) qs(item, left, j);
    if(i<right) qs(item, i, right);
}

int comp(const void *a, const void *b)
{
   return *(int *) a - *(int *)b;
}
```

As mentioned earlier, the reason that the standard library version of quicksort runs more slowly than the template version is that **qsort( )** incurs substantial, unnecessary overhead each time it is called because of the need for the parameters that specify the size of the data being sorted and the address of the comparison function. Since the quicksort is usually implemented as a recursive function, these extra parameters add overhead not just once, but repeatedly because of the recursive invocations. However, since each instantiation of a template function creates a data-specific version, the size of the data being sorted is already known and the comparison operation is built in. Thus, there is no need for the size or comparison function parameters, and no additional overhead is created.

The difference in the run times between the two approaches to creating a generic function emphasizes why template functions are changing the face of programming.

Sorting User-Defined Types

Since the main reason for creating a template function is to apply it to all types of data, you might be wondering how the preceding sorting functions can be applied to user-defined types. For example, you might prudently ask how an array of class objects can be sorted. Consider the following simple class.

```
class address {
  char name[40];
  char street[40];
  char city[20];
  char state[3];
  char zip[11];
  // ...
};
```

If you were to try to use one of the preceding generic sorts to sort an array of **address** objects, you would receive compile-time errors because the relational operators such as **<** or **>**, used by the sorts to compare the array elements, have not been defined for **address** objects. Thus, even though the generic sorts are capable of sorting any type of data, they cannot do so if one or more operators used within the function have not been defined for the type of data being sorted. Fortunately, it is easy to correct this problem. Simply overload the needed operators. Once this has been done, the generic sorts can sort user-defined types as readily as any built-in type. If you think about it, it is clear that defining the necessary relational operators for a class type that you wish to sort is no great inconvenience, because you will typically need to overload several operator functions when defining a new type, anyway. Also, overloading the relational operators is usually a simple matter.

To see how to sort user-defined types, examine the following sample program. It uses the generic quicksort to sort an array of **address** objects, using the ZIP code as the sort key.

```cpp
// Applying the generic quicksort of user-defined classes.
#include <iostream.h>
#include <string.h>
#include <stdlib.h>
#include <time.h>

const int NUM_ITEMS = 4;

class address {
  char name[40];
  char street[40];
  char city[20];
  char state[3];
  char zip[11];
public:
  address(char *n, char *s, char *c, char *st, char *z);
  address() {}; // null constructor

  int operator<(address &ob)
  {
    return strcmp(zip, ob.zip) < 0;
  }
  friend ostream &operator<<(ostream &stream, address &ob);
};

// Address constructor
address::address(char *n, char *s, char *c,
                 char *st, char *z)
```

```
{
  strcpy(name, n);
  strcpy(street, s);
  strcpy(city, c);
  strcpy(state, st);
  strcpy(zip, z);
}

// Inserter for address class.
ostream &operator<<(ostream &stream, address &ob)
{
  cout << ob.name << endl;
  cout << ob.street << endl;
  cout << ob.city << " " << ob.state << " ";
  cout << ob.zip << endl << endl;
  return stream;
}

address addrs[NUM_ITEMS] = {
  address("A. Alexander", "101 1st St", "Olney", "Ga", "55555"),
  address("B. Bertrand", "22 2nd Ave", "Oakland", "Pa", "34232"),
  address("C. Carlisle", "33 3rd Blvd", "Ava", "Or", "92000"),
  address("D. Dodger", "4 Fourth Dr", "Fresno", "Mi", "45678")
};

template <class Stype> void quick(Stype *item, int count);
template <class Stype> void qs(Stype *item, int left, int right);

main()
{
  int i;

  cout << "Unsorted Addresses:\n\n";
  for(i=0; i<NUM_ITEMS; i++) cout << addrs[i];

  quick(addrs, NUM_ITEMS);
  cout << "Addresses sorted by ZIP code:\n\n";
  for(i=0; i<NUM_ITEMS; i++) cout << addrs[i];

  return 0;
}

// Quicksort entry function.
template <class Stype> void quick(Stype *item, int count)
{
  qs(item, 0, count-1);
}
```

```
// The generic quicksort.
template <class Stype> void qs(Stype *item, int left, int right)
{
  register int i, j;
  Stype x, y;

  i = left; j = right;
  x = item[(left+right)/2];

  do {
    while(item[i]<x && i<right) i++;
    while(x<item[j] && j>left) j--;

    if(i<=j) {
      y = item[i];
      item[i] = item[j];
      item[j] = y;
      i++; j--;
    }
  } while(i<=j);

  if(left<j) qs(item, left, j);
  if(i<right) qs(item, i, right);
}
```

As you can see, the **address** class overloads the **<** operator. This is the only relational operator used by the **quick( )** function. (Of course, if you want to use a different sort, you may need to overload other relational operators.) Overloading **<** allows the generic quicksort to operate unmodified on **address** objects.

The preceding special case can be generalized. When you want to sort user-defined objects, simply overload the necessary relational operators. Once you have done this, any of the generic sorts can be used without alteration.

Choosing a Sort

Every programmer should have a wide selection of sorts from which to choose. Although quicksort is the optimal sort for the average case, it will not be the best sort in all cases. For example, when only very small lists are sorted (with say, fewer than 100 items), the overhead created by quicksort's recursive calls may offset the benefits of its superior algorithm. In rare cases like this, one of the simpler sorts—perhaps even the bubble sort—may be quicker. Also, if you know that a list is already nearly ordered or if you don't want like keys to be exchanged, then one of the other sorts may out perform quicksort. The point is that just because quicksort is the best general-purpose sorting algorithm does not mean that you cannot do better with another approach in special situations.

Searching

Databases of information exist so that, from time to time, a user can locate a record by entering its key. There is one method of finding information in an unsorted array and another for a sorted array. All C++ compilers supply search functions as part of the standard library. However, as with sorting, these general-purpose routines are usually holdovers from C and are simply too inefficient for use in demanding situations because of the extra overhead. In this section, you will see how to implement two template search functions.

Searching Methods

Finding information in an unsorted array requires a sequential search starting at the first element and stopping either when a match is found or at the end of the array. However, if the data has been sorted, you can use a binary search, which helps you locate the data much more quickly.

The Sequential Search

The sequential search is simple to implement. The template function shown in the following program searches an array of known length until a match of the specified key is found.

```
// Using a generic sequential search.
#include <iostream.h>

template <class Stype> int seq_search(Stype *item,
                              int count, Stype key);

main()
{
  char str[] = "acbedfg";
  int nums[] = {1, 7, 3, 5, 4, 6, 2};
  int index;

  index = seq_search(str, (int) sizeof(str), 'd');
  if(index >= 0)
    cout << "Match found at " << index << endl;
  else
    cout << "No match found\n";
```

```
  index = seq_search(nums, 7, 2);
  if(index >= 0)
    cout << "Match found at " << index << endl;
  else
    cout << "No match found\n";

  return 0;
}

// A generic sequential search.
template <class Stype>
int seq_search(Stype *item, int count, Stype key)
{
  register int t;

  for(t=0; t<count; ++t)
    if(key==item[t]) return t;
  return -1; // no match
}
```

The **seq_search( )** function returns the index number of the matching entry if there is one; otherwise, it returns –1.

It is easy to see that a sequential search will, on the average, test $1/2n$ elements. In the best case, it tests only one element; in the worst case, it tests n elements. For small amounts of data, this performance will be acceptable. But if large amounts of data are searched, the sequential approach is painfully slow. Of course, if the data is unsorted, the sequential search is your only option.

The Binary Search

If the data to be searched is sorted, you can use a vastly superior method of searching. It is the *binary search,* which uses the divide-and-conquer approach. To employ this method, test the middle element. If it is larger than the key, then test the middle element of the first half; otherwise, test the middle element of the second half. Repeat this procedure until a match is found, or there are no more elements to test.

For example, to find the number 4 given the array

123456789

a binary search first tests the middle, which is 5. Since this is greater than 4, the search continues with the first half, or

12345

The middle element is now 3. This is less than 4, so the first half is discarded. The search continues with

4 5

This time the match is found.

In a binary search, the number of comparisons in the worst case is

$\log_2 n$

In the average case, the number is somewhat lower; in the best case, the number of comparisons is one.

The following program implements a generic binary search.

```cpp
// Using a generic binary search.
#include <iostream.h>

template <class Stype> int binary_search(Stype *item,
                                int count, Stype key);

main()
{
  char str[] = "abcdefg";
  int nums[] = {1, 2, 3, 4, 5, 6, 7};
  int index;

  index = binary_search(str, (int) sizeof(str), 'd');
  if(index >= 0)
    cout << "Match found at " << index << endl;
  else
    cout << "No match found\n";

  index = binary_search(nums, 7, 2);
  if(index >= 0)
    cout << "Match found at " << index << endl;
  else
    cout << "No match found\n";

  return 0;
}

// A generic binary search.
template <class Stype>
int binary_search(Stype *item, int count, Stype key)
{
  int low, high, mid;
```

```
low = 0; high = count-1;
while(low<=high) {
  mid = (low+high)/2;
  if(key<item[mid]) high = mid-1;
  else if(key>item[mid]) low = mid+1;
  else return mid; // found
}
return -1;
}
```

Some Things to Try

Since templates are relatively new to C++, most C++ programmers are not yet taking full advantage of them. One of the first things that you might want to do is to examine your own library of custom functions, looking for functions which are good candidates for conversion into templates. You might be surprised by how many such functions there will be.

Since an instantiated version of a template function is as efficient as a "normal" function and much more efficient than old-style generalized functions, you might also want to look for old-style functions that can be converted into templates. Remember, the old approach to generalized functions added overhead because of the need for extra parameters. This overhead is completely eliminated when templates are used.

Finally, you might want to begin building a new template function library from scratch. Since templates let you separate the method from the data, such a library could be widely applied.

Chapter 2

Harnessing the Power of Template Classes

This chapter continues the exploration of templates by examining template classes. As mentioned in Chapter 1, a class template is used to create a generic class. When you create a generic class, you are creating a class framework which may be applied to any type of data. That is, the type of data operated upon by the class is specified as a parameter when an object of that class is created. As you can guess, the principal advantage of a generic class is that it allows you to define the members of a class once, but to apply that class to a variety of data types.

The most common application of class templates is to create container classes. In fact, as mentioned in Chapter 1, the creation of container classes is one of the main reasons for the invention of templates. A *container class* is a general name given to classes that hold organized data. For example, arrays and linked lists are both containers. The advantage of defining generic container classes is that once the logic necessary to support a container has been defined, it can be applied to any type of data without rewriting. This makes it possible to write and debug a container class once, but use it repeatedly. For example, a generic linked-list container could be used to create lists that hold mailing addresses, book titles, or auto parts information. Because of the importance and historical significance of container classes, they will be used to illustrate the power of class templates.

This chapter will look at five types of containers:

♦   Bounded (or "safe") array

♦   Queue

♦   Stack

♦   Linked list

♦   Binary tree

Each of these containers performs a specific storage-and-retrieval operation on the information that it is given and the requests that it receives. Specifically, they all store an item and retrieve an item, where an item is one informational unit. The rest of this chapter shows you how to build generic versions of these containers.

A Review of Template Classes

Before you begin to build generic container classes, a brief review of template classes is in order. When you define a template class, you create a class that defines all algorithms used by that class, but the actual type of the data being manipulated will be specified as a parameter when objects of that class are instantiated. The compiler will automatically generate an appropriate object based upon the type that you specify.

The general form of a generic class declaration is shown here:

```
template <class Ttype> class class-name {
    .
    .
    .
}
```

Here, *Ttype* is a placeholder type name which will be replaced by the actual data type when a class is instantiated. If necessary, you may define more than one generic data type using a comma-separated list. *Ttype* may be used anywhere inside the class definition.

Once you have created a generic class, you create a specific instance of that class using the following general form:

class-name <*type*> *ob*;

Here, *type* is the type name of the actual data that the class will be operating upon and is substituted for *Ttype*.

One last point: Member functions of a generic class are automatically generic. They need not be explicitly specified as such by use of **template**.

2

Bounded Arrays

By far, the simplest container class is a bounded, or "safe," array. As you know, in C++, it is possible to overrun (or underrun) an array boundary at run time without generating a run-time error message. Although this lack of boundary checking allows C++ to generate extremely fast executable code, it has also been a source of errors and frustration for programmers ever since C++ (and its predecessor, C) was invented. However, it is possible to eliminate this problem. To do so, create a class that contains the array, and allow access to that array only through the overloaded **[ ]** subscripting operator. Inside the **operator[ ]( )** function, you can intercept an out-of-range index. Since the bounds-checking mechanism will be the same for all types of data, it makes sense to create a generic bounded array which you can use whenever you need a safe array. As you will see, even though a generic bounded array is the simplest container class, it is one of the most useful.

As mentioned, the creation of a bounded array requires the overloading of the **[ ]** operator. If you are unfamiliar with the overloading of this operator, the following review will help.

Overloading the [ ]

In C++, the **[ ]** is considered a binary operator when overloading it. The **[ ]** may only be overloaded by a member function. Therefore, the general form of a member **operator[ ]( )** function is as shown here:

```
type class-name::operator[ ](int index)
{
  // ...
}
```

Technically, the parameter does not have to be of type **int**, but **operator[ ]( )** functions are typically used to provide array subscripting, and as such an integer value is generally used. Typically, the return type of the **operator[ ]( )**

function will be the same as the type of data stored in the array that it is indexing.

To understand how the **[ ]** operator works, assume an object called **ob** is indexed as shown here:

```
ob[9]
```

This index will translate into the following call to the **operator[ ]( )** function:

```
operator[](9)
```

That is, the value of the expression within the subscripting operator is passed to the **operator[ ]( )** function in its explicit parameter. The **this** pointer will point to **ob**, the object that generated the call.

It is possible to design the **operator[ ]( )** function in such a way that the **[ ]** can be used on both the left and right sides of an assignment statement. To do this, specify the return value of **operator[ ]( )** to be a reference, and return a reference to the specified array element. When this is the case, the following types of statements will be correct:

```
ob[9] = 10;
x = ob[9];
```

Creating a Generic Bounded Array

The following program creates a generic, bounded array and illustrates its use. Notice that the **operator[ ]( )** function returns a reference which allows it to be used on either side of an assignment statement.

```
// A generic bounded array.
#include <iostream.h>
#include <stdlib.h>

// A generic bounded array class.
template <class AType> class atype {
  AType *a;
  int length;
public:
  atype(int size);
  ~atype() { delete [] a; }
  AType &operator[](int i);
};
```

```
// Constructor for atype.
template <class AType> atype<AType>::atype(int size)
{
  register int i;

  length = size;
  a = new AType[size]; // dynamically allocate storage
  if(!a) {
    cout << "Cannot allocate array.\n";
    exit(1);
  }

  // initialize to zero
  for(i=0; i<size; i++) a[i] = 0;
}


// Provide range checking for atype.
template <class AType> AType &atype<AType>::operator[](int i)
{
  if(i<0 || i> length-1) {
    cout << "\nIndex value of ";
    cout << i << " is out-of-bounds.\n";
    exit(1);
  }
  return a[i];
}

main()
{
  atype<int> intob(20); // integer array
  atype<double> doubleob(10); // double array
  int i;

  cout << "Integer array: ";
  for(i=0; i<20; i++) intob[i] = i;
  for(i=0; i<20; i++) cout << intob[i] << " ";
  cout << endl;

  cout << "Double array: ";
  cout.precision(4);
  for(i=0; i<10; i++) doubleob[i] = (double) i * 3.14;
  for(i=0; i<10; i++) cout << doubleob[i] << " ";
  cout << endl;

  intob[45] = 100; // generates run-time error

  return 0;
}
```

This program implements a generic safe array type and then demonstrates its use by creating an array of integers and an array of **double**s. (You might want to try creating other types of arrays.) As this example shows, part of the power of generic classes is that they allow you to write the code once, debug it, and then apply it to any type of data without having to re-engineer it for each specific application.

The operation of the generic array class is straightforward. Space for the array is dynamically allocated, and a pointer to that memory is stored in **a**. The size of the array is passed as a parameter to the **atype** constructor and is stored in **length**. Thus, you must specify the size of each array when it is created. Because differently sized arrays may be created, **atype** can be applied to the widest variety of applications. However, if you know in advance that you will always be dealing with same-sized arrays, then you might want to use a fixed array size for **atype**. This would mean slightly faster run times.

Queues

A *queue* is simply a linear list of information that is accessed in *first-in, first-out* order, which is sometimes called FIFO. That is, the first item placed on the queue is the first item removed, the second item put in is the second item removed, and so on. This is the only means of storage and retrieval in a queue; unlike an array, random access of any specific item is not allowed.

Queues are very common in real life. For example, lines at a bank or a fast-food restaurant are queues. Queues are used in many programming situations. One of the most common is in simulations. Queues are also used by the task scheduler of an operating system and for I/O buffering.

To visualize how a queue works, consider two functions: **qstore( )** and **qretrieve( )**. The **qstore( )** function places an item onto the end of the queue, and **qretrieve( )** removes the first item from the queue and returns its value. Table 2-1 shows the effect of a series of these operations. Keep in mind that a retrieval operation removes an item from the queue and

A Queue in Action

Table 2-1.

Action	Contents of Queue
qstore(A)	A
qstore(B)	A B
qstore(C)	A B C
qretrieve( ) returns **A**	B C
qstore(D)	B C D
qretrieve( ) returns **B**	C D
qretrieve( ) returns **C**	D

destroys it if it is not stored elsewhere. Therefore, a queue may be empty because all items have been removed.

In the following program, a generic queue is created. In the example, an integer queue and a floating-point queue are demonstrated, but any data type may be used.

```
// A generic queue class.
#include <iostream.h>
#include <stdlib.h>

// A generic queue class.
template <class QType> class queue {
  QType *q;
  int sloc, rloc;
  int length;
public:
   queue(int size);
  ~queue() { delete [] q; }
  void qstore(QType i);
  QType qretrieve();
};

template <class QType> queue<QType>::queue(int size)
{
  size++;

  q = new QType[size];
  if(!q) {
    cout << "Cannot allocate queue.\n";
    exit(1);
  }
  length = size;
  sloc = rloc = 0;
}


// Put an object into the queue.
template <class QType> void queue<QType>::qstore(QType i)
{
  if(sloc+1==length) {
    cout << "Queue is full.\n";
    return;
  }
  sloc++;
  q[sloc] = i;
}

// Get an object from the queue.
```

```
template <class QType> QType queue<QType>::qretrieve()
{
  if(rloc == sloc) {
    cout << "Queue underflow.\n";
    return 0;
  }
  rloc++;
  return q[rloc];
}

main()
{
  queue<int> a(5), b(5);   // create two integer queues

  a.qstore(100);
  b.qstore(200);

  a.qstore(300);
  b.qstore(400);

  cout << a.qretrieve() << " ";
  cout << a.qretrieve() << " ";
  cout << b.qretrieve() << " ";
  cout << b.qretrieve() << endl;

  queue<double> c(5), d(5);   // create two double queues

  c.qstore(8.12);
  d.qstore(9.99);

  c.qstore(-2.0);
  d.qstore(0.986);

  cout << c.qretrieve() << " ";
  cout << c.qretrieve() << " ";
  cout << d.qretrieve() << " ";
  cout << d.qretrieve() << endl;

  return 0;
}
```

The output from this program is shown here:

```
100 300 200 400
8.12 -2 9.99 0.986
```

Each queue is held in a dynamically allocated array pointed to by **q**. The size of the queue is passed as a parameter to the **queue** class' constructor. This size is stored in the **length** member of **queue**. Notice that the size of the array allocated to support the queue is one greater than the size of the queue. The reason for this is that in the simplest implementation of a queue, one array location is always empty. Therefore, if you wish to store 10 items in a queue, the array supporting the queue must actually be 11 elements long, for example.

The member variables **rloc** and **sloc** are used to index the queue. **sloc** contains the location at which the next item will be stored. **rloc** specifies the index at which point the next item will be removed. Each time a new item is stored, **sloc** is incremented. Each time an item is retrieved, **rloc** is incremented. Thus, **rloc** chases **sloc**. The queue is empty when **rloc** and **sloc** contain the same value. One last point: Even though the information stored in the queue is not actually destroyed by **qretrieve( )**, it is effectively destroyed because it can never be accessed again.

The Circular Queue

In studying the preceding program, an improvement may have occurred to you. Instead of having the program stop when the limit of the array used to store the queue is reached, you could have both the store index (**sloc**) and the retrieve index (**rloc**) loop back to the start of the array. In this way, any number of items could be placed on the queue, so long as items were also being taken off. This implementation of a queue is called a *circular queue,* because it uses its storage array as if it were a circle instead of a linear list.

To create a circular queue, you need to change the functions **qstore( )** and **qretrieve( )** as shown in the following program.

```
// A generic circular queue class.
#include <iostream.h>
#include <stdlib.h>

// A generic circular queue class.
template <class QType> class queue {
  QType *q;
  int sloc, rloc;
  int length;
public:
   queue(int size);
  ~queue() { delete [] q; }
  void qstore(QType i);
  QType qretrieve();
};

template <class QType> queue<QType>::queue(int size)
```

```
{
  size++;

  q = new QType[size];
  if(!q) {
    cout << "Cannot allocate queue.\n";
    exit(1);
  }
  length = size;
  sloc = rloc = 0;
}

// Put an object into the queue.
template <class QType> void queue<QType>::qstore(QType i)
{
  if(sloc+1==rloc || (sloc+1==length && !rloc)) {
    cout << "Queue is full.\n";
    return;
  }
  q[sloc] = i;
  sloc++;
  if(sloc==length) sloc = 0; // loop around
}

// Get an object from the queue.
template <class QType> QType queue<QType>::qretrieve()
{
  if(rloc==length) rloc = 0; // loop around
  if(rloc == sloc) {
    cout << "Queue underflow.\n";
    return 0;
  }
  rloc++;
  return q[rloc-1];
}

main()
{
  queue<int> a(10);  // create an integer queue
  int i;

  // demonstrate integer circular queue
  for(i=0; i<10; i++) a.qstore(i);
  cout << a.qretrieve() << endl;
  a.qstore(10);
  cout << a.qretrieve() << endl;
  a.qstore(11);
  cout << a.qretrieve() << endl;
```

```
     a.qstore(12);
     for(i=0; i<10; i++) cout << a.qretrieve() << " ";
     cout << endl;

     queue<double> b(10);   // create double queue

     // demonstrate double circular queue
     for(i=0; i<10; i++) b.qstore((double) i * 1.1);
     cout << b.qretrieve() << endl;
     b.qstore(10.0);
     cout << b.qretrieve() << endl;
     b.qstore(11.1);
     cout << b.qretrieve() << endl;
     b.qstore(12.2);
     for(i=0; i<10; i++) cout << b.qretrieve() << " ";

     return 0;
}
```

2

The output produced by this program is shown here:

```
0
1
2
3 4 5 6 7 8 9 10 11 12
0
1.1
2.2
3.3 4.4 5.5 6.6 7.7 8.8 9.9 10 11.1 12.2
```

In this version, the queue is full only when the retrieve index is 1 greater than the store index. The queue is empty when **rloc** equals **sloc**. Otherwise, there is room in the queue for another item.

Stacks

A stack is the opposite of a queue, because it uses *last-in, first-out* accessing, which is sometimes called LIFO. To visualize a stack, just imagine a stack of plates. The first plate on the table is the last to be used, and the last plate placed on the stack is the first to be used. Stacks are used a great deal in system software, including compilers and interpreters. In fact, C++ compilers use the stack for passing arguments to functions.

The two basic operations—store and retrieve—are traditionally called *push* and *pop,* respectively. Therefore, to implement a stack you need two functions: **push( )** (which places a value on the stack) and **pop( )** (which

Action	Contents of Stack
push(A)	A
push(B)	B A
push(C)	C B A
pop( ) retrieves **C**	B A
push(F)	F B A
pop( ) retrieves **F**	B A
pop( ) retrieves **B**	A
pop( ) retrieves **A**	*empty*

A Stack in
Action
Table 2-2.

retrieves a value from the stack). You also need a region of memory to use as the stack. You can use an array for this purpose or allocate a region of memory using **new**. As in the queue, the retrieval function takes a value off the list and destroys it if it is not stored elsewhere. To see how a stack works, see Table 2-2.

The following program creates a generic stack class.

```cpp
// Demonstrate a generic stack class.
#include <iostream.h>
#include <stdlib.h>

// This creates the generic class stack.
template <class SType> class stack {
  SType *stck;
  int tos;
  int length;
public:
  stack(int size);
  ~stack() { delete [] stck; }
  void push(SType i);
  SType pop();
};

// stack's constructor function.
template <class SType> stack<SType>::stack(int size)
{
  stck = new SType[size];

  if(!stck) {
    cout << "Cannot allocate stack.\n";
    exit(1);
  }
  length = size;
```

```
    tos = 0;
  }

  // Push an object onto the stack.
  template <class SType> void stack<SType>::push(SType i)
  {
    if(tos==length) {
      cout << "Stack is full.\n";
      return;
    }
    stck[tos] = i;
    tos++;
  }

  // Pop an object off the stack.
  template <class SType> SType stack<SType>::pop()
  {
    if(tos==0) {
      cout << "Stack underflow.\n";
      return 0;
    }
    tos—;
    return stck[tos];
  }

  main()
  {
    stack<int> a(10); // create integer stack
    stack<double> b(10); // create a double stack
    stack<char> c(10); // create a character stack

    int i;

    // use the integer and double stacks
    a.push(10);
    b.push(100.1);
    a.push(20);
    b.push(10-3.3);

    cout << a.pop() << " ";
    cout << a.pop() << " ";
    cout << b.pop() << " ";
    cout << b.pop() << endl;

    // demonstrate the character stack
    for(i=0; i<10; i++) c.push((char) 'A'+i);
    for(i=0; i<10; i++) cout << c.pop();
```

```
    cout << endl;

    return 0;
}
```

The output produced by this program is shown here:

```
20 10 6.7 100.1
JIHGFEDCBA
```

The stack is held in a dynamically allocated array pointed to by **stck**. The size of the stack is passed as a parameter to the **stack** class' constructor. This size is stored in the **length** member of **stack**. The member variable **tos** is the index of the next open stack location, which is the top of the stack. An empty stack is signaled by **tos** being zero, and a full stack by **tos** being greater than the last storage location.

An excellent example of stack usage is a four-function calculator. Most calculators today accept a standard form of an expression called *infix notation,* which takes the general form *operand-operator-operand.* For example, to add 200 to 100, enter **100**, then press the plus (+) key, then **200**, and press the equal (=) key. In contrast, many early calculators (and some still made today) use *postfix notation,* in which both operands are entered first and then the operator is entered. For example, to add 200 to 100 by using postfix notation, you enter 100, then 200, and then press the plus (+) key. As operands are entered, they are placed on a stack. Each time an operator is entered, two operands are removed from the stack, and the result is pushed back on the stack. One advantage of the postfix form is that long, complex expressions can be easily entered by the user. The following example demonstrates a stack by implementing a postfix calculator.

The entire postfix-based calculator program is shown here:

```
// A simple four-function calculator that uses the generic stack.

#include <iostream.h>
#include <stdlib.h>

void calculator();

// This creates the generic class stack.
template <class SType> class stack {
  SType *stck;
  int tos;
  int length;
public:
  stack(int size);
```

```
  ~stack() { delete [] stck; }
  void push(SType i);
  SType pop();
};

// stack's constructor function.
template <class SType> stack<SType>::stack(int size)
{
  stck = new SType[size];

  if(!stck) {
    cout << "Cannot allocate stack.\n";
    exit(1);
  }
  length = size;

  tos = 0;
}

// Push an object onto the stack.
template <class SType> void stack<SType>::push(SType i)
{
  if(tos==length) {
    cout << "Stack is full.\n";
    return;
  }
  stck[tos] = i;
  tos++;
}

// Pop an object off the stack.
template <class SType> SType stack<SType>::pop()
{
  if(tos==0) {
    cout << "Stack underflow.\n";
    return 0;
  }
  tos—;
  return stck[tos];
}

main()
{
  calculator();

  return 0;
}
```

```
// A four-function calculator.
void calculator()
{
  stack<double> calc(100);
  double a, b;
  char str[80];

  cout << "Four Function Calculator\n";
  cout << "Enter 'q' to quit\n";

  do {
    cout << ": ";
    cin >> str;
    switch(*str) {
      case '+':
        a = calc.pop();
        b = calc.pop();
        cout << a+b << endl;
        calc.push(a+b);
        break;
      case '-':
        a = calc.pop();
        b = calc.pop();
        cout << b-a << endl;
        calc.push(b-a);
        break;
      case '*':
        a = calc.pop();
        b = calc.pop();
        cout << a*b << endl;
        calc.push(b*a);
        break;
      case '/':
        a = calc.pop();
        b = calc.pop();
        if(!a) {
          cout << "divide by 0\n";
          break;
        }
        cout << b/a << endl;
        calc.push(b/a);
        break;
      case '.': // show contents of top of stack
        a = calc.pop();
        calc.push(a);
        cout << "Current value on top of stack: ";
        cout << a << endl;
        break;
```

```
      default:
         calc.push(atof(str));
      }
   } while(*str != 'q');
}
```

Linked Lists

Queues and stacks share two common traits. First, they both have very strict rules for referencing the data stored in them. That is, a queue may only be accessed in FIFO order, and a stack in LIFO order. Second, their retrieval operations are, by nature, consumptive. In other words, accessing an item in a stack or queue requires its removal, and unless the item is stored elsewhere, it is destroyed. However, the next container class to be examined does not share these constraints. Unlike a stack or a queue, a *linked list* may be accessed in a flexible fashion, because each piece of information carries with it a link to the next data item in the chain. In addition, a linked-list retrieval operation does not remove and destroy an item from the list. In fact, you need to add a specific deletion operation to do this. In this section a generic linked-list class is developed.

Linked lists can be either singly linked or doubly linked. In a *singly linked* list each item contains a link to the next data item. In a *doubly linked* list each item contains links to both the next and the previous element in the list. Although singly linked lists are not uncommon, doubly linked lists are more valuable because of three main factors. First, a doubly linked list may be read in both directions, that is, front to back or back to front. A singly linked list may only be read in one direction. Second, because there are two links associated with each member of the list, a damaged list may be more easily reconstructed when it is doubly linked. Third, certain types of list operations (such as deletion) are easier to perform on a doubly linked list. Since doubly linked lists provide more flexibility and require only a small amount of extra work, they are the type of linked list examined here. (If you are interested in singly linked lists, see my book *C: The Complete Reference, 3rd Ed.*, Osborne/McGraw-Hill.)

As you probably know, doubly linked lists are dynamic data structures which may grow or shrink in length during the execution of your program. In fact, the principal advantage of a dynamic data structure is that its size does not need to be fixed at compile time. Rather, it is free to expand or contract, as needed, during run time. As stated, each object in the list contains a link to the preceding object and to the following object. Objects are inserted into or deleted from the list by rearranging the links appropriately. Because doubly linked lists are dynamic data structures, most commonly each object in the list is dynamically allocated. This is the case with the doubly linked list class developed in this section.

Each item stored in a doubly linked list contains three parts: a pointer to the next element in the list, a pointer to the previous element in the list, and the information that is stored in the list. Figure 2-1 depicts a doubly linked list.

Creating a Generic Doubly Linked List Class

To create a generic doubly linked list, let's use a simple class hierarchy. One class, called **listob**, defines the nature of the objects that will be stored in the list. This class is then inherited by another class, called **dllist**, that actually implements the doubly linked list mechanism.

The **listob** class is shown here:

```
template <class DataT> class listob {
public:
  DataT info; // information
  listob<DataT> *next;  // pointer to next object
  listob<DataT> *prior; // pointer to previous object
  listob() {
    info = 0;
    next = NULL;
    prior = NULL;
  };
  listob(DataT c) {
    info = c;
    next = NULL;
    prior = NULL;
  }
  listob<DataT> *getnext() {return next;}
  listob<DataT> *getprior() {return prior;}
  void getinfo(DataT &c) { c = info;}
  void change(DataT c) { info = c; }   // change an element
  friend ostream &operator<<(ostream &stream, listob<DataT> o);
  friend ostream &operator<<(ostream &stream, listob<DataT> *o);
  friend istream &operator>>(istream &stream, listob<DataT> &o);
};

// Overload << for object of type listob.
template <class DataT>
ostream &operator<<(ostream &stream, listob<DataT> o)
{
  stream << o.info << endl;
  return stream;
}
```

```
// Overload << for pointer to object of type listob.
template <class DataT>
ostream &operator<<(ostream &stream, listob<DataT> *o)
{
  stream << o->info << endl;
  return stream;
}

// Overload >> for listob references.
template <class DataT>
istream &operator>>(istream &stream, listob<DataT> &o)
{
  cout << "Enter information: ";
  stream >> o.info;
  return stream;
}
```

As you can see, **listob** has three data members. The member **info** holds the information stored by the list, which is specified by the generic type **DataT**. The **next** pointer will point to the next element in the list, and **prior** will point to the previous element in the list. Notice that the data members of **listob** are public. They are declared as public only for the sake of illustration and to allow all aspects of a linked list to be easily demonstrated. However, you might want to make them private or protected for your own application.

Also defined within **listob** are a number of operations that can be performed on **listob** objects. Specifically, the information associated with an object can be retrieved or modified, and pointers to the next or previous elements can be obtained. In addition, objects of type **listob** can be input or output by use of the overloaded **<<** and **>>** operators. Keep in mind that the operations defined within **listob** are independent of the list-keeping mechanism. **listob** only defines the nature of the data to be stored in the list.

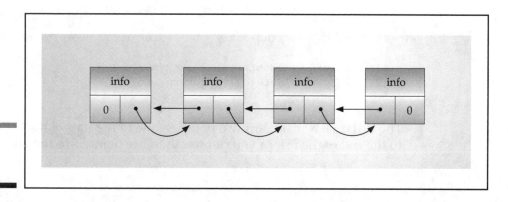

A doubly
linked list
Figure 2-1.

2

When each object is constructed, the **prior** and **next** fields are initialized to **NULL**. These pointers are null until the object is put into a list. If an initializer is included, it is copied into **info**. Otherwise, **info** is initialized to zero.

The **getnext( )** function returns a pointer to the next element in the list. This will be **NULL** if the end of the list has been reached. The **getprior( )** function returns the previous element in the list, if it exists; it returns **NULL** otherwise. These functions are technically unnecessary since both **next** and **prior** are public. However, they will be needed if you make **next** and **prior** private in your own application.

Notice that the << operator is overloaded for both objects of type **listob** and pointers to objects of type **listob**. This is because it is extremely common, when using a linked list, to access members of the list using a pointer. Therefore it is useful to overload << so that it operates when given a pointer to the object. However, since there is no reason to preclude an object being output, the second form, which operates directly on an object, is also included. Alternatively, you might want to overload << for **listob** references, instead.

While **listob** defines the nature of doubly linked objects, it does not create a linked list. Instead, the linked list mechanism is implemented by **dllist**, shown here. As you can see, it inherits **listob** and operates on objects of that type.

```
template <class DataT> class dllist : public listob<DataT> {
  listob<DataT> *start, *end;
public:
  dllist() { start = end = NULL; }
  ~dllist(); // destructor for the list

  void store(DataT c);
  void remove(listob<DataT> *ob); // delete entry
  void frwdlist(); // display the list from beginning
  void bkwdlist(); // display the list from the end

  listob<DataT> *find(DataT c); // return pointer to match

  listob<DataT> *getstart() { return start; }
  listob<DataT> *getend() { return end; }
};
```

The **dllist** class maintains two pointers: one to the start of the list and one to the end of the list. As you can see, these are pointers to **listob** objects.

These pointers are initialized to **NULL** when a list is first created. The **dllist** class supports several doubly linked list operations, including

♦ Putting an item in the list

♦ Removing an item from the list

♦ Following the list in either the forward or backward direction

♦ Finding a specific element

♦ Obtaining pointers to the start and end of the list

Each of these procedures is examined next.

The store( ) Function

Information is added to the list using the **store( )** function. It is implemented as shown here:

```
// Add the next entry.
template <class DataT> void dllist<DataT>::store(DataT c)
{
  listob<DataT> *p;

  p = new listob<DataT>;
  if(!p) {
    cout << "Allocation error.\n";
    exit(1);
  }

  p->info = c;

  if(start==NULL) { // first element in list
    end = start = p;
  }
  else { // put on end
    p->prior = end;
    end->next = p;
    end = p;
  }
}
```

Before a new item can be put into the list, a **listob** object is needed to hold it. Since linked lists are dynamic data structures, it makes sense that **store( )** obtains an object dynamically, using **new**. After a **listob** object has been allocated, **store( )** assigns the information passed in **c** to the **info** member of the new object and then adds the object to the end of the list. Notice that the **start** and **end** pointers are updated as needed. In this way, **start** and **end** will always point to the beginning and end of the list.

Because objects are always added to the end of the list, the list is not sorted. However, you can modify **store( )** so that it maintains a sorted list if you like.

As the **store( )** function makes clear, the linked list managed by the **dllist** class maintains a list of *objects of type* **listob**. The type of data stored within an object of type **listob** is irrelevant to the **store( )** function.

The remove( ) Function

The **remove( )** function removes an object from the list. It is shown here:

```
/* Remove an element from the list and update start and
   end pointers.
*/
template <class DataT> void dllist<DataT>::remove(listob<DataT> *ob)
{
  if(ob->prior) { // not deleting first element
    ob->prior->next = ob->next;
    if(ob->next) // not deleting last element
      ob->next->prior = ob->prior;
    else // otherwise, are deleting last element
      end = ob->prior;  // update end pointer
  }
  else {  // deleting first element
    if(ob->next) { // list not empty
      ob->next->prior = NULL;
      start = ob->next;
    }
    else // list now empty
      start = end = NULL;
  }
}
```

The **remove( )** function deletes the object pointed to by its parameter, **ob**. (**ob** must be a valid pointer to a **listob** object.) There are three places where an item to be deleted can be located (see Figure 2-2). It can be the first item, the last item, or somewhere in between. The **remove( )** function handles all three cases.

Keep in mind that **remove( )** removes an object from the list, but that object is not destroyed. It is simply "delinked." (Of course, you can destroy it if you like, using **delete**.)

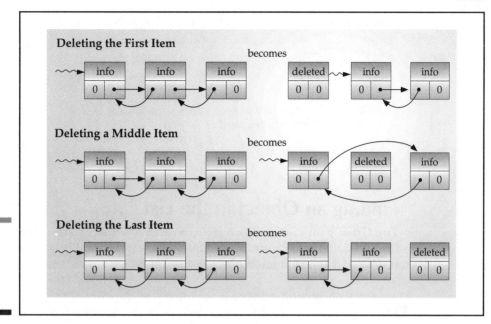

Removing an object from a doubly linked list

Figure 2-2.

Like **store( )**, the operation of **remove( )** does not depend upon the type of data actually stored in the list.

Displaying the List

The functions **frwdlist( )** and **bkwdlist( )** display the contents of the list in a forward and backward direction, respectively. These functions are included to illustrate how the **dllist** class works. They also make convenient debugging aids.

```
// Walk through list in forward direction.
template <class DataT> void dllist<DataT>::frwdlist()
{
  listob<DataT> *temp;

  temp = start;
  while(temp) {
    cout << temp->info << " ";
    temp = temp->getnext();
  }
  cout << endl;
}

// Walk through list in backward direction.
```

2

```
template <class DataT> void dllist<DataT>::bkwdlist()
{
  listob<DataT> *temp;

  temp = end;
  while(temp) {
    cout << temp->info << " ";
    temp = temp->getprior();
  }
  cout << endl;
}
```

Finding an Object in the List

The **find( )** function, shown here, returns a pointer to the object in the list
that contains information that matches that specified in its parameter. It will
return **NULL** if no matching object is found.

```
// Find an object given info.
template <class DataT> listob<DataT> *dllist<DataT>::find(DataT c)
{
  listob<DataT> *temp;

  temp = start;

  while(temp) {
    if(c==temp->info) return temp; // found
    temp = temp->getnext();
  }
  return NULL; // not in list
}
```

The Complete Generic Doubly Linked List Class

The entire generic doubly linked list class and sample **main( )** function are
shown here. Take note of the way the generic data type is used throughout the
function definitions. As you can see, in all cases, the data operated on by the
list has been specified using the generic **DataT** type. It is not until an actual
list is instantiated in **main( )** that the specific nature of the data is resolved.

```
// A generic doubly linked list class.

#include <iostream.h>
#include <string.h>
#include <stdlib.h>
```

2

```cpp
template <class DataT> class listob; // forward reference listob

// Overload << for object of type listob.
template <class DataT>
ostream &operator<<(ostream &stream, listob<DataT> o)
{
  stream << o.info << endl;
  return stream;
}

// Overload << for pointer to object of type listob.
template <class DataT>
ostream &operator<<(ostream &stream, listob<DataT> *o)
{
  stream << o->info << endl;
  return stream;
}

// Overload >> for listob references.
template <class DataT>
istream &operator>>(istream &stream, listob<DataT> &o)
{
  cout << "Enter information: ";
  stream >> o.info;
  return stream;
}

// Generic list object class.
template <class DataT> class listob {
public:
  DataT info; // information
  listob<DataT> *next;  // pointer to next object
  listob<DataT> *prior; // pointer to previous object
  listob() {
    info = 0;
    next = NULL;
    prior = NULL;
  };
  listob(DataT c) {
    info = c;
    next = NULL;
    prior = NULL;
  }
  listob<DataT> *getnext() {return next;}
  listob<DataT> *getprior() {return prior;}
  void getinfo(DataT &c) { c = info;}
  void change(DataT c) { info = c; }  // change an element
  friend ostream &operator<<(ostream &stream, listob<DataT> o);
```

```
    friend ostream &operator<<(ostream &stream, listob<DataT> *o);
    friend istream &operator>>(istream &stream, listob<DataT> &o);
};

// Generic list class.
template <class DataT> class dllist : public listob<DataT> {
  listob<DataT> *start, *end;
public:
  dllist() { start = end = NULL; }
  ~dllist(); // destructor for the list

  void store(DataT c);
  void remove(listob<DataT> *ob); // delete entry
  void frwdlist(); // display the list from beginning
  void bkwdlist(); // display the list from the end

  listob<DataT> *find(DataT c); // return pointer to match

  listob<DataT> *getstart() { return start; }
  listob<DataT> *getend() { return end; }
};

// dllist destructor.
template <class DataT> dllist<DataT>::~dllist()
{
  listob<DataT> *p, *p1;

  // free all elements in the list
  p = start;
  while(p) {
    p1 = p->next;
    delete p;
    p = p1;
  }
}

// Add the next entry.
template <class DataT> void dllist<DataT>::store(DataT c)
{
  listob<DataT> *p;

  p = new listob<DataT>;
  if(!p) {
    cout << "Allocation error.\n";
    exit(1);
  }
```

2

```
  p->info = c;

  if(start==NULL) { // first element in list
    end = start = p;
  }
  else { // put on end
    p->prior = end;
    end->next = p;
    end = p;
  }
}

/* Remove an element from the list and update start and
   end pointers.
*/
template <class DataT> void dllist<DataT>::remove(listob<DataT> *ob)
{
  if(ob->prior) { // not deleting first element
    ob->prior->next = ob->next;
    if(ob->next) // not deleting last element
      ob->next->prior = ob->prior;
    else // otherwise, are deleting last element
      end = ob->prior;  // update end pointer
  }
  else {  // deleting first element
    if(ob->next) { // list not empty
      ob->next->prior = NULL;
      start = ob->next;
    }
    else // list now empty
      start = end = NULL;
  }
}

// Walk through list in forward direction.
template <class DataT> void dllist<DataT>::frwdlist()
{
  listob<DataT> *temp;

  temp = start;
  while(temp) {
    cout << temp->info << " ";
    temp = temp->getnext();
  }
  cout << endl;
}

// Walk through list in backward direction.
```

```
template <class DataT> void dllist<DataT>::bkwdlist()
{
  listob<DataT> *temp;

  temp = end;
  while(temp) {
    cout << temp->info << " ";
    temp = temp->getprior();
  }
  cout << endl;
}

// Find an object given info.
template <class DataT> listob<DataT> *dllist<DataT>::find(DataT c)
{
  listob<DataT> *temp;

  temp = start;

  while(temp) {
    if(c==temp->info) return temp; // found
    temp = temp->getnext();
  }
  return NULL; // not in list
}

main()
{
  // First, demonstrate an integer list.
  dllist<int> list;
  int i;
  listob<int> *p;

  list.store(1);
  list.store(2);
  list.store(3);

  // use member functions to display the list
  cout << "Integer list forwards: ";
  list.frwdlist();
  cout << "Integer list backwards: ";
  list.bkwdlist();

  cout << endl;

  // "manually" follow the list
  cout << "Manually follow the list: ";
```

```
p = list.getstart();
while(p) {
  p->getinfo(i);
  cout << i << " ";
  p = p->getnext(); // get next one
}

cout << endl << endl;

// look for an item
cout << "Searching for item 2.\n";
p = list.find(2);
if(p) {
  p->getinfo(i);
  cout << "Found item " << i << endl;
}

cout << endl;

// remove an item
p->getinfo(i);
cout << "Deleting item " << i << ".\n";
list.remove(p);
cout << "List after deletion: ";
list.frwdlist();

cout << endl;

// add another entry
cout << "Inserting an item.\n";
list.store(4);
cout << "List after insertion: ";
list.frwdlist();

cout << endl;

// change information
p = list.find(1);
if(!p) {
  cout << "Error, item not found.\n";
  return 1; // error
}

p->getinfo(i);
cout << "Changing " << i << " to 5.\n";
p->change(5);
cout << "Integer list forwards: ";
list.frwdlist();
```

```
    cout << "Integer list backwards: ";
    list.bkwdlist();

    cout << endl;

    // demonstrate << and >>
    cin >> *p;
    cout << "Item now contains: " << *p;

    cout << "Integer list forwards: ";
    list.frwdlist();

    cout << endl;

    // remove head of list
    cout << "After removing head of list: ";
    p = list.getstart();
    list.remove(p);
    list.frwdlist();

    cout << endl;

    // remove end of list
    cout << "After removing tail of list: ";
    p = list.getend();
    list.remove(p);
    list.frwdlist();

    cout << endl;

    // Create a list of doubles.
    dllist<double> dlist;

    dlist.store(98.6);
    dlist.store(212.0);
    dlist.store(88.9);

    // use member functions to display the list
    cout << "Here is the list of doubles ";
    cout << "forwards and backwards.\n";
    dlist.frwdlist();
    dlist.bkwdlist();

    return 0;
}
```

The output produced by this program is shown here:

Integer list forwards: 1 2 3
Integer list backwards: 3 2 1

Manually follow the list: 1 2 3

Searching for item 2.
Found item 2

Deleting item 2.
List after deletion: 1 3

Inserting an item.
List after insertion: 1 3 4

Changing 1 to 5.
Integer list forwards: 5 3 4
Integer list backwards: 4 3 5

Enter information: 10
Item now contains: 10
Integer list forwards: 10 3 4

After removing head of list: 3 4

After removing tail of list: 3

Here is the list of doubles forwards and backwards.
98.6 212 88.9
88.9 212 98.6

This example creates a doubly linked list of integer data and demonstrates the various functions that can be applied to it. The program then creates a list of **double**s to show the generic nature of the linked-list class. On your own, you should try creating lists of other types of data. Remember, even compound data types, such as a structure that contains a mailing address, can be stored in the list.

Binary Trees

The final data structure to be examined is the *binary tree*. Although there can be many types of trees, binary trees are special because, when sorted, they lend themselves to rapid searches, insertions, and deletions. Each item in a tree consists of information along with a link to the left member and a link to the right member. Figure 2-3 shows a small tree.

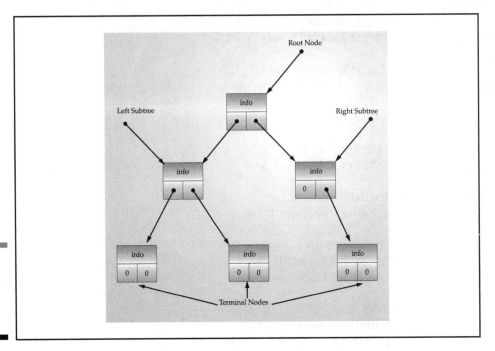

A sample
binary tree
with height of
three

Figure 2-3.

Special terminology is needed when discussing trees. Computer scientists are not known for their grammar, and terminology for trees is a classic case of a confused metaphor. The *root* is the first item in the tree. Each data item is called a *node* (or sometimes a *leaf*) of the tree, and any piece of the tree is called a *subtree*. A node that has no subtrees attached to it is called a *terminal node*. The *height* of the tree is equal to the number of layers deep that its roots grow. When working with trees, you can think of them existing in memory looking the way they do on paper. But remember: a tree is only a way to logically organize data in memory, and memory is linear.

In a sense, the binary tree is a special form of linked list. Items can be inserted, deleted, and accessed in any order. Also, the retrieval operation is nondestructive. Although trees are easy to visualize, they present some very difficult programming problems. This discussion only scratches the surface.

Most functions that use trees are recursive, because the tree is a recursive data structure. That is, each subtree is a tree. Therefore, the routines that this discussion develops will be recursive. Remember, nonrecursive versions of these functions exist, but their code is much harder to understand.

How a tree is ordered depends on how it is going to be accessed. The process of accessing each node in a tree is called a *tree traversal*. Consider the following tree:

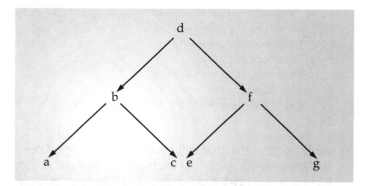

There are three ways to traverse a tree: *inorder, preorder,* and *postorder.* Using inorder, you visit the left subtree, the root, and then the right subtree. In preorder, you visit the root, the left subtree, and then the right subtree. With postorder, you visit the left subtree, the right subtree, and then the root. The order of access for the tree shown using each method is

inorder	a b c d e f g
preorder	d b a c f e g
postorder	a c b e g f d

Although a tree need not be sorted, most uses require this. Of course, what constitutes a sorted tree depends on how you will be traversing the tree. The rest of this chapter assumes inorder. Therefore, a sorted binary tree is one where the subtree on the left contains nodes that are less than the root, and those on the right are greater than the root.

Now that the necessary terminology has been defined, let's create a generic binary tree class. In the interest of space, only a very simple tree class is created. However, on your own you might want to try enhancing and expanding it. (See "Things to Try" later in this chapter for some ideas.)

The Generic Tree Class

To create a generic binary tree class, the following class template, called **tree**, will be used.

```
template <class DataT> class tree {
  DataT info;
  tree *left;
  tree *right;
public:
  tree *root;
  tree() { root = NULL; }
```

```
    void stree(tree *r, tree *previous, DataT info);
    tree *dtree(tree *r, DataT key);
    void preorder(tree *r);
    void inorder(tree *r);
    void postorder(tree *r);
    void print_tree(tree *r, int l);
    tree *search_tree(tree *r, DataT key);
};
```

Each node in the tree will be an object of type **tree**. The **info** member holds
the information stored at each node. For each object, **left** is a pointer to the
left subtree, **right** is a pointer to the right subtree, and **root** is a pointer to
the root of the entire tree. Keep in mind that **root** is not necessary (the root
of the tree could have been stored elsewhere), but it is included as a
convenience. It enables any node in the tree to know where the entire tree
begins. This can be a benefit in some circumstances.

Storing Items in a Tree

To insert items into a tree, use the **stree( )** function. It is shown here:

```
template <class DataT> void tree<DataT>::stree(
        tree *r, tree *previous, DataT info)
{
  if(!r) {
    r = new tree;
    if(!r) {
      cout << "Out of memory.\n";
      exit(1);
    }
    r->left = NULL;
    r->right = NULL;
    r->info = info;
    if(!root) root = r; // first entry
    else {
      if(info < previous->info) previous->left = r;
      else previous->right = r;
    }
    return;
  }

  if(info<r->info)
    stree(r->left, r, info);
  else
    stree(r->right, r, info);
}
```

This function inserts an object into a binary tree. It does so by following the links through the tree, going left or right based on the **info** field, until the correct location in the tree is found. The function **stree( )** is a recursive algorithm, as are most tree routines. The same routine would be several times longer if you were to employ iterative methods. The function must be called with the following arguments (proceeding left to right): a pointer to the root of the tree or subtree to be searched, a pointer to the previous node, and the information to be stored. When called the first time, the second parameter may be **NULL**.

This function is actually sorting the information that you give it as it stores it in the tree. It is essentially a variation of the insertion sort that you saw in the previous chapter. In the average case, its performance can be quite good, but the quicksort is still a better general-purpose sorting method, because it uses less memory and has lower processing overhead. However, if you have to build a tree from scratch or maintain an already sorted tree, you should always insert new entries in sorted order by using the **stree( )** function.

Traversing a Tree

To traverse in order the tree built by using **stree( )**, and to print the **info** field of each node, you could use the **inorder( )** function shown here:

```
template <class DataT> void tree<DataT>::inorder(tree *r)
{
  if(!r) return;

  inorder(r->left);
  if(r->info) cout << r->info << " ";
  inorder(r->right);
}
```

To use the function, call it with a pointer to the root node of the subtree that you want to traverse. If you wish to traverse the entire tree, call it with a pointer to the root of the tree. This recursive function returns when a terminal node (a null pointer) is encountered.

Here are the functions for traversing the tree in preorder and postorder:

```
template <class DataT> void tree<DataT>::preorder(tree *r)
{
  if(!r) return;

  if(r->info) cout << r->info << " ";
  preorder(r->left);
  preorder(r->right);
```

```
}

template <class DataT> void tree<DataT>::postorder(tree *r)
{
  if(!r) return;

  postorder(r->left);
  postorder(r->right);
  if(r->info) cout << r->info << " ";
}
```

Now consider a short but interesting program that builds a sorted binary tree and then prints that tree inorder, sideways on your screen. The program requires only a small modification to the function **inorder( )** to print the tree. Because the tree is printed sideways on the screen, the right subtree must be printed before the left subtree for the tree to look correct. (This is technically the opposite of an inorder traversal.) This new function is called **print_tree( )** and is shown here:

```
template <class DataT> void tree<DataT>::print_tree(tree *r, int l)
{
  int i;

  if(!r) return;

  print_tree(r->right, l+1);
  for(i=0; i<l; ++i) cout << " ";
  cout << r->info << endl;
  print_tree(r->left, l+1);
}
```

The entire tree-printing program follows. Try entering various trees to see how each one is built.

```
// This program displays a binary tree.

#include <iostream.h>
#include <stdlib.h>

template <class DataT> class tree {
  DataT info;
  tree *left;
  tree *right;
public:
  tree *root;
  tree() { root = NULL; }
  void stree(tree *r, tree *previous, DataT info);
```

```
    void print_tree(tree *r, int l);
};

template <class DataT> void tree<DataT>::stree(
  tree *r, tree *previous, DataT info)
{
  if(!r) {
    r = new tree;
    if(!r) {
      cout << "Out of Memory\n";
      exit(1);
    }
    r->left = NULL;
    r->right = NULL;
    r->info = info;
    if(!root) root = r; // first entry
    else {
      if(info < previous->info) previous->left = r;
      else previous->right = r;
    }
    return;
  }

  if(info<r->info)
    stree(r->left, r, info);
  else
    stree(r->right, r, info);
}

// Display a tree.
template <class DataT> void tree<DataT>::print_tree(tree *r, int l)
{
  int i;

  if(!r) return;

  print_tree(r->right, l+1);
  for(i=0; i<l; ++i) cout << " ";
  cout << r->info << endl;
  print_tree(r->left, l+1);
}

main()
{
  char s[80];
  tree<char> chTree;
```

2

```
do {
   cout << "Enter a letter (period to stop): ";
   cin >> s;
   if(*s!='.') chTree.stree(chTree.root, NULL, *s);
} while(*s!='.');

chTree.print_tree(chTree.root, 0);

return 0;
}
```

If you have run the tree-printing program, you have probably noticed that some trees are *balanced*—that is, each subtree is the same or nearly the same height as any other—and that others are very far out of balance. In fact, if you entered the tree **abcd**, it would have looked like this:

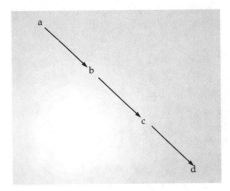

There would have been no left subtrees. This is called a *degenerate tree*, because it has degenerated into a linear list. In general, if the data you are using as input to build a binary tree is fairly random, the tree produced approximates a balanced tree. However, if the information is already sorted, a degenerate tree results. (It is possible to readjust the tree with each insertion to keep the tree in balance, but this process is fairly complex and beyond the scope of this chapter.)

Searching a Tree

Search functions are easy to implement for binary trees. The following function returns a pointer to the node in the tree that matches the key; otherwise, it returns a null.

```
template <class DataT>
tree<DataT> *tree<DataT>::search_tree(tree *r, DataT key)
{
  if(!r) return r;   // empty tree
  while(r->info != key) {
    if(key<r->info) r = r->left;
    else r = r->right;
    if(r==NULL) break;
  }
  return r;
}
```

You must call this function with a pointer to the start of the subtree that you want to search and the information that you are looking for. To search the entire tree, pass a pointer to the root node of the tree.

Deleting an Item from a Tree

Unfortunately, deleting a node from a tree is not as simple as searching a tree. The deleted node may be either the root, a left node, or a right node. Also, the node may have from zero to two subtrees attached to it. The process of rearranging the pointers lends itself to a recursive algorithm, which is shown here:

```
template <class DataT>
tree<DataT> *tree<DataT>::dtree(tree *r, DataT key)
{
  tree *p,*p2;

  if(!r) return r; // not found

  if(r->info==key) { // delete root
    // this means an empty tree
    if(r->left==r->right){
      free(r);
      if(r==root) root = NULL;
      return NULL;
    }
    // or if one subtree is null
    else if(r->left==NULL) {
      p = r->right;
      free(r);
      if(r==root) root = p;
      return p;
    }
    else if(r->right==NULL) {
      p = r->left;
```

```
      free(r);
      if(r==root) root = p;
      return p;
    }
    // or both subtrees present
    else {
      p2 = r->right;
      p = r->right;
      while(p->left) p = p->left;
      p->left = r->left;
      free(r);
      if(r==root) root = p2;
      return p2;
    }
  }
  if(r->info<key) r->right = dtree(r->right, key);
  else r->left = dtree(r->left, key);
  return r;
}
```

You must call this function with a pointer to the start of the subtree that you want to search and the information that you want to delete. To search the entire tree, pass a pointer to the root node of the tree.

Binary trees offer tremendous power, flexibility, and efficiency. Because a balanced binary tree has, as a worst case, $\log_2 n$ comparisons in searching, it is far better than a linked list, which must rely on a sequential search.

Things to Try

One of the first things that you will want to try is using the containers described in this chapter to store user-defined data types. For example, you might want to experiment by creating your own mailing list program. You could create a mailing list class that holds the name and address information, and overloads the necessary operators. You might store the mailing list using a linked list or a binary tree.

As mentioned earlier, the **tree** class is intentionally simplified in the interest of space. Therefore, you may want to expand and enhance the binary tree class for your own use. One of the first things that you will want to do is to separate tree objects from tree operations (in much the same way that the linked list class separates list objects from list operations). For example, define a **treeob** class that defines the nature of tree objects and then have **tree** inherit that class. You may also want to overload the input and output operators relative to the tree classes.

Although the five containers examined are the most common and elemental, there are several other types. You might want to try creating some on your own. Here are a few ideas.

♦ A priority queue, in which items are added to the queue in order of their priority

♦ An associative linked list, in which list items also contain links to related items

♦ A multiway tree (such as a Bayer tree) instead of a binary tree

2

Because of the power of generic classes, the effort you expend creating a container will be repaid several times over throughout your life as a programmer.

Chapter

3

An Object-Oriented Expression Parser

This chapter applies C++ to one of programming's more mysterious processes: *expression parsing.* Here, you will learn how to create an object-oriented expression parser. An expression parser is used to evaluate an algebraic expression, such as (10 − 8) * 3. Expression parsers are quite useful and are applicable to a wide range of applications. They are also one of programming's more elusive entities. For various reasons, the procedures used to create an expression parser are not widely taught or disseminated. Indeed, many otherwise accomplished programmers are mystified by the process of expression parsing.

Although mysterious, expression parsing is actually very straightforward and is, in many ways, easier than other programming tasks. The reason is that the task is well-defined and works according to the strict rules of algebra. This chapter will develop what is commonly referred to as a *recursive-descent parser* and all the necessary support routines that enable you to evaluate complex numeric expressions. Three versions of the parser will be created. The first two are nongeneric versions. The final version is generic and may be applied to any numeric type. However, before any parser can be developed, a brief overview of expressions and parsing is necessary.

Expressions

Since an expression parser evaluates an algebraic expression, it is important to understand what the constituent parts of an expression are. Although expressions can be made up of all types of information, this chapter deals only with numeric expressions. For purposes of this chapter *numeric expressions* are composed of the following items:

♦ Numbers
♦ Operators (+, –, /, *, ^, %, =)
♦ Parentheses
♦ Variables

The operator ^ indicates exponentiation, as it does in BASIC, and = is the assignment operator. These items can be combined in expressions according to the rules of algebra. Here are some examples:

```
10 – 8
(100 – 5) * 14/6
a + b – c
10^5
a = 10 – b
```

Assume this precedence for each operator:

highest	+ – (unary)
	^
	* / %
	+ –
lowest	=

Operators of equal precedence evaluate from left to right.

In the examples in this chapter, all variables are single letters (in other words, 26 variables, **A** through **Z**, are available). The variables are not case sensitive (**a** and **A** are treated as the same variable). For the first version of the parser, all numeric values are elevated to **double**, although you could easily write the routines to handle other types of values. Finally, to keep the logic clear and easy to understand, only a minimal amount of error checking is included.

Parsing Expressions: The Problem

If you have not thought much about the problem of expression parsing, you might assume that it is a simple task. However, to better understand the problem, try to evaluate this sample expression:

10 – 2 * 3

You know that this expression is equal to the value 4. Although you could easily create a program that would compute that *specific* expression, the question is how to create a program that gives the correct answer for any *arbitrary* expression. At first you might think of a routine something like this:

3

```
a = get first operand
while(operands present) {
    op = get operator
    b = get second operand
    a = a op b
}
```

This routine gets the first operand, the operator, and the second operand to perform the first operation, then gets the next operator and operand—if any—to perform the next operation, and so on. However, if you use this basic approach, the expression 10 – 2 * 3 evaluates to 24 (that is, 8 * 3) instead of 4, because this procedure neglects the precedence of the operators. You cannot just take the operands and operators in order from left to right, because the rules of algebra dictate that multiplication must be done before subtraction. Some beginners think that this problem can be easily overcome, and sometimes—in very restricted cases—it can. But the problem only gets worse when you add parentheses, exponentiation, variables, unary operators, and the like.

Although there are a few ways to write a routine that evaluates expressions, the one developed here is the one most easily written by a person. It is also the most common. The method used here is called a *recursive-descent parser*, and in the course of this chapter you will see how it got its name. (Some of the other methods used to write parsers employ complex tables that must be generated by another computer program. These are sometimes called *table-driven parsers*.)

Parsing an Expression

There are a number of ways to parse and evaluate an expression. For use with a recursive-descent parser, think of expressions as *recursive data structures*—that is, expressions that are defined in terms of themselves. If, for the moment, you assume that expressions can only use +, –, *, /, and parentheses, all expressions can be defined with the following rules:

expression → term [+ term] [– term]
term → factor [* factor] [/ factor]
factor → variable, number, or (expression)

The square brackets designate an optional element, and the → means "produces." In fact, these rules are usually called the *production rules* of an expression. Therefore, you could say: "Term produces factor times factor or factor divided by factor" for the definition of *term*. Notice that the precedence of the operators is implicit in the way an expression is defined.

For example, the expression

10 + 5 * B

has two terms: 10 and 5 * B. The second term contains two factors: 5 and B. These factors consist of one number and one variable.

On the other hand, the expression

14 * (7 – C)

has two factors: 14 and (7 – C). The factors consist of one number and one parenthesized expression. The parenthesized expression contains two terms: one number and one variable.

A recursive-descent parser is a set of mutually recursive functions that work in a chain-like fashion to implement the production rules. At each appropriate step, the parser performs the specified operations in the algebraically correct sequence. To see how the production rules are used to parse an expression, let's work through an example using the following expression.

9/3 – (100 + 56)

Here is the sequence that you will follow.

1. Get the first term, 9/3.
2. Get each factor and divide the integers. The resulting value is 3.

3. Get the second term, (100 + 56). At this point, start recursively analyzing the second subexpression.

4. Get each term and add. The resulting value is 156.

5. Return from the recursive call and subtract 156 from 3. The answer is –153.

If you are a little confused at this point, don't feel bad. This is a fairly complex concept that takes some getting used to. There are two basic things to remember about this recursive view of expressions. First, the precedence of the operators is implicit in the way the production rules are defined. Second, this method of parsing and evaluating expressions is very similar to the way humans evaluate mathematical expressions.

The remainder of this chapter develops three parsers. The first will parse and evaluate floating-point expressions of type **double** which consist of only constant values. Next, this parser is enhanced to support the use of variables. Finally, in the third version, the parser is implemented as a template class which can be used to parse expressions of any type.

The Parser Class

The expression parser is built upon the **parser** class. In the course of this chapter, three versions of the **parser** class will be used. The first expression parser uses the version of **parser** shown here. Subsequent versions of the parser build upon it.

```
class parser {
  char *exp_ptr;  // points to the expression
  char token[80]; // holds current token
  char tok_type;  // holds token's type

  void eval_exp2(double &result);
  void eval_exp3(double &result);
  void eval_exp4(double &result);
  void eval_exp5(double &result);
  void eval_exp6(double &result);
  void atom(double &result);
  void get_token();
  void serror(int error);
  int isdelim(char c);
public:
  parser();
  double eval_exp(char *exp);
};
```

The **parser** class contains three private member variables. The expression to be evaluated is contained in a null-terminated string pointed to by **exp_ptr**. Thus, the parser evaluates expressions that are contained in standard ASCII strings. For example, the following strings contain expressions that the parser can evaluate.

```
"10 – 5"
"2 * 3.3 / (3.1416 * 3.3)"
```

When the parser begins execution, **exp_ptr** must point to the first character in the expression string. As the parser executes, it works its way through the string until the null-terminator is encountered.

The meanings of the other two member variables, **token** and **tok_type**, are described in the next section.

The entry point to the parser is through **eval_exp( )**, which must be called with a pointer to the expression to be analyzed. The functions **eval_exp2( )** through **eval_exp6( )** along with **atom( )** form the recursive-descent parser. They implement an enhanced set of the expression production rules discussed earlier. In subsequent versions of the parser, a function called **eval_exp1( )** will also be added.

The **serror( )** function handles syntax errors in the expression. The functions **get_token( )** and **isdelim( )** are used to dissect the expression into its component parts, as described in the next section.

Dissecting an Expression

To evaluate expressions, you need to be able to break an expression into its components. Since this operation is fundamental to parsing, let's look at it before examining the parser.

Each component of an expression is called a *token*. For example, the expression

```
A * B – (W + 10)
```

contains the tokens A, *, B, –, (, W, +, 10, and   ). Each token represents an indivisible unit of the expression. In general, you need a function that sequentially returns each token in the expression individually. The function must also be able to skip over spaces and tabs and detect the end of the expression. The function that will be used to perform this task is called **get_token( )**, which is a member function of the **parser** class.

Besides the token itself, you will also need to know what type of token is being returned. For the parser developed in this chapter, you need only three types: **VARIABLE, NUMBER,** and **DELIMITER. (DELIMITER** is used for both operators and parentheses.)

The **get_token( )** function is shown here. It obtains the next token from the expression pointed to by **exp_ptr** and puts it into the member variable **token**. It puts the type of the token into the member variable **tok_type**.

```
// Obtains the next token.
void parser::get_token()
{
  register char *temp;

  tok_type = 0;
  temp = token;
  *temp = '\0';

  if(!*exp_ptr) return; // at end of expression

  while(isspace(*exp_ptr)) ++exp_ptr; // skip over white space

  if(strchr("+-*/%^=()", *exp_ptr)){
    tok_type = DELIMITER;
    // advance to next char
    *temp++ = *exp_ptr++;
  }
  else if(isalpha(*exp_ptr)) {
    while(!isdelim(*exp_ptr)) *temp++ = *exp_ptr++;
    tok_type = VARIABLE;
  }
  else if(isdigit(*exp_ptr)) {
    while(!isdelim(*exp_ptr)) *temp++ = *exp_ptr++;
    tok_type = NUMBER;
  }

  *temp = '\0';
}

// Return true if c is a delimiter.
int parser::isdelim(char c)
{
  if(strchr(" +-/*%^=()", c) || c==9 || c=='\r' || c==0)
    return 1;
  return 0;
}
```

Look closely at the preceding functions. After the first few initializations, **get_token( )** checks to see if the null terminating the expression has been found. It does so by checking the character pointed to by **exp_ptr**. Since **exp_ptr** is a pointer to the expression being analyzed, if it points to a null, the end of the expression has been reached. If there are still more tokens to retrieve from the expression, **get_token( )** first skips over any leading spaces. Once the spaces have been skipped, **exp_ptr** is pointing to either a number, a variable, an operator, or—if trailing spaces end the expression—a null. If the next character is an operator, it is returned as a string in **token**, and **DELIMITER** is placed in **tok_type**. If the next character is a letter instead, it is assumed to be one of the variables. It is returned as a string in **token**, and **tok_type** is assigned the value **VARIABLE**. If the next character is a digit, the entire number is read and placed in its string form in **token** and its type is **NUMBER**. Finally, if the next character is none of the preceding, it is assumed that the end of the expression has been reached. In this case, **token** is null, which signals the end of the expression.

As stated earlier, to keep the code in this function clean, a certain amount of error checking has been omitted, and some assumptions have been made. For example, any unrecognized character may end an expression. Also, in this version, variables may be any length, but only the first letter is significant. You can add more error checking and other details as your specific application dictates.

To better understand the tokenization process, study what it returns for each token and type in the following expression:

A + 100 – (B * C) /2

Token	Token Type
A	VARIABLE
+	DELIMITER
100	NUMBER
–	DELIMITER
(	DELIMITER
B	VARIABLE
*	DELIMITER
C	VARIABLE
)	DELIMITER
/	DELIMITER
2	NUMBER
null	Null

Remember that **token** always holds a null-terminated string, even if it contains just a single character.

A Simple Expression Parser

Here is the first version of the parser. It can evaluate expressions that consist solely of constants, operators, and parentheses. It cannot accept expressions that contain variables.

```cpp
/* This module contains the recursive descent
   parser that does not use variables.
*/

#include <iostream.h>
#include <stdlib.h>
#include <ctype.h>
#include <string.h>

enum types { DELIMITER = 1, VARIABLE, NUMBER};

class parser {
  char *exp_ptr;  // points to the expression
  char token[80]; // holds current token
  char tok_type;  // holds token's type

  void eval_exp2(double &result);
  void eval_exp3(double &result);
  void eval_exp4(double &result);
  void eval_exp5(double &result);
  void eval_exp6(double &result);
  void atom(double &result);
  void get_token();
  void serror(int error);
  int isdelim(char c);
public:
  parser();
  double eval_exp(char *exp);
};

// parser constructor
parser::parser()
{
  exp_ptr = NULL;
}

// Parser entry point.
double parser::eval_exp(char *exp)
{
  double result;
```

```
    exp_ptr = exp;

    get_token();
    if(!*token) {
      serror(2); // no expression present
      return 0.0;
    }
    eval_exp2(result);
    if(*token) serror(0); // last token must be null
    return result;
}

// Add or subtract two terms.
void parser::eval_exp2(double &result)
{
  register char op;
  double temp;

  eval_exp3(result);
  while((op = *token) == '+' || op == '-') {
    get_token();
    eval_exp3(temp);
    switch(op) {
      case '-':
        result = result - temp;
        break;
      case '+':
        result = result + temp;
        break;
    }
  }
}

// Multiply or divide two factors.
void parser::eval_exp3(double &result)
{
  register char op;
  double temp;

  eval_exp4(result);
  while((op = *token) == '*' || op == '/' || op == '%') {
    get_token();
    eval_exp4(temp);
    switch(op) {
      case '*':
        result = result * temp;
        break;
```

```cpp
      case '/':
        result = result / temp;
        break;
      case '%':
        result = (int) result % (int) temp;
        break;
    }
  }
}

// Process an exponent
void parser::eval_exp4(double &result)
{
  double temp, ex;
  register int t;

  eval_exp5(result);
  if(*token== '^') {
    get_token();
    eval_exp4(temp);
    ex = result;
    if(temp==0.0) {
      result = 1.0;
      return;
    }
    for(t=(int)temp-1; t>0; --t) result = result * (double)ex;
  }
}

// Evaluate a unary + or -.
void parser::eval_exp5(double &result)
{
  register char  op;

  op = 0;
  if((tok_type == DELIMITER) && *token=='+' || *token == '-') {
    op = *token;
    get_token();
  }
  eval_exp6(result);
  if(op=='-') result = -result;
}

// Process a parenthesized expression.
void parser::eval_exp6(double &result)
{
```

```cpp
  if((*token == '(')) {
    get_token();
    eval_exp2(result);
    if(*token != ')')
      serror(1);
    get_token();
  }
  else atom(result);
}

// Get the value of a number.
void parser::atom(double &result)
{
  switch(tok_type) {
    case NUMBER:
      result = atof(token);
      get_token();
      return;
    default:
      serror(0);
  }
}

// Display a syntax error.
void parser::serror(int error)
{
  static char *e[]= {
      "Syntax Error",
      "Unbalanced Parentheses",
      "No Expression Present"
  };
  cout << e[error] << endl;
}

// Obtain the next token.
void parser::get_token()
{
  register char *temp;

  tok_type = 0;
  temp = token;
  *temp = '\0';

  if(!*exp_ptr) return; // at end of expression

  while(isspace(*exp_ptr)) ++exp_ptr; // skip over white space
```

```
    if(strchr("+-*/%^=()", *exp_ptr)){
      tok_type = DELIMITER;
      // advance to next char
      *temp++ = *exp_ptr++;
    }
    else if(isalpha(*exp_ptr)) {
      while(!isdelim(*exp_ptr)) *temp++ = *exp_ptr++;
      tok_type = VARIABLE;
    }
    else if(isdigit(*exp_ptr)) {
      while(!isdelim(*exp_ptr)) *temp++ = *exp_ptr++;
      tok_type = NUMBER;
    }

    *temp = '\0';
}

// Return true if c is a delimiter.
int parser::isdelim(char c)
{
  if(strchr(" +-/*%^=()", c) || c==9 || c=='\r' || c==0)
    return 1;
  return 0;
}
```

The parser as it is shown can handle the following operators: **+, –, *, /, %**. In addition, it can handle integer exponentiation (^) and the unary minus. The parser can also deal with parentheses correctly. The actual evaluation of an expression takes place in the mutually recursive functions **eval_exp2( )** through **eval_exp6( )**, plus the **atom( )** function, which returns the value of a number. The comments at the start of each function describe what role it plays in parsing the expression.

The simple **main( )** function that follows demonstrates the use of the parser.

```
main()
{
  char expstr[80];

  cout << "Enter a period to stop.\n";

  parser ob; // instantiate a parser

  for(;;) {
    cout << "Enter expression: ";
    cin.getline(expstr, 79);
    if(*expstr=='.') break;
    cout << "Answer is: " << ob.eval_exp(expstr) << "\n\n";
  };
```

```
    return 0;
}
```

A sample run is shown here.

    Enter a period to stop.
    Enter expression: 10–2*3
    Answer is: 4

    Enter expression: (10–2)*3
    Answer is: 24

    Enter expression: 10/3
    Answer is: 3.33333

    Enter expression: .

Understanding the Parser

To understand exactly how the parser evaluates an expression, work through the following expression. (Assume that **exp_ptr** points to the start of the expression.)

    10 – 3 * 2

When **eval_exp( )**, the entry point into the parser, is called, it gets the first token. If the token is null, the function prints the message **No Expression Present** and returns. However, in this case, the token contains the number **10**. Since the first token is not null, **eval_exp2( )** is called. As a result, **eval_exp2( )** calls **eval_exp3( )**, and **eval_exp3( )** calls **eval_exp4( )**, which in turn calls **eval_exp5( )**. Then **eval_exp5( )** checks whether the token is a unary plus or minus, which in this case, it is not, so **eval_exp6( )** is called. At this point **eval_exp6( )** either recursively calls **eval_exp2( )** (in the case of a parenthesized expression) or **atom( )** to find the value of a number. Since the token is not a left parenthesis, **atom( )** is executed and **result** is assigned the value 10. Next, another token is retrieved, and the functions begin to return up the chain. The token is now the operator –, and the functions return up to **eval_exp2( )**.

What happens next is very important. Because the token is –, it is saved in **op**. The parser then gets the next token, which is **3**, and the descent down the chain begins again. As before, **atom( )** is entered. The value 3 is returned in **result**, and the token * is read. This causes a return back up the chain to **eval_exp3( )**, where the final token 2 is read. At this point, the first arithmetic operation occurs—the multiplication of 2 and 3. The result is returned to **eval_exp2( )**, and the subtraction is performed. The subtraction yields the answer 4. Although the process may at first seem complicated, work through some other examples to verify that this method functions correctly every time.

This parser would be suitable for use by a desktop calculator, as is illustrated by the previous program. Before it could be used in a computer language, database, or in a sophisticated calculator, however, it would need the ability to handle variables. This is the subject of the next section.

Adding Variables to the Parser

All programming languages, many calculators, and spreadsheets use variables to store values for later use. Before the parser can be used for such applications, it needs to be expanded to include variables. To accomplish this, you need to add several things to the parser. First, of course, are the variables. As stated earlier, the letters **A** through **Z** will be used for variables. The variables will be stored in an array inside the **parser** class. Each variable uses one array location in a 26-element array of **double**s. Therefore, add the following to the **parser** class:

```
double vars[NUMVARS]; // holds variables' values
```

You will also need to change the **parser** constructor, as shown here:

```
// parser constructor
parser::parser()
{
  int i;

  exp_ptr = NULL;

  for(i=0; i<NUMVARS; i++) vars[i] = 0.0;
}
```

As you can see, the variables are initialized to 0 as a courtesy to the user.

You will also need a function to look up the value of a given variable. Because the variables are named **A** through **Z**, they can easily be used to index the array **vars** by subtracting the ASCII value for **A** from the variable name. The member function **find_var( )**, shown here, accomplishes this:

```
// Return the value of a variable.
double parser::find_var(char *s)
{
```

```
  if(!isalpha(*s)){
    serror(1);
    return 0.0;
  }
  return vars[toupper(*token)-'A'];
}
```

As this function is written, it will actually accept long variable names, but only the first letter is significant. You may change this to fit your needs.

You must also modify the **atom( )** function to handle both numbers and variables. The new version is shown here:

```
// Get the value of a number or a variable.
void parser::atom(double &result)
{
  switch(tok_type) {
    case VARIABLE:
      result = find_var(token);
      get_token();
      return;
    case NUMBER:
      result = atof(token);
      get_token();
      return;
    default:
      serror(0);
  }
}
```

Technically, these additions are all that is needed for the parser to use variables correctly; however, there is no way for these variables to be assigned a value. Often this is done outside the parser, but you can treat the equal sign as an assignment operator (which is the way that it is handled in C++) and make it part of the parser. There are various ways to do this. One method is to add another function, called **eval_exp1( )**, to the **parser** class. This function will now begin the recursive-descent chain. This means that it, not **eval_exp2( )**, must be called by **eval_exp( )** to begin parsing the expression. **eval_exp1( )** is shown here:

```
// Process an assignment.
void parser::eval_exp1(double &result)
{
  int slot;
  char ttok_type;
  char temp_token[80];
```

```
if(tok_type==VARIABLE) {
  // save old token
  strcpy(temp_token, token);
  ttok_type = tok_type;

  // compute the index of the variable
  slot = toupper(*token) - 'A';

  get_token();
  if(*token != '=') {
    putback(); // return current token
    // restore old token - not assignment
    strcpy(token, temp_token);
    tok_type = ttok_type;
  }
  else {
    get_token(); // get next part of exp
    eval_exp2(result);
    vars[slot] = result;
    return;
  }
}

eval_exp2(result);
}
```

As you can see, the function needs to look ahead to determine whether an assignment is actually being made. This is because a variable name always precedes an assignment, but a variable name alone does not guarantee that an assignment expression follows. That is, the parser will accept A = 100 as an assignment, but is also smart enough to know that A/10 is not an assignment. To accomplish this, **eval_exp1( )** reads the next token from the input stream. If it is not an equal sign, the token is returned to the input stream for later use by calling **putback( )**. The **putback( )** function must also be included in the **parser** class. It is shown here:

```
// Return a token to the input stream.
void parser::putback()
{
  char *t;

  t = token;
  for(; *t; t++) exp_ptr--;
}
```

After making all the necessary changes, the parser will now look like this:

```cpp
/* This module contains the recursive descent
   parser that recognizes variables.
*/

#include <iostream.h>
#include <stdlib.h>
#include <ctype.h>
#include <string.h>

enum types { DELIMITER = 1, VARIABLE, NUMBER};

const int NUMVARS = 26;

class parser {
  char *exp_ptr;  // points to the expression
  char token[80]; // holds current token
  char tok_type;  // holds token's type
  double vars[NUMVARS]; // holds variables' values

  void eval_exp1(double &result);
  void eval_exp2(double &result);
  void eval_exp3(double &result);
  void eval_exp4(double &result);
  void eval_exp5(double &result);
  void eval_exp6(double &result);
  void atom(double &result);
  void get_token();
  void putback();
  void serror(int error);
  double find_var(char *s);
  int isdelim(char c);
public:
  parser();
  double eval_exp(char *exp);
};

// parser constructor
parser::parser()
{
  int i;

  exp_ptr = NULL;

  for(i=0; i<NUMVARS; i++) vars[i] = 0.0;
}

// Parser entry point.
double parser::eval_exp(char *exp)
```

```
{
  double result;

  exp_ptr = exp;

  get_token();
  if(!*token) {
    serror(2); // no expression present
    return 0.0;
  }
  eval_exp1(result);
  if(*token) serror(0); // last token must be null
  return result;
}

// Process an assignment.
void parser::eval_exp1(double &result)
{
  int slot;
  char ttok_type;
  char temp_token[80];

  if(tok_type==VARIABLE) {
    // save old token
    strcpy(temp_token, token);
    ttok_type = tok_type;

    // compute the index of the variable
    slot = toupper(*token) - 'A';

    get_token();
    if(*token != '=') {
      putback(); // return current token
      // restore old token - not assignment
      strcpy(token, temp_token);
      tok_type = ttok_type;
    }
    else {
      get_token(); // get next part of exp
      eval_exp2(result);
      vars[slot] = result;
      return;
    }
  }

  eval_exp2(result);
}
```

```cpp
// Add or subtract two terms.
void parser::eval_exp2(double &result)
{
  register char op;
  double temp;

  eval_exp3(result);
  while((op = *token) == '+' || op == '-') {
    get_token();
    eval_exp3(temp);
    switch(op) {
      case '-':
        result = result - temp;
        break;
      case '+':
        result = result + temp;
        break;
    }
  }
}

// Multiply or divide two factors.
void parser::eval_exp3(double &result)
{
  register char op;
  double temp;

  eval_exp4(result);
  while((op = *token) == '*' || op == '/' || op == '%') {
    get_token();
    eval_exp4(temp);
    switch(op) {
      case '*':
        result = result * temp;
        break;
      case '/':
        result = result / temp;
        break;
      case '%':
        result = (int) result % (int) temp;
        break;
    }
  }
}

// Process an exponent
void parser::eval_exp4(double &result)
{
```

```
    double temp, ex;
    register int t;

    eval_exp5(result);
    if(*token== '^') {
      get_token();
      eval_exp4(temp);
      ex = result;
      if(temp==0.0) {
        result = 1.0;
        return;
      }
      for(t=(int)temp-1; t>0; --t) result = result * (double)ex;
    }
}

// Evaluate a unary + or -.
void parser::eval_exp5(double &result)
{
  register char  op;

  op = 0;
  if((tok_type == DELIMITER) && *token=='+' || *token == '-') {
    op = *token;
    get_token();
  }
  eval_exp6(result);
  if(op=='-') result = -result;
}

// Process a parenthesized expression.
void parser::eval_exp6(double &result)
{
  if((*token == '(')) {
    get_token();
    eval_exp2(result);
    if(*token != ')')
      serror(1);
    get_token();
  }
  else atom(result);
}

// Get the value of a number or a variable.
void parser::atom(double &result)
{
  switch(tok_type) {
    case VARIABLE:
```

3

```
          result = find_var(token);
          get_token();
          return;
        case NUMBER:
          result = atof(token);
          get_token();
          return;
        default:
          serror(0);
    }
}

// Return a token to the input stream.
void parser::putback()
{
  char *t;

  t = token;
  for(; *t; t++) exp_ptr--;
}

// Display a syntax error.
void parser::serror(int error)
{
  static char *e[]= {
      "Syntax Error",
      "Unbalanced Parentheses",
      "No Expression Present"
  };
  cout << e[error] << endl;
}

// Obtain the next token.
void parser::get_token()
{
  register char *temp;

  tok_type = 0;
  temp = token;
  *temp = '\0';

  if(!*exp_ptr) return; // at end of expression

  while(isspace(*exp_ptr)) ++exp_ptr; // skip over white space

  if(strchr("+-*/%^=()", *exp_ptr)){
    tok_type = DELIMITER;
    // advance to next char
```

```
    *temp++ = *exp_ptr++;
  }
  else if(isalpha(*exp_ptr)) {
    while(!isdelim(*exp_ptr)) *temp++ = *exp_ptr++;
    tok_type = VARIABLE;
  }
  else if(isdigit(*exp_ptr)) {
    while(!isdelim(*exp_ptr)) *temp++ = *exp_ptr++;
    tok_type = NUMBER;
  }

  *temp = '\0';
}


// Return true if c is a delimiter.
int parser::isdelim(char c)
{
  if(strchr(" +-/*%^=()", c) || c==9 || c=='\r' || c==0)
    return 1;
  return 0;
}


// Return the value of a variable.
double parser::find_var(char *s)
{
  if(!isalpha(*s)){
    serror(1);
    return 0.0;
  }
  return vars[toupper(*token)-'A'];
}
```

3

To try the enhanced parser, you may use the same **main( )** function that you used for the simple parser. With the enhanced parser, you can now enter expressions like

    A = 10/4
    A – B
    C = A * (F – 21)

Syntax Checking in a Recursive-Descent Parser

Before moving on to the template version of the parser, let's briefly look at syntax checking. In expression parsing, a syntax error is simply a situation in which the input expression does not conform to the strict rules required by the parser. Most of the time, this is caused by human error—usually typing mistakes. For example, the following expressions are not valid for the parsers in this chapter:

```
10 ** 8
(10 – 5) * 9)
/8
```

The first contains two operators in a row, the second has unbalanced parentheses, and the last has a division sign at the start of an expression. None of these conditions is allowed by the parsers. Because syntax errors can cause the parser to give erroneous results, you need to guard against them.

As you studied the code of the parsers, you probably noticed the **serror( )** function, which is called under certain situations. Unlike many other parsers, the recursive-descent method makes syntax checking easy because, for the most part, it occurs in **atom( )**, **find_var( )**, or **eval_exp6( )**, where parentheses are checked. The only problem with the syntax checking as it now stands is that the entire parser is not aborted on syntax error. This can lead to multiple error messages.

The best way to implement the **serror( )** function is to have it execute some sort of reset. For example, all C++ compilers come with a pair of companion functions called **setjmp( )** and **longjmp( )**. These two functions allow a program to branch to a *different* function. Therefore, **serror( )** could execute a **longjmp( )** to some safe point in your program outside the parser.

Depending upon the use you put the parser to, you might also find that C++'s exception handling mechanism (implemented through **try**, **catch**, and **throw**) will be beneficial when handling errors.

If you leave the code the way it is, multiple syntax-error messages may be issued. This can be an annoyance in some situations, but it can be a blessing in others, because multiple errors may be caught. Generally, however, you will want to enhance the syntax checking before using it in commercial programs.

Building a Generic Parser

The two preceding parsers operated on numeric expressions in which all values were assumed to be of type **double**. While this is fine for applications that use **double** values, it is certainly excessive for applications that use only integer values, for example. Also, by hard-coding the type of values being evaluated, the application of the parser is unnecessarily restricted. Fortunately, using a class template it is an easy task to create a generic version of the parser that can work with any type of data for which algebraic-style expressions are defined. Once this has been done, the parser can be used with both built-in types and with numeric types that you create.

Here is the generic version of the expression parser:

```
// A generic parser.

#include <iostream.h>
#include <stdlib.h>
#include <ctype.h>
#include <string.h>

enum types { DELIMITER = 1, VARIABLE, NUMBER};

const int NUMVARS = 26;

template <class PType> class parser {
  char *exp_ptr;  // points to the expression
  char token[80]; // holds current token
  char tok_type;  // holds token's type
  PType vars[NUMVARS]; // holds variable's values

  void eval_exp1(PType &result);
  void eval_exp2(PType &result);
  void eval_exp3(PType &result);
  void eval_exp4(PType &result);
  void eval_exp5(PType &result);
  void eval_exp6(PType &result);
  void atom(PType &result);
  void get_token(), putback();
  void serror(int error);
  PType find_var(char *s);
  int isdelim(char c);
public:
  parser();
  PType eval_exp(char *exp);
};

// parser constructor
template <class PType> parser<PType>::parser()
{
  int i;

  exp_ptr = NULL;

  for(i=0; i<NUMVARS; i++) vars[i] = (PType) 0;
}
```

```cpp
// Parser entry point.
template <class PType> PType parser<PType>::eval_exp(char *exp)
{
  PType result;

  exp_ptr = exp;

  get_token();
  if(!*token) {
    serror(2); // no expression present
    return (PType) 0;
  }
  eval_exp1(result);
  if(*token) serror(0); // last token must be null
  return result;
}

// Process an assignment.
template <class PType> void parser<PType>::eval_exp1(PType &result)
{
  int slot;
  char ttok_type;
  char temp_token[80];

  if(tok_type==VARIABLE) {
    // save old token
    strcpy(temp_token, token);
    ttok_type = tok_type;

    // compute the index of the variable
    slot = toupper(*token) - 'A';

    get_token();
    if(*token != '=') {
      putback(); // return current token
      // restore old token - not assignment
      strcpy(token, temp_token);
      tok_type = ttok_type;
    }
    else {
      get_token(); // get next part of exp
      eval_exp2(result);
      vars[slot] = result;
      return;
    }
  }
```

```cpp
    eval_exp2(result);
}

// Add or subtract two terms.
template <class PType> void parser<PType>::eval_exp2(PType &result)
{
  register char op;
  PType temp;

  eval_exp3(result);
  while((op = *token) == '+' || op == '-') {
    get_token();
    eval_exp3(temp);
    switch(op) {
      case '-':
        result = result - temp;
        break;
      case '+':
        result = result + temp;
        break;
    }
  }
}

// Multiply or divide two factors.
template <class PType> void parser<PType>::eval_exp3(PType &result)
{
  register char op;
  PType temp;

  eval_exp4(result);
  while((op = *token) == '*' || op == '/' || op == '%') {
    get_token();
    eval_exp4(temp);
    switch(op) {
      case '*':
        result = result * temp;
        break;
      case '/':
        result = result / temp;
        break;
      case '%':
        result = (int) result % (int) temp;
        break;
    }
  }
}
```

3

```cpp
// Process an exponent
template <class PType> void parser<PType>::eval_exp4(PType &result)
{
  PType temp, ex;
  register int t;

  eval_exp5(result);
  if(*token== '^') {
    get_token();
    eval_exp4(temp);
    ex = result;
    if(temp==0.0) {
      result = (PType) 1;
      return;
    }
    for(t=(int)temp-1; t>0; --t) result = result * ex;
  }
}

// Evaluate a unary + or -.
template <class PType> void parser<PType>::eval_exp5(PType &result)
{
  register char  op;

  op = 0;
  if((tok_type == DELIMITER) && *token=='+' || *token == '-') {
    op = *token;
    get_token();
  }
  eval_exp6(result);
  if(op=='-') result = -result;
}

// Process a parenthesized expression.
template <class PType> void parser<PType>::eval_exp6(PType &result)
{
  if((*token == '(')) {
    get_token();
    eval_exp2(result);
    if(*token != ')')
      serror(1);
    get_token();
  }
```

```cpp
    else atom(result);
}

// Get the value of a number or a variable.
template <class PType> void parser<PType>::atom(PType &result)
{
  switch(tok_type) {
    case VARIABLE:
      result = find_var(token);
      get_token();
      return;
    case NUMBER:
      result = (PType) atof(token);
      get_token();
      return;
    default:
      serror(0);
  }
}

// Return a token to the input stream.
template <class PType> void parser<PType>::putback()
{
  char *t;

  t = token;
  for(; *t; t++) exp_ptr--;
}

// Display a syntax error.
template <class PType> void parser<PType>::serror(int error)
{
  static char *e[]= {
      "Syntax Error",
      "Unbalanced Parentheses",
      "No Expression Present"
  };
  cout << e[error] << endl;
}

// Obtain the next token.
template <class PType> void parser<PType>::get_token()
{
  register char *temp;
```

```
      tok_type = 0;
      temp = token;
      *temp = '\0';

      if(!*exp_ptr) return; // at end of expression

      while(isspace(*exp_ptr)) ++exp_ptr; // skip over white space

      if(strchr("+-*/%^=()", *exp_ptr)){
        tok_type = DELIMITER;
        // advance to next char
        *temp++ = *exp_ptr++;
      }
      else if(isalpha(*exp_ptr)) {
        while(!isdelim(*exp_ptr)) *temp++ = *exp_ptr++;
        tok_type = VARIABLE;
      }
      else if(isdigit(*exp_ptr)) {
        while(!isdelim(*exp_ptr)) *temp++ = *exp_ptr++;
        tok_type = NUMBER;
      }

      *temp = '\0';
    }

    // Return true if c is a delimiter.
    template <class PType> int parser<PType>::isdelim(char c)
    {
      if(strchr(" +-/*%^=()", c) || c==9 || c=='\r' || c==0)
        return 1;
      return 0;
    }

    // Return the value of a variable.
    template <class PType> PType parser<PType>::find_var(char *s)
    {
      if(!isalpha(*s)){
        serror(1);
        return (PType) 0;
      }
      return vars[toupper(*token)-'A'];
    }
```

As you can see, the type of data now operated upon by the parser is specified by the generic type **PType**. The following **main( )** function demonstrates the generic parser:

```
main()
{
  char expstr[80];

  // Demonstrate floating-point parser.
  parser<double> ob;

  cout << "Floating-point parser.  ";
  cout << "Enter a period to stop\n";
  for(;;) {
    cout << "Enter expression: ";
    cin.getline(expstr, 79);
    if(*expstr=='.') break;
    cout << "Answer is: " << ob.eval_exp(expstr) << "\n\n";
  }
  cout << endl;

  // Demonstrate integer-based parser.
  parser<int> Iob;

  cout << "Integer parser.  ";
  cout << "Enter a period to stop\n";
  for(;;) {
    cout << "Enter expression: ";
    cin.getline(expstr, 79);
    if(*expstr=='.') break;
    cout << "Answer is: " << Iob.eval_exp(expstr) << "\n\n";
  }

  return 0;
}
```

Here is a sample run.

    Floating-point parser. Enter a period to stop
    Enter expression: a=10.1
    Answer is: 10.1

    Enter expression: b=3.2
    Answer is: 3.2

    Enter expression: a/b
    Answer is: 3.15625

    Enter expression: .

Integer parser. Enter a period to stop
Enter expression: a=10
Answer is: 10

Enter expression: b=3
Answer is: 3

Enter expression: a/b
Answer is: 3

Enter expression: .

As you can see, the floating-point parser uses floating-point values, and the integer parser uses integer values.

Some Things to Try

As mentioned early on in this chapter, only minimal error checking is performed by the parser. You might want to add detailed error reporting. For example, you could highlight the point in the expression at which an error was detected. This would allow the user to find and correct a syntax error.

As the parser now stands, it can evaluate only numeric expressions. However, with a few additions, it is possible to enable the parser to evaluate other types of expressions, such as strings, spatial coordinates, or complex numbers. For example, to allow the parser to evaluate string objects, you must make the following changes:

1. Define a string class, including all necessary operators.
2. Define a new token type called STRING.
3. Enhance **get_token( )** so that it recognizes double-quoted strings.
4. Add a new case inside **atom( )** that handles STRING type tokens.

After implementing these steps, the parser could handle string expressions like these:

```
a = "one"
b = "two"
c = a + b
```

The result in **c** should be the concatenation of **a** and **b**, or "onetwo".

Here is one good application for the parser: create a simple, pop-up application that accepts an expression entered by the user and then displays the result. This would make an excellent addition to nearly any commercial application. If you are programming for Windows, this would be especially easy to do.

3

Chapter

4

Sparse Arrays C++ Style

One of the more intriguing programming problems is the implementation of a sparse array. A *sparse array* is one in which not all the elements of the array are actually in use, present, or needed. Sparse arrays are valuable when both of the following conditions are met: the size of the array required by an application is quite large (possibly exceeding available memory), and not all array locations will be used. Thus, a sparse array is typically a thinly populated, large array. As you will see, there are several ways in which sparse arrays can be implemented. While important in their own right, the sparse-array techniques presented in this chapter have a second purpose: they show the way that some of C++'s most sophisticated features can be used to provide simple, elegant solutions to a classic programming problem. Also, because of C++'s ability to overload the [ ] operator, sparse arrays can be fully integrated into your programming environment.

This chapter examines four distinct techniques for creating a generic sparse array: the linked list, the binary tree, the pointer array, and hashing. Each approach is implemented as a template class. Thus, each approach can be used to create sparse arrays of any type of data. The sparse-array classes are constructed by modifying and enhancing the bounded-array container class described in Chapter 2.

However, before beginning, let's restate the problem that sparse arrays are designed to solve.

Understanding the Reason for Sparse Arrays

To understand the need for sparse arrays, consider the following two points.

♦ When you declare a normal C++ array, all of the memory required by the array is allocated at that time.

♦ Large arrays—especially multidimensional arrays—can consume vast quantities of memory.

Let's examine the implication of these statements. The fact that memory for an array is allocated when the array is created means that the largest array you can declare within your program is limited (in part) by the amount of available memory. If you need an array larger than will fit within the physical confines of your computer, you must use some other mechanism to support the array. (For example, a fully populated large array typically uses some form of virtual memory.) Even if the large array will fit in memory, it may not always be a good idea, because it may have a negative impact on the rest of your program or the computer system in general. As just stated, when you declare an array in C++, all of the memory required by that array is set aside. This means that none of it can be used by other parts of your program or any other processes running in the system. In situations where not all array locations will actually be used, allocating memory for a large array is especially wasteful of system resources.

To solve the problems caused by large, thinly populated arrays, several sparse-array techniques have been invented. All sparse-array techniques share one thing in common: they allocate memory for elements of the array only as needed. Therefore, the advantage of a sparse array is that it only requires memory for elements actually in use. This leaves the rest of memory free for other uses. It also allows extremely large arrays—larger than would normally be allowed by the system—to be employed.

There are numerous examples of applications that require sparse-array processing. Many apply to matrix operations or to scientific and engineering problems that are easily understood only by experts in those fields. However, there is one very familiar application that typically uses a sparse array: a spreadsheet program. Even though the matrix of the average spreadsheet is very large, only a portion of the matrix is actually in use at any one time. Spreadsheets use the matrix to hold formulas, values, and strings associated with each location. Using a sparse array, storage for each element is allocated from the pool of free memory as it is needed. Because only a small portion of the array elements is actually being used, the array (that is, the spreadsheet) may appear very large while only requiring memory for those cells actually in use.

There are two terms which will be used repeatedly in this chapter: *logical array* and *physical array*. The logical array is the array that you think of as existing in the system. The physical array is the array that actually exists inside the computer. For example, if you define the following sparse array:

ArrayType arrayob[100000];

the logical array consists of 100,000 elements—even if this array does not physically exist within the computer. Thus, if only 100 elements of this array were actually in use, then only 100 elements would be taking up physical memory space inside the computer. The sparse-array techniques developed in this chapter provide the link between the logical and physical arrays.

4

Sparse-Array Objects

Most implementations of sparse arrays, including those in this chapter, utilize some type of object to hold those elements of the array that are actually in use. Most often, this object contains at least two pieces of information: the logical index of the element and the value of the element. However, different approaches may require more or less information. The sparse-array classes developed in this chapter will use objects of type **ArrayOb**. The version of this class that will be used by three of the four implementations is shown here. (A slightly altered version is required for the fourth approach to sparse arrays.)

```
/* This class defines the type of object
   stored in the sparse array.
*/
template <class DataT> class ArrayOb {
public:
  long index; // index of array element
  DataT info; // information
};
```

Here, **index** will contain the logical index of the element, and **info** will contain its value. For example, assuming a sparse array called **Sparse**, then

```
Sparse[987343] = 10;
```

would store an **ArrayOb** object in the physical array in which **index** contains the value 987,343 (which is the logical index), and **info** contains the value 10.

As you can see, **ArrayOb** is a template class in which the type of the data is specified by the generic type **DataT**. The type of **index** is **long** so that large arrays can be supported. This class will be inherited by the sparse-array classes described in the remainder of this chapter.

The Linked-List Sparse Array

One of the easiest ways to implement a sparse array is to use a linked list to store those elements of the array that are actually in use. That is, the physical array is implemented as a linked list. Using this approach, whenever the logical array is indexed, the list is searched and the value associated with that index is returned. To support the linked-list approach, the linked-list class developed in Chapter 2 is reworked and optimized for sparse arrays.

The entire linked-list sparse-array class is shown here, along with a short **main( )** function that demonstrates it.

```
/*
   A generic sparse array class
   that uses a linked list.
*/
#include <iostream.h>
#include <stdlib.h>

/* This class defines the type of object
   stored in the sparse array.
*/
template <class DataT> class ArrayOb {
public:
  long index; // index of array element
  DataT info; // information
};

// Linked list array object for sparse arrays.
template <class DataT>
class SparseOb: public ArrayOb<DataT> {
public:
```

```
    SparseOb<DataT> *next;  // pointer to next object
    SparseOb<DataT> *prior; // pointer to previous object

    SparseOb() {
      info = 0;
      index = -1;
      next = NULL;
      prior = NULL;
    };
};

// A generic doubly linked list class for sparse arrays.
template <class DataT>
class SparseList : public SparseOb<DataT> {
  SparseOb<DataT> *start, *end;
public:
  SparseList() { start = end = NULL; }
  ~SparseList();

  void store(long ix, DataT c); // store element
  void remove(long ix); // delete element

  // return pointer to element given index
  SparseOb<DataT> *find(long ix);
};

// SparseList destructor.
template <class DataT> SparseList<DataT>::~SparseList()
{
  SparseOb<DataT> *p, *p1;

  // free all elements in the list
  p = start;
  while(p) {
    p1 = p->next;
    delete p;
    p = p1;
  }
}

// Add element to array.
template <class DataT>
void SparseList<DataT>::store(long ix, DataT c)
{
  SparseOb<DataT> *p;

  p = new SparseOb<DataT>;
  if(!p) {
```

```
    cout << "Allocation error.\n";
    exit(1);
  }

  p->info = c;
  p->index = ix;

  if(start==NULL) { // first element in list
    end = start = p;
  }
  else { // put on end
    p->prior = end;
    end->next = p;
    end = p;
  }
}

/* Remove an element from the array given its index
   and update start and end pointers.
*/
template <class DataT>
void SparseList<DataT>::remove(long ix)
{
  SparseOb<DataT> *ob;

  ob = find(ix); // get pointer to element
  if(!ob) return; // array element does not exist

  if(ob->prior) { // not deleting first element
    ob->prior->next = ob->next;
    if(ob->next) // not deleting last element
      ob->next->prior = ob->prior;
    else // otherwise, deleting last element
      end = ob->prior;   // update end pointer
  }
  else {  // deleting first element
    if(ob->next) { // list not empty
      ob->next->prior = NULL;
      start = ob->next;
    }
    else // list now empty
      start = end = NULL;
  }
}

// Find an array element given its index.
```

```cpp
template <class DataT>
SparseOb<DataT> *SparseList<DataT>::find(long ix)
{
  SparseOb<DataT> *temp;

  temp = start;

  while(temp) {
    if(ix==temp->index) return temp; // found
    temp = temp->next;
  }
  return NULL; // not in list
}

// A generic sparse array class.
template <class DataT>
class SparseArray : public SparseList<DataT>{
  long length; // dimension of array
public:
  SparseArray(long size) { length = size; }
  DataT &operator[](long i);
};

// Index into the sparse array
template <class DataT>
DataT &SparseArray<DataT>::operator[](long ix)
{
  if(ix<0 || ix>length-1) {
    cout << "\nIndex value of ";
    cout << ix << " is out-of-bounds.\n";
    exit(1);
  }

  SparseOb<DataT> *o;

  o = find(ix); // get pointer to element
  if(!o) { // new entry into array
    store(ix, 0); // store new element
    o = find(ix); // get pointer to the new element
  }

  return o->info;
}

main()
{
```

```
SparseArray<int> iob(100000);
SparseArray<double> dob(100000);
int i;

cout << "Here is an array of integers: " << endl;
// put some values into the array
for(i=0; i<5; i++) iob[i] = i;
for(i=0; i<5; i++) cout << iob[i] << " ";
cout << endl;

// assign one array element to another
iob[2] = iob[3];
for(i=0; i<5; i++) cout << iob[i] << " ";
cout << endl;

// add some more elements
iob[1000] = 9345;
iob[2000] = iob[1000] + 100;

cout << iob[1000] << " " << iob[2000] << endl;

cout << "Here is an array of doubles: " << endl;
for(i=0; i<5; i++) dob[i*100] = (double) i *1.19;
for(i=0; i<5; i++) cout << dob[i*100] << " ";
cout << endl;

// access a location that has not been given a value
dob[200] = dob[999];
cout << dob[200] << " " << dob[999] << endl;

return 0;
}
```

A Closer Look at the Linked-List Approach

The linked-list approach to a sparse array is implemented using a multilevel class hierarchy of template classes. The topmost class is **ArrayOb**. **ArrayOb** is inherited by **SparseOb**, which is then inherited by **SparseList**, which is finally inherited by **SparseArray**. This hierarchy is shown here:

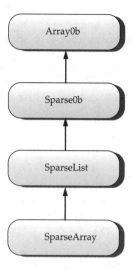

The linked-list classes **SparseOb** and **SparseList** are slightly modified versions of **listob** and **dllist** from Chapter 2. For example, the **find( )** function now searches the linked list for an array index. However, their basic logic is unchanged, and they should present no surprises. (If you are unsure about how the linked-list classes operate, refer to Chapter 2.) Although the sparse-array class **SparseArray** does not make use of the **remove( )** member function of **SparseList**, this function might be useful in your own applications. It could be used, for example, to perform garbage collection to reclaim deleted elements.

Sparse arrays are declared by instantiating objects of type **SparseArray**, specifying the type of data and the size of the array (as shown in the program). Since the linked list used to support the sparse array is technically unbounded, there is no theoretical need to actually specify the size of the logical array when creating a sparse array. However, by storing the size of the logical array, **SparseArray** is able to detect an out-of-bounds index.

The most interesting portion of the program is found in the **SparseArray** class. It is shown here for your convenience:

```
// A generic sparse array class.
template <class DataT>
class SparseArray : public SparseList<DataT>{
  long length; // dimension of array
public:
  SparseArray(long size) { length = size; }
  DataT &operator[](long i);
};

// Index into the sparse array
```

4

```
template <class DataT>
DataT &SparseArray<DataT>::operator[](long ix)
{
  if(ix<0 || ix>length-1) {
    cout << "\nIndex value of ";
    cout << ix << " is out-of-bounds.\n";
    exit(1);
  }

  SparseOb<DataT> *o;

  o = find(ix); // get pointer to element
  if(!o) { // new entry into array
    store(ix, 0); // store new element
    o = find(ix); // get pointer to the new element
  }

  return o->info;
}
```

The key to the operation of the sparse array is found in the **operator[ ]( )** function. Remember, each time the array is indexed, this function is invoked. Inside the function, the range of the index is checked to prevent boundary errors. Next, the function attempts to find the element in the list given its index. If the element is already in the list, a reference to its information is returned. If the element is not currently in the list, then a new entry for it is created and put into the list. Next, a pointer to the new element is obtained, and the function returns a reference to its information. This simple, yet effective mechanism works in all cases. For example, consider the following code fragment:

```
SparseArray<int> ob(100000);
int x;

aob[1] = 10; // statement 1
x = ob[1];  // statement 2
```

In the first statement, **operator[ ]( )** is invoked with the index of 1 as its **ix** parameter. Inside **operator[ ]( )** the list is searched for this index. Since this is the first reference to index 1, it is not found. This causes the index to be added to the list with an initial value of zero. Next, a pointer to this object is obtained. Finally, a reference to the **info** member of this object is returned. This reference is then used to assign the **info** member associated with index 1 the value 10. When the second statement executes, the **operator[ ]( )** function is again executed with **ix** containing the index 1. This time, 1 is found in the list, and a reference to its **info** member is returned. Since 1's

info member now contains the value 10, it is this value that is assigned to **x**. As you can see, memory for array elements is only allocated when they are actually used.

Before moving on, you might want to add several **cout** statements to the example program, observing what happens each time **operator[ ]( )** is invoked.

Analysis of the Linked-List Approach

The principal advantage of the linked-list approach to sparse arrays is that it makes efficient use of memory—memory is only used for those elements in the array that actually contain information. It is also simple to implement. However, it has one major drawback: it must use a linear search to access elements in the list. This means that the search time will be proportional to *n*/2, where *n* is the number of elements in the list. For very sparse arrays, this will not be a problem. If the physical array contains several elements, then the search time may be unacceptable. However, you can improve access time by using a binary tree to support the sparse array, as shown next.

The Binary-Tree Approach to Sparse Arrays

In essence, a binary tree is simply a modified doubly linked list. Its major advantage over a list is that it can be searched quickly, which means that insertions and lookups can be very fast. In applications where you want a linked-list structure but need fast search times, the binary tree is the answer. The following program implements a sparse array using a binary tree to store the physical array.

```
/*
    A generic sparse array class
    that uses a binary tree.
*/
#include <iostream.h>
#include <stdlib.h>

/* This class defines the type of object
    stored in the sparse array.
*/
template <class DataT> class ArrayOb {
public:
  long index; // index of array element
  DataT info; // information
};

// A generic binary tree for sparse arrays.
```

```
template <class DataT>
class SparseTree : public ArrayOb<DataT> {
public:
  SparseTree *left;
  SparseTree *right;
  SparseTree *root;

  SparseTree() { root = NULL; }
  void store(SparseTree *r, SparseTree *previous,
             long ix, DataT info);
  SparseTree *dtree(SparseTree *r, long ix);
  SparseTree *find(SparseTree *r, long ix);
};

// Store an element in the array.
template <class DataT>
void SparseTree<DataT>::store(SparseTree *r,
                              SparseTree *previous,
                              long ix, DataT info)
{
  if(!r) {
    r = new SparseTree;
    if(!r) {
      cout << "Out of Memory\n";
      exit(1);
    }
    r->left = NULL;
    r->right = NULL;
    r->info = info;
    r->index = ix;
    if(!root) root = r; // first entry
    else {
      if(ix < previous->index) previous->left = r;
      else previous->right = r;
    }
    return;
  }

  if(ix<r->index)
    store(r->left, r, ix, info);
  else
    store(r->right, r, ix, info);
}

// Remove an element from the array.
template <class DataT>
SparseTree<DataT> *SparseTree<DataT>::dtree(
                        SparseTree *r, long ix)
```

```
     {
       SparseTree *p, *p2;

       if(!r) return r; // not found

       if(r->index==ix) { // delete root
         // this means an empty tree
         if(r->left==r->right){
           free(r);
           if(r==root) root = NULL;
           return NULL;
         }
         // or if one subtree is null
         else if(r->left==NULL) {
           p = r->right;
           free(r);
           if(r==root) root = p;
           return p;
         }
         else if(r->right==NULL) {
           p = r->left;
           free(r);
           if(r==root) root = p;
           return p;
         }
         // or both subtrees present
         else {
           p2 = r->right;
           p = r->right;
           while(p->left) p = p->left;
           p->left = r->left;
           free(r);
           if(r==root) root = p2;
           return p2;
         }
       }
       if(r->index < ix) r->right = dtree(r->right, ix);
       else r->left = dtree(r->left, ix);
       return r;
     }

     // Find an element given an index.
     template <class DataT>
     SparseTree<DataT> *
     SparseTree<DataT>::find(SparseTree *r, long ix)
     {
       if(!r) return r;  // empty tree
       while(r->index != ix) {
```

```
      if(ix < r->index) r = r->left;
      else r = r->right;
      if(r==NULL) break;
    }
    return r;
}

// A generic sparse array class.
template <class DataT>
class SparseArray : public SparseTree<DataT>{
  long length; // dimension of array
public:
  SparseArray(long size) { length = size; }
  DataT &operator[](long i);
};

// Index into the sparse array
template <class DataT>
DataT &SparseArray<DataT>::operator[](long ix)
{
  if(ix<0 || ix>length-1) {
    cout << "\nIndex value of ";
    cout << ix << " is out-of-bounds.\n";
    exit(1);
  }

  SparseTree<DataT> *o;

  o = find(this->root, ix); // get pointer to element
  if(!o) { // new entry into array
    store(this->root, NULL,  ix, 0); // store new element
    o = find(this->root, ix); // get pointer to the new element
  }

  return o->info;
}

main()
{
  SparseArray<int> iob(100000);
  SparseArray<double> dob(100000);
  int i;

  cout << "Here is an array of integers: " << endl;
  // put some values into the array
  for(i=0; i<5; i++) iob[i] = i;
  for(i=0; i<5; i++) cout << iob[i] << " ";
  cout << endl;
```

```
    // assign one array element to another
    iob[2] = iob[3];
    for(i=0; i<5; i++) cout << iob[i] << " ";
    cout << endl;

    // add some more elements
    iob[1000] = 9345;
    iob[2000] = iob[1000] + 100;

    cout << iob[1000] << " " << iob[2000] << endl;

    cout << "Here is an array of doubles: " << endl;
    for(i=0; i<5; i++) dob[i*100] = (double) i *1.19;
    for(i=0; i<5; i++) cout << dob[i*100] << " ";
    cout << endl;

    // access a location that has not been given a value
    dob[200] = dob[999];
    cout << dob[200] << " " << dob[999] << endl;

    return 0;
}
```

4

A Closer Look at the Binary-Tree Approach

Like the linked-list, the binary-tree approach to a sparse array is
implemented by use of a multilevel class hierarchy of template classes. As
before, the topmost class is **ArrayOb**. **ArrayOb** is inherited by
SparseTree, which is finally inherited by **SparseArray**. This hierarchy is
shown here:

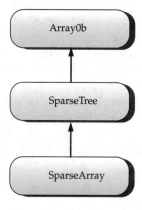

The binary-tree class **SparseTree** is a slightly modified version of the **tree** class from Chapter 2. However, its basic logic is the same and should present no surprises. (If you are unsure about how the **SparseTree** class operates, refer to Chapter 2.) The **SparseArray** class is essentially unchanged except that its **operator[ ]( )** function now uses the **store( )** and **find( )** functions defined by **SparseTree( )**.

Analysis of the Binary-Tree Approach

A binary tree results in much faster search times than a linked list. Remember, a sequential search requires, on average, $n/2$ comparisons, where n is the number of elements in the list. A binary search, in contrast, requires only $\log_2 n$ comparisons. However, such search times assume a balanced tree. Thus, you may need to add a mechanism to balance a severely out-of-balance tree in some applications. This, of course, will add overhead.

The Pointer-Array Approach to Sparse Arrays

Both the linked-list and binary-tree approaches to implementing a sparse array require a search phase each time an array element is accessed. Although the binary-tree approach is faster, neither approach approximates the fast access time that is achieved by indexing a normal array. However, there are two approaches to sparse arrays that can narrow this gap. The first method to be examined involves the use of a pointer array.

Let's begin with a short thought experiment. Imagine that you need a 1,000-element array of objects, with each object being 1,000 bytes long. Further, assume that the array will not be fully populated. If you declared this as a normal array, it would occupy 1 million bytes of memory. However, if you declared a 1,000-element array of *pointers to the objects,* then the resulting pointer array would only be 4,000 bytes long (assuming 4-byte addresses). Therefore, this array of pointers would require significantly less permanent storage than the array objects. To use the pointer array to store information, use the following method. To put an object into the array, allocate memory for that object, and then set the appropriate element in the pointer array so that it points to that object. This scheme offers superior performance over the linked-list and binary-tree methods. In fact, it is only one level of indirection worse than the direct addressing utilized by normal arrays. Figure 4-1 shows how this might appear in memory, with the pointer array providing support for the sparse array.

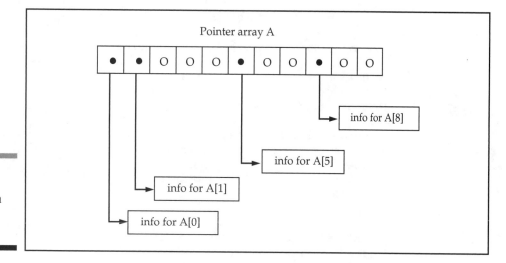

A pointer
array as
support for a
sparse array
Figure 4-1.

Here is a version of **SparseArray** that uses the pointer-array approach:

4

```
/*
   A generic sparse array class that uses
   a pointer array.
*/
#include <iostream.h>
#include <stdlib.h>

/* This class defines the type of object
   stored in the sparse array.
*/
template <class DataT> class ArrayOb {
public:
  /* For pointer array approach, the index
     no longer needs to be part of ArrayOb. */
  DataT info; // information
};

// A generic sparse array class.
template <class DataT>
class SparseArray : public ArrayOb<DataT>{
  long length; // dimension of array
  ArrayOb<DataT> **ptr; // pointer to array of pointers
public:
  SparseArray(long size);
  DataT &operator[](long i);
};
```

```cpp
// Constructor for SparseArray.
template <class DataT>
SparseArray<DataT>::SparseArray(long size)
{
  long i;

  length = size;

  // dynamically allocate array of pointers
  ptr = new ArrayOb<DataT> *[size];
  if(!ptr) {
    cout << "Cannot allocate pointer array.\n";
    exit(1);
  }

  // initialize pointer array to zero
  for(i=0; i<size; i++) {
    ptr[i] = NULL;
  }
}

// Index into the sparse array
template <class DataT>
DataT &SparseArray<DataT>::operator[](long ix)
{
  if(ix<0 || ix>length-1) {
    cout << "\nIndex value of ";
    cout << ix << " is out-of-bounds.\n";
    exit(1);
  }

  // if not currently in array, add it
  if(!ptr[ix]) {
    ptr[ix] = new ArrayOb<DataT>;
    if(ptr[ix]) ptr[ix]->info = 0;
  }

  return ptr[ix]->info;
}

main()
{
  SparseArray<int> iob(1000);
  SparseArray<double> dob(1000);
  int i;

  cout << "Here is an array of integers: " << endl;
  // put some values into the array
```

```
for(i=0; i<1000; i++) iob[i] = i;
for(i=0; i<1000; i++) cout << iob[i] << " ";
cout << endl;

// assign one array element to another
iob[2] = iob[3];
iob[91] = iob[103] = 9345;
iob[92] = iob[103] + 100;
for(i=0; i<5; i++) cout << iob[i] << " ";
cout << endl;
cout << iob[91] << " " << iob[92] << " " << iob[103] << endl;

cout << "Here is an array of doubles: " << endl;
for(i=0; i<5; i++) dob[i*10] = (double) i *1.19;
for(i=0; i<5; i++) dob[i*11] = (double) i *1.29;
for(i=0; i<5; i++)
  cout << dob[i*10] << " " << dob[i*11] << " ";

cout << endl;

// access a location that has not been given a value
dob[20] = dob[9];
cout << dob[20] << " " << dob[9];

return 0;
}
```

4

A Closer Look at the Pointer-Array Approach

As you can easily see, the code for the pointer-array method of implementing a sparse array is much shorter than the two preceding approaches. Inside the private portion of **SparseArray**, a pointer to an array of **ArrayOb** pointers, called **ptr**, has been declared. Inside the **SparseArray** constructor an array of pointers is allocated, and a pointer to this array is assigned to **ptr**. The size of the array is specified by the **size** parameter when an array object is declared. Notice that each pointer in the array is initialized to **NULL** when the **SparseArray** object is constructed. A **NULL** pointer indicates that an array location is empty.

Each time the sparse array is indexed, the **operator[ ]( )** function simply uses the same index to access the pointer array, returning a reference to the **info** member of the **ArrayOb** object pointed to by that element in the pointer array. If the pointer associated with that array location is currently **NULL**, then a new object is allocated, and a pointer to the object is stored in the pointer array.

Analysis of the Pointer-Array Approach

The pointer-array method of sparse-array handling provides much faster accessing to array elements than either the linked-list or binary-tree method. In fact, as mentioned, this approach is nearly as fast as normal array addressing. Further, all elements in the array are accessed in the same time. When you use the linked-list or binary-tree methods, elements near the end of the list will be accessed more slowly than those near the front.

The main disadvantage to the pointer-array approach is that it cannot be used in all cases. First, it can only be used in situations in which an array will be largely unpopulated. Remember, as the number of elements actually in use grows, the memory requirements of a pointer array will approach those of a normal array of the same size. Second, for very large arrays, even the pointer array will be too large to allocate.

Hashing

As you have seen, all of the preceding approaches to implementing sparse arrays have advantages and disadvantages. This naturally gives rise to the thought "Is there some way to get the best of each?" As you will see, in some cases, there is. This section will implement an approach to sparse arrays that combines the pointer array and the linked list—getting the best of both.

To begin, consider the main advantage to the pointer array: speed. Consider its main disadvantage: the entire pointer array must be allocated. For very large arrays, this restriction will prevent its use. Consider the main advantage of the linked list: memory is only used as needed. However, the linked list performs quite poorly if it contains too many elements. Fortunately, there is a way to combine these two approaches and obtain the benefits of each without their detriments. Here is how.

Each time a sparse array is created, a smaller array (say 10 percent the size of the original) is allocated. This smaller array, called the *primary array*, consists of objects which hold the index of the item, the value associated with that index, and a pointer to an overflow list. Each logical index is mapped onto the smaller, primary array and, if possible, the information associated with that logical index is stored in the primary array. Since (in this example) the primary array is one-tenth the size of the logical array, 10 logical indexes will map onto the same physical index. This means that collisions may occur. When they do, the overflow will be put into the *collision list*. Using this scheme, a relatively unpopulated sparse array will achieve very good performance, because most values will be immediately available from the primary array. In cases where collisions occur, no list will be more than 9 elements long, so search times will also be very short.

To implement the preceding approach, you need a method by which an index into the logical array is transformed into an index into the smaller primary array. The means by which this is accomplished is commonly called *hashing*. Hashing is the process of computing an index at which information will be stored from the information, itself. Traditionally, hashing has been applied to disk files as a means of decreasing access time. However, you can use the same general methods to implement sparse arrays. When applied to sparse arrays, the information that will be hashed is the element's index in the logical array. The outcome of the hash will be an index into the smaller primary array at which point the element is actually stored.

As applied to sparse arrays, the hashing algorithm can be quite simple. One easy method (and the approach used in this chapter) is simply to divide the logical index by the ratio of the size of the logical array to the primary array. For example, if the primary array is 10 percent the size of the logical array, then the logical index is divided by 10 to produce the physical index.

Applying the scheme just described, the following procedure will be used to store an element in the physical array. First, the logical index is transformed into a physical index by use of the hashing function. If that location in the primary array is free, the logical index and the value are stored there. However, since ten logical locations actually map onto one physical location, hash collisions can occur. When this happens, the entry will be put onto the collision list. A separate collision list is associated with each element in the primary array. Of course, these lists are zero length until a collision occurs. This situation is depicted in Figure 4-2. To find an element in the physical array—given its logical array index—first, transform the logical index into its hash value. Next, check the primary array at the index generated by the hash to see if the logical index stored there matches the one you are searching for. If it does, return the information. Otherwise, follow the collision list until either the proper index is found, or the end of the chain is reached. The following program implements this approach.

4

```
/*
   A generic sparse array class that uses hashing.
*/
#include <iostream.h>
#include <stdlib.h>

/* This class defines the type of object
   stored in the sparse array.
*/
template <class DataT> class ArrayOb {
public:
  long index; // index of array element
  DataT info; // information
```

```cpp
};

// Linked list array object for sparse arrays.
template <class DataT>
class SparseOb: public ArrayOb<DataT> {
public:
  SparseOb<DataT> *next;   // pointer to next object
  SparseOb<DataT> *prior; // pointer to previous object

  SparseOb() {
    info = 0;
    index = -1;
    next = NULL;
    prior = NULL;
  }
};

// A generic doubly linked list class for sparse arrays.
template <class DataT>
class SparseList : public SparseOb<DataT> {
  SparseOb<DataT> *start, *end;
public:
  SparseList() { start = end = NULL; }
  ~SparseList();

  void store(long ix, DataT c); // store element
  void remove(long ix); // delete element

  // return pointer to element given index
  SparseOb<DataT> *find(long ix);
};

// SparseList destructor.
template <class DataT> SparseList<DataT>::~SparseList()
{
  SparseOb<DataT> *p, *p1;

  // free all elements in the list
  p = start;
  while(p) {
    p1 = p->next;
    delete p;
    p = p1;
  }
}

// Add the next element.
template <class DataT>
```

```
void SparseList<DataT>::store(long ix, DataT c)
{
  SparseOb<DataT> *p;

  p = new SparseOb<DataT>;
  if(!p) {
    cout << "Allocation error.\n";
    exit(1);
  }

  p->info = c;
  p->index = ix;

  if(start==NULL) { // first element in list
    end = start = p;
  }
  else { // put on end
    p->prior = end;
    end->next = p;
    end = p;
  }
}


/* Remove an element from the list given its index
   and update start and end pointers.
*/
template <class DataT>
void SparseList<DataT>::remove(long ix)
{
  SparseOb<DataT> *ob;

  ob = find(ix); // get pointer to element
  if(!ob) return; // array element does not exist

  if(ob->prior) { // not deleting first element
    ob->prior->next = ob->next;
    if(ob->next) // not deleting last element
      ob->next->prior = ob->prior;
    else // otherwise, deleting last element
      end = ob->prior;  // update end pointer
  }
  else {  // deleting first element
    if(ob->next) { // list not empty
      ob->next->prior = NULL;
      start = ob->next;
    }
    else // list now empty
      start = end = NULL;
```

```
  }
}

// Find an array element given its index.
template <class DataT>
SparseOb<DataT> *SparseList<DataT>::find(long ix)
{
  SparseOb<DataT> *temp;

  temp = start;

  while(temp) {
    if(ix==temp->index) return temp; // found
    temp = temp->next;
  }
  return NULL; // not in list
}

// A generic sparse array class.
template <class DataT>
class SparseArray : public ArrayOb<DataT>{
  long length; // dimension of array
  ArrayOb<DataT> *primary;
  SparseList<DataT> *chains;
  int hash(long ix); // hashing function
public:
  SparseArray(long size);
  DataT &operator[](long i);
};

// Constructor for SparseArray using hashing.
template <class DataT>
SparseArray<DataT>::SparseArray(long size)
{
  long i;

  length = size;

  // dynamically allocate storage for primary array
  primary = new ArrayOb<DataT>[hash(size)+1];
  if(!primary) {
    cout << "Cannot allocate primary array.\n";
    exit(1);
  }

  // initialize primary array to zero
  for(i=0; i < (hash(size)+1); i++) {
    primary[i].index = -1;
```

```
      primary[i].info = 0;
    }

    // allocate hash chain objects
    chains = new SparseList<DataT>[hash(size)+1];
}

// Index into the sparse array
template <class DataT>
DataT &SparseArray<DataT>::operator[](long ix)
{
  if(ix<0 || ix>length-1) {
    cout << "\nIndex value of ";
    cout << ix << " is out-of-bounds.\n";
    exit(1);
  }

  // first, see if index in primary array
  if(ix == primary[hash(ix)].index)
    return primary[hash(ix)].info;

  // if not, add element to primary array
  if(primary[hash(ix)].index == -1) {
    primary[hash(ix)].index = ix; // put in primary array
    return primary[hash(ix)].info; // return pointer to it
  }

  // otherwise, see if in hash chain
  SparseOb<DataT> *o;

  o = chains[hash(ix)].find(ix); // get pointer to element
  if(!o) { // new entry into array
    chains[hash(ix)].store(ix, 0); // store new element in chain
    o = chains[hash(ix)].find(ix); // get pointer to new element
  }

  return o->info;
}

// Define hash function here.
template <class DataT>
int SparseArray<DataT>::hash(long ix)
{
  return ix/10;
}

main()
```

```
{
  SparseArray<int> iob(1000);
  SparseArray<double> dob(100);
  int i;

  cout << "Here is an array of integers: " << endl;
  // put some values into the array
  for(i=0; i<1000; i++) iob[i] = i;
  for(i=0; i<1000; i++) cout << iob[i] << " ";
  cout << endl;

  // assign one array element to another
  iob[2] = iob[3];
  iob[91] = iob[103] = 9345;
  iob[92] = iob[103] + 100;
  for(i=0; i<5; i++) cout << iob[i] << " ";
  cout << endl;
  cout << iob[91] << " " << iob[92] << " " << iob[103] << endl;

  cout << "Here is an array of doubles: " << endl;
  for(i=0; i<5; i++) dob[i*10] = (double) i *1.19;
  for(i=0; i<5; i++) dob[i*11] = (double) i *1.29;
  for(i=0; i<5; i++)
    cout << dob[i*10] << " " << dob[i*11] << " ";

  cout << endl;

  // access a location that has not been given a value
  dob[20] = dob[9];
  cout << dob[20] << " " << dob[9];

  return 0;
}
```

A Closer Look at Hashing

To understand how the hashing approach to sparse arrays works, let's start at the beginning with the **SparseArray** class. It is shown here for your convenience.

```
// A generic sparse array class.
template <class DataT>
class SparseArray : public ArrayOb<DataT>{
  long length; // dimension of array
  ArrayOb<DataT> *primary;
  SparseList<DataT> *chains;
  int hash(long ix); // hashing function
```

```
public:
  SparseArray(long size);
  DataT &operator[](long i);
};
```

Notice that three new private members have been added. The first is the pointer **primary**. This pointer will point to the smaller, primary array that is allocated when a **SparseArray** object is created. Next is **chains**. It will point to an array of **SparseList** objects which will hold the collision lists associated with each index in the primary array. Finally, the hash value is computed by **hash( )**, shown here:

```
// Define hash function here.
template <class DataT>
int SparseArray<DataT>::hash(long ix)
{
  return ix/10;
}
```

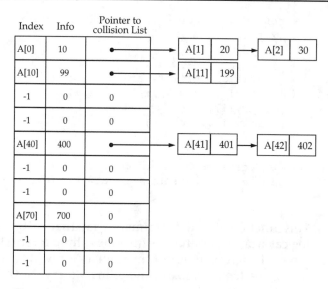

Given elements stored in the following order:

```
A[0] = 10;
A[1] = 20;
A[2] = 30;
A[10] = 99;
A[11] = 199;
A[40] = 400;
A[41] = 401;
A[42] = 402;
A[70] = 700;
```

A hashing example

Figure 4-2.

4

In this case, 10 logical indexes map onto the same physical index. This means that the primary array must be one-tenth the size of the logical array. Thus, the **hash( )** function reduces a logical index by a factor of 10 to produce a physical index. Although this hashing function is quite simple, a more complex approach may be required by your own application.

When an object of type **SparseList** is created, its constructor, shown here, is executed:

```
// Constructor for SparseArray using hashing.
template <class DataT>
SparseArray<DataT>::SparseArray(long size)
{
  long i;

  length = size;

  // dynamically allocate storage for primary array
  primary = new ArrayOb<DataT>[hash(size)+1];
  if(!primary) {
    cout << "Cannot allocate primary array.\n";
    exit(1);
  }

  // initialize primary array to zero
  for(i=0; i < (hash(size)+1); i++) {
    primary[i].index = -1;
    primary[i].info = 0;
  }

  // allocate hash chain objects
  chains = new SparseList<DataT>[hash(size)+1];
}
```

This function allocates a primary array that is 10 percent the size of the logical array and initializes it. Note: calling **hash(size)** causes **hash( )** to return the largest index of the primary array. By adding 1 to this value, you obtain the required size of the primary array. Next, the array of **SparseList** objects is allocated.

Each time a logical array element is indexed, the **operator[ ]( )** function shown here is called:

```
// Index into the sparse array
template <class DataT>
DataT &SparseArray<DataT>::operator[](long ix)
{
```

```
if(ix<0 || ix>length-1) {
  cout << "\nIndex value of ";
  cout << ix << " is out-of-bounds.\n";
  exit(1);
}

// first, see if index in primary array
if(ix == primary[hash(ix)].index)
  return primary[hash(ix)].info;

// if not, add element to primary array
if(primary[hash(ix)].index == -1) {
  primary[hash(ix)].index = ix;
  return primary[hash(ix)].info;
}

// otherwise, see if in hash chain
SparseOb<DataT> *o;

o = chains[hash(ix)].find(ix); // get pointer to element
if(!o) { // new entry into array
  chains[hash(ix)].store(ix, 0);
  o = chains[hash(ix)].find(ix);
}

return o->info;
}
```

4

After performing a bounds check, the function first looks for the index in the primary array. If it is not in the primary array, and that index of the primary array is unused, the element is put into the primary array. Otherwise, the collision list associated with that index is searched. If the element is not found in the list, then the element is created and put into the list. In all cases, a reference to the **info** member is returned.

Analysis of Hashing

In its best case (quite rare), each physical index created by the hash is unique, and access times approximate that of direct indexing. This means that no collision lists are created, and all lookups are essentially direct accesses. However, this will seldom be the case, because it requires that the logical indexes be evenly distributed throughout the logical index space. In a worst case (also rare), a hashed scheme degenerates into a linked list. This can happen when the hashed values of the logical indexes are all the same. In the average (and the most likely) case, the hash method can access any specific element in the amount of time it takes to use a direct index plus some value that is proportional to the average length of the hash chains. The most critical factor in using hashing to support a sparse array is to make sure that the hashing algorithm spreads the physical index evenly so that long collision lists are avoided.

Choosing an Approach

You must consider speed and the efficient use of memory when deciding whether to use a linked-list, a binary-tree, a pointer-array, or a hashing approach to implement a sparse array. Further, you must consider whether your sparse array will most likely be thinly populated or thickly populated.

When the logical array is very sparse, the most memory-efficient approaches are the linked lists and binary trees, because only array elements that are actually in use have memory allocated to them. The links require very little additional memory and generally have a negligible effect. The pointer-array design requires that the entire pointer array exist, even if some of its elements are not used. Not only must the entire pointer array fit in memory, but also enough memory must be left over for the application to use. This could be a serious problem for certain applications, but may not be a problem at all for others. Usually you can calculate the approximate amount of free memory and determine whether it is sufficient for your program. The hashing method lies somewhere between the pointer-array and the linked-list/binary-tree approaches. Although it requires that all of the primary array exist even if it is not all used, it will still be smaller than a pointer array.

When the logical array is fairly full, the situation changes substantially. In this case, the pointer array and hashing become more appealing. Further, the time it takes to find an element in the pointer array is constant no matter how full the logical array is. While not constant, the search time for the hashing approach is bounded by some low value. However, for the linked list and binary tree, average search time increases as the array becomes more heavily populated. If consistent access times are important, then you will want to keep this in mind.

Some Things to Try

As they are currently written, the sparse-array classes do not overload the assignment operator. They also do not define copy constructors. If you will be using these classes in situations in which you will be assigning one sparse array to another, you will need to implement these operations. If you don't, then when you assign one array to another, a bitwise copy will take place. However, since all four approaches to a sparse array shown in this chapter contain pointers to dynamically allocated objects, performing a bitwise copy means that both arrays will have pointers pointing to the same elements, and changing one will imply changing the other! You will usually want to avoid this.

Here is another thing to try. In some applications you will want to delete unused elements. Although this can be done on an individual basis as each element is determined to be no longer needed, there is another approach that is sometimes helpful. When an element is no longer needed, mark it as deleted. (To do this, add another member to the **ArrayOb** class that determines an element's status.) Then, periodically, execute a garbage collection function which frees all deleted elements. The advantage to this approach is that the overhead of deleting an element is not added to the routines in your program that are actually accessing the sparse array. It is deferred until there is idle time.

Finally, in the hashing approach, the collision lists are implemented as linked lists. Try implementing them as binary trees. Doing so will ensure excellent performance in most situations.

4

Chapter

5

Understanding and Using Run-time Type Information

One of the most important yet misunderstood advanced features of C++ is *run-time type information (RTTI)*. RTTI is the subsystem that allows your program to know the type of an object during execution. RTTI was not part of the original specification for C++. However, its inclusion had long been expected because there is a small, but important, class of problems that greatly benefits from its presence. Today, all mainstream C++ compilers support RTTI, and its use is finding its way into a wide variety of programs.

Run-time type information is supported in C++ by two keywords: **typeid** and **dynamic_cast**. RTTI also makes use of the built-in class **type_info**. For the most part, RTTI is supported in C++ relative to polymorphic classes. (A polymorphic class contains at least one virtual function.) This chapter will look at these features in detail. It will also show how they can be applied. Let's begin by examining why RTTI is needed in the first place.

Understanding the Need for RTTI

Run-time type information may be new to you because it is not found in nonpolymorphic languages such as C, Pascal, BASIC, or FORTRAN. In nonpolymorphic languages there is no need for run-time type information because the type of each object is known at compile time (that is, when the program is written). However, in polymorphic languages such as C++, there can be situations in which the type of an object is unknown at compile time because the precise nature of that object is not determined until the program is executed. As you know, C++ implements polymorphism through the use of class hierarchies, virtual functions, and base class pointers. In this approach, a base class pointer may be used to point to objects of the base class or *to any object derived from that base*. Thus, it is not always possible to know in advance what type of object will be pointed to by a base pointer at any moment. This determination must be made at run time. Usually, this mechanism is trouble-free and does not require RTTI. However, there are times when it is less than perfect. Let's see how such a situation might occur.

To understand the essence of the problem, consider the following. First, assume a polymorphic base class called B and several classes derived from B. Further, assume that you want to write some function called F that operates on objects of type B or objects derived from B. To allow this, F defines one parameter of type B* (that is, a base class pointer), which means that it will accept pointers of type B* as well as pointers to any objects derived from B. (Remember, a base pointer can also be used to point to any object derived from that base.) However, what if at a later date, you (or a coworker) define another class derived from B, called D1, that contains features not found in B but that must be taken into account by F? How will F know which of the objects being pointed to are of type D1 and which are not? That is, how will F know which of the objects that its parameter points to are actually valid for it to operate on? To solve this problem, run-time type information was invented.

To better understand the problem, let's construct a real example. It will use a simple class hierarchy that stores X,Y coordinate pairs. The base class for the hierarchy is called **coord** and it is shown here:

```
// This is a polymorphic base class.
class coord {
protected:
  int x, y; // coordinate values
public:
  coord() { x=0; y=0; }
  coord(int i, int j) { x=i; y=j; }
  void get_xy(int &i, int &j) { i=x; j=y; }
  void set_xy(int i, int j) { x=i; y=j; }
```

```
    virtual void show() { cout << x << "," << y; }
};
```

From this base class, two classes, called **translate_coord** and **abs_coord**, are derived. They are shown here:

```
// Create a derived class from coord.
class translate_coord : public coord {
  int deltaX; // translation values
  int deltaY;
public:
  translate_coord() : coord() {deltaX = deltaY = 0; }
  translate_coord(int i, int j) : coord(i, j)
    {deltaX = deltaY = 0; }

  void set_trans(int a, int b)
    { deltaX = a; deltaY = b; }
  void get_trans(int &a, int &b)
    { a = deltaX; b = deltaY; }
};

// Create a second derived class from coord.
class abs_coord : public coord {
public:
  abs_coord() : coord() {}
  abs_coord(int i, int j) : coord(abs(i), abs(j)) {}
};
```

5

The **translate_coord** class expands on **coord** by allowing coordinate translations as specified in the values of **deltaX** and **deltaY**. The **abs_coord** class creates a variation of **coord** that stores the absolute value of the coordinates.

With the preceding class hierarchy as a backdrop, consider the following function, which reports the quadrant in which the coordinate pointed to by **ptr** is located.

```
// Report quadrant of point.  Not quite right!
void quadrant(coord *ptr)
{
  int x, y;

  ptr->get_xy(x, y);

  if(x > 0 && y > 0)
    cout << "Point is in first quadrant\n";
  else if(x < 0 && y > 0)
```

```
      cout << "Point is in second quadrant\n";
   else if(x < 0 && y < 0)
     cout << "Point is in third quadrant\n";
   else if(x > 0 && y <0)
     cout << "Point is in fourth quadrant\n";
   else cout << "Point is at origin\n";
}
```

At first glance, this function seems fine. It obtains the coordinates of the specified point and determines its quadrant. However, since the parameter to this function is a **coord *** pointer, it may also be called with a pointer to an object of any class derived from **coord**. This presents a problem. For example, what if it is called with an object of type **translate_coord**? The function might report the wrong quadrant, since it will not take into consideration the translation values of **deltaX** and **deltaY**. In an attempt to fix this problem, you might try something like this version of **quadrant( )**:

```
// Report quadrant of point.  Still not quite right!
void quadrant(coord *ptr)
{
  translate_coord *p;
  int x, y;
  int dx, dy;

  p = (translate_coord *) ptr;

  p->get_xy(x, y);
  p->get_trans(dx, dy);

  x += dx; // normalize
  y += dy;

  if(x > 0 && y > 0)
    cout << "Point is in first quadrant\n";
  else if(x < 0 && y > 0)
    cout << "Point is in second quadrant\n";
  else if(x < 0 && y < 0)
    cout << "Point is in third quadrant\n";
  else if(x > 0 && y <0)
    cout << "Point is in fourth quadrant\n";
  else cout << "Point is at origin\n";
}
```

This version casts **ptr** into a **translate_coord** pointer, obtains the translation values by calling **get_trans( )**, and then normalizes the coordinates. But now another problem arises. What if **quadrant( )** is called with a pointer to a **coord** or an **abs_coord** object? Neither of these classes defines the member function **get_trans( )**. Depending upon your compiler and environment, one of several things may occur, but one likely scenario is that you will crash your computer! Clearly, a difficult situation has been created. Specifically, how can you construct a version of **quadrant( )** that will be safe for all objects that it can be called with? As you will see in the remainder of this chapter, the C++ run-time type information system provides a way to answer this question.

So that there is a concrete point of reference, the entire (but wrong) coordinates program is shown here. Over the next few sections, this program will be fixed by using C++'s RTTI system.

```cpp
// A troublesome program that will be fixed using RTTI.
#include <iostream.h>
#include <stdlib.h>

// This is a polymorphic base class.
class coord {
protected:
  int x, y; // coordinate values
public:
  coord() { x=0; y=0; }
  coord(int i, int j) { x=i; y=j; }
  void get_xy(int &i, int &j) { i=x; j=y; }
  void set_xy(int i, int j) { x=i; y=j; }
  virtual void show() { cout << x << "," << y; }
};

// Create a derived class from coord.
class translate_coord : public coord {
  int deltaX; // translation values
  int deltaY;
public:
  translate_coord() : coord() {deltaX = deltaY = 0; }
  translate_coord(int i, int j) : coord(i, j)
    {deltaX = deltaY = 0; }

  void set_trans(int a, int b)
    { deltaX = a; deltaY = b; }
  void get_trans(int &a, int &b)
    { a = deltaX; b = deltaY; }
};

// Create a second derived class from coord.
class abs_coord : public coord {
public:
  abs_coord() : coord() {}
```

5

```
    abs_coord(int i, int j) : coord(abs(i), abs(j)) {}
};

/* Report quadrant of point.

   *** Caution: This function will not work in all cases. ***

*/
void quadrant(coord *ptr)
{
  translate_coord *p;
  int x, y;
  int dx, dy;

  p = (translate_coord *) ptr;

  p->get_xy(x, y);

  /* What if the object pointed to by p is not really
     a translate_coord object? */
  p->get_trans(dx, dy); // Possible Error

  x += dx; // normalize
  y += dy;

  if(x > 0 && y > 0)
    cout << "Point is in first quadrant\n";
  else if(x < 0 && y > 0)
    cout << "Point is in second quadrant\n";
  else if(x < 0 && y < 0)
    cout << "Point is in third quadrant\n";
  else if(x > 0 && y <0)
    cout << "Point is in fourth quadrant\n";
  else cout << "Point is at origin\n";
}

main()
{
  coord coordOb(1, 1), *ptr;
  translate_coord tcoordOb(1, 1);
  abs_coord acoordOb(-10, -20);

  ptr = &tcoordOb;
  ptr->show();
  cout << ": ";
  quadrant(ptr); // works OK, ptr points to translatable object

  tcoordOb.set_trans(-10, 5);
```

```
ptr->show();
cout << ": ";
quadrant(ptr); // works OK, ptr points to translatable object

/* ERROR - cannot execute the following lines
  ptr = &coordOb;
  ptr->show();
  cout << ": ";
  quadrant(ptr); // ERROR, non-translatable object

  ptr = &acoordOb;
  ptr->show();
  cout << ": ";
  quadrant(ptr); // ERROR, non-translatable object
*/

  return 0;
}
```

Note that short examples that *require* RTTI are difficult to find. Situations that require RTTI tend to involve complex hierarchies derived from library classes or interactions between producers and consumers of objects in a multitasking environment. In most simpler situations, you will not need to resort to run-time type information because other C++ mechanisms will be sufficient. Such is the case with the preceding example. It is possible to fix this program without using RTTI. (For example, **get_xy( )** could have been made into a virtual function and then overridden by **translate_coord( )** in such a way that it automatically translated the coordinates.) However, this example does illustrate the essence of the problem for which run-time type information was invented, and the subsequent variations that employ the features of RTTI demonstrate the types of situations that can be applied.

5

Using typeid

At the center of the problem presented by the troublesome coordinates program is its inability to determine the type of the object that the **quadrant( )** function is operating upon. Once the type of the object is known, the problems with the function can be easily fixed. Fortunately, C++ provides a mechanism, called **typeid**, which can determine the type of an object at run time. Its general form is shown here:

   typeid(*object*)

Here, *object* is the object whose type you will be obtaining. **typeid** returns a reference to an object of type **type_info** that describes the type of object defined by *object*. You must include the header file TYPEINFO.H in order to use **typeid**.

The **type_info** class defines the following public members:

```
bool operator==(const type_info &ob) const;
bool operator!=(const type_info &ob) const;
bool before(const type_info &ob) const;
const char *name( ) const;
```

The overloaded **==** and **!=** provide for the comparison of types. The **before( )** function returns true if the invoking object is before the object used as a parameter in collation order. (This function is mostly for internal use only. Its return value has nothing to do with inheritance or class hierarchies.) The **name( )** function returns a pointer to the name of the type.

Since **typeid** is evaluated at run time, it can be applied to polymorphic types. This means that it can be used to determine the type of an object that is pointed to by a base class pointer of a polymorphic class. As you will see, this fact will be used to fix the coordinates program.

The following program demonstrates **typeid**:

```
// Demonstrate typeid.
#include <iostream.h>
#include <typeinfo.h>

class BaseClass {
  int a, b;
  virtual void f() {}; // make BaseClass polymorphic
};

class Derived1: public BaseClass {
  int i, j;
};

class Derived2: public BaseClass {
  int k;
};

main()
{
  int i;
  BaseClass *p, baseob;
  Derived1 ob1;
  Derived2 ob2;
```

```
    // First, display type name of a built in type.
    cout << "Typeid of i is ";
    cout << typeid(i).name() << endl;

    // Demonstrate typeid with polymorphic types.
    p = &baseob;
    cout << "p is pointing to an object of type ";
    cout << typeid(*p).name() << endl;

    p = &ob1;
    cout << "p is pointing to an object of type ";
    cout << typeid(*p).name() << endl;

    p = &ob2;
    cout << "p is pointing to an object of type ";
    cout << typeid(*p).name() << endl;

    // Demonstrate == and != with typeid
    if(typeid(baseob) == typeid(ob1))
      cout << "This will not be displayed.\n";

    if(typeid(baseob) != typeid(ob1))
      cout << "baseob and ob1 not of the same type.\n";

    return 0;
}
```

5

The output produced by this program is shown here:

```
Typeid of i is int
p is pointing to an object of type BaseClass
p is pointing to an object of type Derived1
p is pointing to an object of type Derived2
baseob and ob1 not of the same type.
```

As mentioned, when **typeid** is applied to a base class pointer of a polymorphic type, the type of the object pointed to will be determined at run time, as the output produced by the program shows. It is important to understand that this run-time determination only applies to polymorphic classes. For an experiment, comment out the virtual function **f( )** in **BaseClass** and observe the results. This causes **BaseClass** to lose its polymorphic attribute. As a result, the type of the objects pointed to by **p** will all be reported as being of type **BaseClass**.

Using typeid to Fix the Coordinates Program

Since **typeid** obtains type information about an object, you can use this fact to implement one approach to fixing the coordinates program, as shown here:

```cpp
// Using typeid to fix the coordinates program.
#include <iostream.h>
#include <typeinfo.h>
#include <stdlib.h>

// This is a polymorphic base class.
class coord {
protected:
  int x, y; // coordinate values
public:
  coord() { x=0; y=0; }
  coord(int i, int j) { x=i; y=j; }
  void get_xy(int &i, int &j) { i=x; j=y; }
  void set_xy(int i, int j) { x=i; y=j; }
  virtual void show() { cout << x << "," << y; }
};

// Create a derived class from coord.
class translate_coord : public coord {
  int deltaX; // translation values
  int deltaY;
public:
  translate_coord() : coord() {deltaX = deltaY = 0; }
  translate_coord(int i, int j) : coord(i, j)
    {deltaX = deltaY = 0; }

  void set_trans(int a, int b)
    { deltaX = a; deltaY = b; }
  void get_trans(int &a, int &b)
    { a = deltaX; b = deltaY; }
};

// Create a second derived class from coord.
class abs_coord : public coord {
public:
  abs_coord() : coord() {}
  abs_coord(int i, int j) : coord(abs(i), abs(j)) {}
};

// Report quadrant of point -- typeid version.
void quadrant(coord *ptr)
{
```

```
      translate_coord *p;
      int x, y;
      int dx, dy;

      ptr->get_xy(x, y);

      // if translate object, normalize
      if(typeid(*ptr) == typeid(translate_coord)) {
        p = (translate_coord *) ptr;
        cout << "Translation required: ";
        p->get_trans(dx, dy);
        x += dx;
        y += dy;
      }

      if(x > 0 && y > 0)
        cout << "Point is in first quadrant\n";
      else if(x < 0 && y > 0)
        cout << "Point is in second quadrant\n";
      else if(x < 0 && y < 0)
        cout << "Point is in third quadrant\n";
      else if(x > 0 && y <0)
        cout << "Point is in fourth quadrant\n";
      else cout << "Point is at origin\n";
    }

main()
{
    coord coordOb(1, 1), *ptr;
    translate_coord tcoordOb(1, 1);
    abs_coord acoordOb(-10, -20);

    ptr = &tcoordOb;
    ptr->show();
    cout << ": ";
    quadrant(ptr);

    tcoordOb.set_trans(-10, 5);
    ptr->show();
    cout << ": ";
    quadrant(ptr);

    // Following lines now OK
    ptr = &coordOb;
    ptr->show();
    cout << ": ";
    quadrant(ptr);
```

```
ptr = &acoordOb;
ptr->show();
cout << ": ";
quadrant(ptr);

return 0;
}
```

In this version of the program the **quadrant( )** function uses **typeid** to prevent an incorrect cast to **translate_coord**. This version of **quadrant( )** can be safely called using a pointer to a **coord** object or any object derived from **coord**. The call to **get_trans( )** and the coordinate normalization only takes place if **ptr** is a pointer to a **translate_coord** class.

At this point you might be thinking that the use of run-time type information in this example is an unnecessarily complex solution. It would be far easier to simply never call **quadrant( )** with a **translate_coord** object (possibly writing a separate quadrant-reporting function specifically for **translate_coord** objects). In this specific case, you would be right. However, there are situations in which this is not so. For example, what if another part of your program generates pointers to various types of coordinate objects—some are of type **coord**, some of type **abs_coord**, and others of type **translate_coord**? In this case, how could you ensure that **quadrant( )** was never called with an improper object? The key point here is that without a run-time type determination, it is not always possible to prevent a pointer from being improperly cast.

Using dynamic_cast

Although the use of **typeid** as shown in the preceding program provides an adequate solution to the original problem with **quadrant( )**, C++ provides a better means of accomplishing the same thing. This better approach uses **dynamic_cast**, one of C++'s casting operators. Before **dynamic_cast** is used to create an improved solution to the problem with **quadrant( )**, here's a brief review of the C++ casting operators.

The Casting Operators

C++ defines five casting operators. The first is the standard cast which was inherited from C. This is the cast with which you are probably most familiar. (It is also the one used in the preceding example programs.) In addition to the standard casting operator, C++ still defines four additional casting operators. They are **const_cast**, **dynamic_cast**, **reinterpret_cast**, and **static_cast**. Their general forms are shown here:

```
const_cast<type> (object)
reinterpret_cast<type> (object)
static_cast<type> (object)
dynamic_cast<type> (object)
```

Here, *type* specifies the target type of the cast, and *object* is the object being cast into the new type.

The **const_cast** operator is used to explicitly override **const** and/or **volatile** in a cast. The target type must be the same as the source type except for the alteration of its **const** or **volatile** attributes. The most common use of **const_cast** is to remove **const**-ness. The **static_cast** operator performs a nonpolymorphic cast. It can be used for any standard conversion. The **reinterpret_cast** operator changes one type into a fundamentally different type. For example, it can be used to change a pointer into an integer. Thus, **reinterpret_cast** should be used for casting inherently incompatible types.

As it relates to RTTI, the most important cast operator is **dynamic_cast**, because it performs a run-time cast that verifies the validity of the cast. If the cast cannot be made, the cast fails and the expression evaluates to null. Its main use is for performing casts on polymorphic types. For example, **dynamic_cast** can be used to determine if the object pointed to by a pointer is compatible with the target type of the cast. In this usage, if the object pointed to is not an object of the base class or of a derived class of the target type, then **dynamic_cast** fails and evaluates to null. This fact will be used shortly to fix **quadrant( )**.

5

Here is one other point to remember: Only **const_cast** can cast away **const**-ness. That is, neither **dynamic_cast**, **static_cast**, nor **reinterpret_cast** can alter the **const**-ness of an object.

Using dynamic_cast to Fix quadrant( )

As just described, when applied to a polymorphic type, **dynamic_cast** succeeds only if the object being cast is either already an object of the target type or an object derived from the target type. For example, consider this statement:

```
p = dynamic_cast<base *> ptr;
```

Here, if **ptr** is a pointer to an object of type **base**, or an object derived from **base**, then the cast will succeed, and **p** will contain a pointer to the object. Otherwise, the cast will fail and **p** will be assigned the null pointer. Making use of this property of **dynamic_cast**, the quadrant function can be improved as shown here:

```
// Report quadrant of point -- dynamic_cast version.
void quadrant(coord *ptr)
{
  translate_coord *p;
  int x, y;
  int dx, dy;

  ptr->get_xy(x, y);

  // attempt dynamic cast to translate_coord
  p = dynamic_cast<translate_coord *>(ptr);

  // if translate object, normalize
  if(p) {
    cout << "Translation required: ";
    p->get_trans(dx, dy);
    x += dx;
    y += dy;
  }

  if(x > 0 && y > 0)
    cout << "Point is in first quadrant\n";
  else if(x < 0 && y > 0)
    cout << "Point is in second quadrant\n";
  else if(x < 0 && y < 0)
    cout << "Point is in third quadrant\n";
  else if(x > 0 && y <0)
    cout << "Point is in fourth quadrant\n";
  else cout << "Point is at origin\n";
}
```

By using **dynamic_cast**, you can accomplish in one step what took two when using **typeid**. That is, in the **typeid** version of **quadrant( )**, the type of the object pointed to by **ptr** was checked. Then, if the object was of type **translate_coord**, the cast was made. By use of **dynamic_cast**, these two operations take place in one step. For this reason, you will find that **dynamic_cast** provides most of your RTTI solutions.

Applying RTTI

As stated at the outset, short examples that *require* run-time type information are hard to find. However, the short program developed in this section will help illustrate its value. It will also give you a taste of the type of problems to which RTTI is commonly applied. The example creates a list of coordinate objects. This list is implemented as a linked list of **coord** pointers. Since a base pointer can also be used to point to a derived object, this list can also be used to store pointers to objects derived from **coord**, which in this case, means **abs_coord** and **translate_coord**. In the program, pointers to these types of objects are put into the list in random order. Next, the list is read and the quadrant of each coordinate in the list is displayed. Since the pointers are stored in the list randomly, there is no way of knowing which of the pointers in the list actually point to **coord** objects and which point to derived objects. However, since **quadrant( )** makes use of run-time type information, the correct quadrant for each point is displayed.

As stated, pointers to coordinate objects will be stored in a linked list. For this purpose, let's use the linked list class developed in Chapter 2. It will be included in the coordinates program as a header file. Call this file LIST.H. For your convenience, the linked list class is shown here:

```
// A generic doubly linked list class.
#include <iostream.h>
#include <string.h>
#include <stdlib.h>

template <class DataT> class listob; // forward reference listob

// Overload << for object of type listob.
template <class DataT>
ostream &operator<<(ostream &stream, listob<DataT> o)
{
  stream << o.info << endl;
  return stream;
}

// Overload << for pointer to object of type listob.
template <class DataT>
ostream &operator<<(ostream &stream, listob<DataT> *o)
{
  stream << o->info << endl;
  return stream;
}

// Overload >> for listob references.
template <class DataT>
istream &operator>>(istream &stream, listob<DataT> &o)
{
  cout << "Enter information: ";
  stream >> o.info;
  return stream;
}
```

5

```cpp
// Generic list object class.
template <class DataT> class listob {
public:
  DataT info; // information
  listob<DataT> *next;  // pointer to next object
  listob<DataT> *prior; // pointer to previous object
  listob() {
    info = 0;
    next = NULL;
    prior = NULL;
  };
  listob(DataT c) {
    info = c;
    next = NULL;
    prior = NULL;
  }
  listob<DataT> *getnext() {return next;}
  listob<DataT> *getprior() {return prior;}
  void getinfo(DataT &c) { c = info;}
  void change(DataT c) { info = c; }  // change an element
  friend ostream &operator<<(ostream &stream, listob<DataT> o);
  friend ostream &operator<<(ostream &stream, listob<DataT> *o);
  friend istream &operator>>(istream &stream, listob<DataT> &o);
};

// Generic list class.
template <class DataT> class dllist : public listob<DataT> {
  listob<DataT> *start, *end;
public:
  dllist() { start = end = NULL; }
  ~dllist(); // destructor for the list

  void store(DataT c);
  void remove(listob<DataT> *ob); // delete entry
  void frwdlist(); // display the list from beginning
  void bkwdlist(); // display the list from the end

  listob<DataT> *find(DataT c); // return pointer to match

  listob<DataT> *getstart() { return start; }
  listob<DataT> *getend() { return end; }
};

// dllist destructor.
template <class DataT> dllist<DataT>::~dllist()
{
  listob<DataT> *p, *p1;
```

```
    // free all elements in the list
    p = start;
    while(p) {
      p1 = p->next;
      delete p;
      p = p1;
    }
}

// Add the next entry.
template <class DataT> void dllist<DataT>::store(DataT c)
{
  listob<DataT> *p;

  p = new listob<DataT>;
  if(!p) {
    cout << "Allocation error.\n";
    exit(1);
  }

  p->info = c;

  if(start==NULL) { // first element in list
    end = start = p;
  }
  else { // put on end
    p->prior = end;
    end->next = p;
    end = p;
  }
}

/* Remove an element from the list and update start and
   end pointers.
*/
template <class DataT> void dllist<DataT>::remove(listob<DataT> *ob)
{
  if(ob->prior) { // not deleting first element
    ob->prior->next = ob->next;
    if(ob->next) // not deleting last element
      ob->next->prior = ob->prior;
    else // otherwise, are deleting last element
      end = ob->prior;  // update end pointer
  }
  else {  // deleting first element
    if(ob->next) { // list not empty
      ob->next->prior = NULL;
      start = ob->next;
```

```
  }
    else // list now empty
      start = end = NULL;
  }
}

// Walk through list in forward direction.
template <class DataT> void dllist<DataT>::frwdlist()
{
  listob<DataT> *temp;

  temp = start;
  while(temp) {
    cout << temp->info << " ";
    temp = temp->getnext();
  }
  cout << endl;
}

// Walk through list in backward direction.
template <class DataT> void dllist<DataT>::bkwdlist()
{
  listob<DataT> *temp;

  temp = end;
  while(temp) {
    cout << temp->info << " ";
    temp = temp->getprior();
  }
  cout << endl;
}

// Find an object given info.
template <class DataT> listob<DataT> *dllist<DataT>::find(DataT c)
{
  listob<DataT> *temp;

  temp = start;

  while(temp) {
    if(c==temp->info) return temp; // found
    temp = temp->getnext();
  }
  return NULL; // not in list
}
```

Here is the coordinates program that creates a linked list of coordinate objects:

```
// Demonstrate RTTI.
#include <iostream.h>
#include <typeinfo.h>
#include <stdlib.h>
#include "list.h"

// This is a polymorphic base class.
class coord {
protected:
  int x, y; // coordinate values
public:
  coord() { x=0; y=0; }
  coord(int i, int j) { x=i; y=j; }
  void get_xy(int &i, int &j) { i=x; j=y; }
  void set_xy(int i, int j) { x=i; y=j; }
  virtual void show() { cout << x << "," << y; }
};

// Create a derived class from coord.
class translate_coord : public coord {
  int deltaX; // translation values
  int deltaY;
public:
  translate_coord() : coord() {deltaX = deltaY = 0; }
  translate_coord(int i, int j) : coord(i, j)
    {deltaX = deltaY = 0; }

  void set_trans(int a, int b)
    { deltaX = a; deltaY = b; }
  void get_trans(int &a, int &b)
    { a = deltaX; b = deltaY; }
};

// Create a second derived class from coord.
class abs_coord : public coord {
public:
  abs_coord() : coord() {}
  abs_coord(int i, int j) : coord(abs(i), abs(j)) {}
};

// Report quadrant of point.
void quadrant(coord *ptr)
{
  translate_coord *p;
  int x, y;
  int dx, dy;

  ptr->get_xy(x, y);
```

5

```
    // attempt dynamic cast to translate_coord
    p = dynamic_cast<translate_coord *>(ptr);

     // if translate object, normalize
    if(p) {
      cout << "Translation required: ";
      p->get_trans(dx, dy);
      x += dx;
      y += dy;
    }

    if(x > 0 && y > 0)
      cout << "Point is in first quadrant\n";
    else if(x < 0 && y > 0)
      cout << "Point is in second quadrant\n";
    else if(x < 0 && y < 0)
      cout << "Point is in third quadrant\n";
    else if(x > 0 && y <0)
      cout << "Point is in fourth quadrant\n";
    else cout << "Point is at origin\n";
}

main()
{
  coord  *ptr;
  dllist<coord *> list; // create list of coord *
  listob<coord *> *p;
  int i, j, x, y;

  // store randomly generated objects
  for(i=0; i<20; i++) {
    x = (rand() % 500) - 250; // generate random
    y = (rand() % 500) - 250; // coordinates

    j = rand() % 3;  // randomly determine type of object
    switch(j) {
      case 0:
        ptr = new coord(x, y);
        list.store(ptr);
        break;
      case 1:
        ptr = new translate_coord(x, y);
        dynamic_cast<translate_coord *>(ptr)->set_trans(100, 100);
        list.store(ptr);
        break;
      case 2:
        ptr = new abs_coord(x, y);
        list.store(ptr);
```

```
            break;
      }
   }

   // obtain quadrant of each coordinate in list
   p = list.getstart();
   while(p) {
     p->getinfo(ptr); // get pointer to coord-based object
     ptr->get_xy(x, y);
     ptr->show();
     cout << ": ";
     quadrant(ptr);    // report quadrant
     p = p->getnext(); // get next object
   }

   return 0;
}
```

As you can see by looking at **main( )**, various types of pointers are put onto the list at random by use of the standard library function **rand( )**. When the list is read, the coordinates of each object pointed to by each pointer are displayed. Thus, even though the list holds different types of pointers in an unknown order, the **quadrant( )** function can still be used to display the quadrant of any element of the list.

Things to Try

5

As has been mentioned, RTTI is most valuable in situations where complex, polymorphic class hierarchies are involved and when it is not possible to know precisely what type of object any given pointer is pointing to. While these situations may be rare today, they will become more common. For example, as multithreaded multitasking environments (such as Windows 95) become more popular, it will become common to see programs in which one part of the program produces objects and another part consumes them in some asynchronous manner. Programs based upon this type of architecture will usually require some form of RTTI. Also, there is an emerging technology that has to do with the construction of "smart objects" which must rely upon run-time type information for their operation.

The preceding paragraph notwithstanding, there is one good use for **typeid** that you might find valuable right now. When you're debugging complex class hierarchies, it can be very useful to know precisely what type of object a routine is operating upon at any given point. To do this, you can use **typeid** to obtain the class name of any object.

Chapter

6

Supercharged Strings: Using the Standard String Class

C++ defines several standard classes. A number of these deal with I/O. Others form the standard template library (STL). However, one of the most popular of the standard classes defined by C++ is the **string** class. This class stores and manipulates strings. Although standard C++ strings (which are implemented as null-terminated character arrays) are highly efficient, they are not always convenient. For the past several years, most C++ programmers at one time or another have defined their own versions of a string class in an attempt to simplify string handling. Of course, each implementation differed from the next. Because string classes were so common, the ANSI C++ standardization committee decided to define once and for all the **string** class. As such, a **string** class has been incorporated into the draft ANSI C++ standard.

At the time of this writing, C++ is still being defined. This applies to the standard **string** class, too. However, the information presented in this chapter is stable and not likely to change. Also, **string**, as described here, is supported by current versions of both the Borland and Microsoft compilers. Of course, since some changes are possible, it is important that you check your compiler's user manual on this topic.

The **string** class is quite large and contains several features—more than can be covered in a single chapter. This chapter will examine the most important, commonly used, and stable elements of the **string** class and then see how this class can be applied. To begin, let's review why the inclusion of a standard **string** class is an important addition to C++.

Why a String Class?

Standard classes have not been casually added to C++. In fact, a significant amount of thought and debate has accompanied each new addition. Given that C++ already contains some support for strings as null-terminated character arrays, it may at first seem that the inclusion of the **string** class is an exception to this rule. However, this is actually far from the truth. Here is why.

As stated, C++ does not define a built-in string data type. Instead, it implements strings as null-terminated character arrays. This approach to strings allows highly efficient routines to be written. In fact, C++'s implementation of strings as character arrays is often cited as one of its most important "power" features. It enables very fast string manipulations and gives the programmer close, detailed control over those operations. However, null-terminated character arrays are less than ideal when such a high level of speed and efficiency is not required. In these cases, the null-terminated string loses much of its appeal. The reason for this is easy to understand: standard, null-terminated strings cannot be manipulated by any of the C++ operators. Nor can they take part in normal C++ expressions. For example, consider this fragment:

```
char str1[80], str2[80], str3[80];

// You can't do this:
//    str1 = "this is a test";
// or
//    str2 = str1;
// you must instead using the following:
strcpy(str1, "this is a test");
strcpy(str2, str1);

// And, you can't do this:
//    str3 = str2 + str1;
// instead, you must write:
```

```
strcpy(str3, str2);
strcat(str3, str1);

// Finally, you can't do this, either
//    if(str2 < str3)
//       cout << "str2 comes before str3 in the dictionary\n";
// instead, you must write:
if(strcmp(str2, str3) < 0)
    cout << "str2 comes before str3 in the dictionary\n";
```

As these examples show, standard, null-terminated strings are operated on only through library functions. Since they are not technically data types in their own right, the C++ operators cannot be applied to them. This makes even the most rudimentary string operations clumsy. More than anything else, it is the inability to operate on null-terminated strings using the C++ operators that has driven the development of a standard string class. Remember, when you define a class in C++, you are defining a new data type which may be fully integrated into the C++ environment. This, of course, means that the operators can be overloaded relative to the new class. Therefore, by adding a standard string class, it becomes possible to manage strings in the same way as any other type of data: through the use of operators.

There is, however, one other reason for the standard **string** class: safety. In the hands of an inexperienced or careless programmer, it is very easy to overrun the end of an array that holds a null-terminated string. For example, consider the standard string copy function **strcpy( )**. This function contains no provision for checking the boundary of the target array. If the source array contains more characters than the target array can hold, then a program error or system crash is possible (likely). As you will see, the standard **string** class prevents such errors.

In the final analysis, there are three reasons for the inclusion of the standard **string** class: consistency (a string now defines a data type), convenience (you may use the standard C++ operators), and safety (array boundaries will not be overrun). Keep in mind that there is no reason that you should abandon normal, null-terminated strings altogether. They are still the most efficient way to implement strings. However, when speed is not an overriding concern, using the new **string** class gives you access to a safe and fully integrated way to manage strings.

6

String Constructors

The **string** class supports several constructors. The prototypes for two of its most commonly used constructors are shown here:

```
string( );
string(const char *str);
```

The first form creates an empty **string** object. The second creates an object that contains the string pointed to by *str*. This form provides a conversion from null-terminated strings to **string** objects.

At the time of this writing, the draft ANSI C++ standard has defined an additional parameter for all **string** constructors. This parameter determines the allocator used by the object. (An *allocator* is a class-specific memory allocation function.) As defined by the current draft of the ANSI C++ standard, the preceding constructors have the following forms:

```
string(const Allocator &= Allocator( ));
string(const char *str, const Allocator &= Allocator( ));
```

Since the *Allocator* defaults to the standard **string** class allocator, you can usually ignore this parameter. Further, at the time of this writing, no commonly available implementation of the **string** class supports the allocator parameter. However, future versions will.

The **string** class also supports the following copy constructor:

```
string(const string &strob);
```

It constructs a **string** object and initializes it using a copy of the object specified by *strob*.

String Class Operators

A number of operators that apply to strings are defined for **string** objects, including

Operator	Meaning
=	Assignment
+	Concatenation
==	Equality
!=	Inequality
<	Less than
<=	Less than or equal
>	Greater than
>=	Greater than or equal
[]	Subscripting
<<	Output
>>	Input

These operators allow the use of **string** objects in normal expressions and eliminate the need for calls to functions such as **strcpy( )** or **strcat( )**, for example. In general, you can mix **string** objects with normal, null-terminated strings in expressions. For example, a **string** object can be assigned a null-terminated string.

As specified in the latest draft of the ANSI C++ standard, the header file required for the standard **string** class is **string**. However, at the time of this writing, no commonly available compilers recognize this name. Instead, Borland C++ uses the header file CSTRING.H, and Microsoft Visual C++ uses the header file BSTRING.H. (For Visual C++, BSTRING.H is part of the standard template library (STL) and is not automatically installed.)

The following program illustrates the use of the **string** class:

```
/* A short demonstration of the standard string class.

   You will need to define either BORLAND or MICROSOFT,
   depending upon which compiler you are using.  At the time
   of this writing, the string class header file used by
   BORLAND is called CSTRING.H.  This file is called
   BSTRING.H by Microsoft.  Other compilers may use a
   different name.  In any case, check your compiler's user
   manual to see what the standard string class header file
   is called.
*/

#define BORLAND

#ifdef BORLAND
#include <cstring.h>
#endif
#ifdef MICROSOFT
#include <bstring.h>
#endif
#include <iostream.h>

main()
{
  string str1("Demonstrating Strings");
  string str2("String Two");
  string str3;

  // assign a string
  str3 = str1;
  cout << str1 << "\n" << str3 << "\n";

  // concatenate two strings
```

6

```
str3 = str1 + str2;
cout << str3 << "\n";

// compare strings
if(str3 > str1) cout << "str3 > str1\n";
if(str3 == str1+str2)
  cout << "str3 == str1+str2\n";

/* A string object can also be
   assigned a normal string. */
str1 = "This is a normal string.\n";
cout << str1;

// create a string object using another string object
string str4(str1);
cout << str4;

// input a string
cout << "Enter a string: ";
cin >> str4;
cout << str4;

return 0;
}
```

This program produces the following output.

```
Demonstrating Strings
Demonstrating Strings
Demonstrating StringsString Two
str3 > str1
str3 == str1+str2
This is a normal string.
This is a normal string.
Enter a string: Hello
Hello
```

As you can see, objects of type **string** may be manipulated in ways similar to C++'s built-in data types. In fact, this is the main advantage to the **string** class.

There is something important to notice in the preceding program: the sizes of the strings are not specified. **string** objects are automatically sized to hold the string that they are given. Thus, when assigning or concatenating strings, the target string will grow as needed to accommodate the size of the new string. It is not possible to overrun the end of the string. This dynamic aspect to **string** objects is one of the ways that they are better than standard null-terminated strings (which *are* subject to boundary overruns).

Notice that you may subscript a **string** object using **[ ]**. Doing so returns either the character at the specified index or a reference to the character, depending upon how the operator is used. Thus, using **[ ]** you can gain access to the individual characters in a string. Here is a short program that demonstrates the **[ ]** operator:

```
// Demonstrate []
#define BORLAND

#ifdef BORLAND
#include <cstring.h>
#endif
#ifdef MICROSOFT
#include <bstring.h>
#endif
#include <iostream.h>

main()
{
  string str1("This is a test");

  cout << "char at [0]: " << str1[0] << endl;
  cout << "char at [3]: " << str1[3] << endl;
  cout << "char at [5]: " << str1[5] << endl;

  return 0;
}
```

The output produced by this program is shown here:

```
char at [0]: T
char at [3]: s
char at [5]: i
```

6

One last point: the assignment operator has the three forms shown here:

string &operator=(const string &*strob*);
string &operator=(const char **str*);
string &operator=(const char *ch*);

These forms allow you to assign a **string** object, a null-terminated string, or a character to a **string** object. Thus, the following types of statements are valid:

```
strob1 = strob2; // string object assigned to string object
strob = "standard string"; // null-terminated string assigned to string object
strob = 'c'; // character assigned to string object
```

Some String Class Member Functions

Although most simple string operations can be accomplished by use of the string operators, more complex or subtle ones are accomplished by use of **string** class member functions. This section will examine several of the most common.

Assigning and Appending Partial Strings

To assign one string to another, use the **assign( )** function. Its prototype is shown here:

string &assign(const string &*strob*, size_t *start* = 0, size_t *num* = NPOS);

Here, *strob* is the **string** object that will be assigned to the invoking object. If *start* is present, it specifies the index in *strob,* at which point the assignment will begin. Otherwise, the assignment begins with the first character of *strob*. If *num* is present, it specifies the number of characters that will be assigned. Otherwise, the assignment ends with the last character of *strob*. **NPOS** is a value that cannot be a valid count and is typically defined as –1. It is defined by the header file that supports the **string** class. You will see that **NPOS** is used frequently by the **string** member functions.

Note: At the time of this writing, the draft ANSI C++ standard has changed the name of **NPOS** to **npos**. However, no commonly available implementation currently recognizes this change. Also, the value of **npos** is still specified as –1.

If neither *start* nor *num* is specified, then **assign( )** copies the entire string and works exactly like the = operator. Of course, it is much easier to use the = to assign one entire string to another. You will only need to use the **assign( )** function when assigning a partial string.

You can append part of one string to another by using the **append( )** member function. Its prototype is shown here:

string &append(const char &*strob*, size_t *start* = 0, size_t *num* = NPOS);

Here, *strob* is the **string** object that will be appended to the invoking object. If *start* is present, it specifies the index at which point the concatenation will begin. Otherwise, the concatenation begins with the first character of *strob*. If *num* is present, it specifies the number of characters that will be appended. Otherwise, the concatenation ends with the last character of *strob*.

If neither *start* nor *num* is specified, then **append( )** concatenates the entire string and works exactly like the **+** operator. Of course, it is much easier to use the **+** to append one entire string to another. You will only need to use the **append( )** function when appending a partial string.

As a general rule, you can also invoke **assign( )** and **append( )** using null-terminated strings for their first arguments. They will automatically be converted into **string** objects.

The following program demonstrates the **assign( )** and **append( )** functions:

```
// Demonstrate assign() and append().
#define BORLAND

#ifdef BORLAND
#include <cstring.h>
#endif
#ifdef MICROSOFT
#include <bstring.h>
#endif
#include <iostream.h>

main()
{
  string str1("This is a test");
  string str2;

  str2.assign(str1, 5, 6);
  cout << str2 << endl;

  str2.assign("123456789", 3, 6);
  cout << str2 << endl;

  str2 = "ABCDEFG";
  str1.append(str2, 3, 4);
  cout << str1 << endl;

  str2.append("normal string", 0, 10);
  cout << str2 << endl;
```

6

```
    return 0;
}
```

The output produced by this program is shown here:

```
is a t
456789
This is a testDEFG
ABCDEFGnormal str
```

Inserting, Removing, and Replacing

The **string** class defines three types of member functions that can alter the characters contained in a string. They are **insert( )**, **remove( )**, and **replace( )**. The prototypes for their most common forms are shown here:

string &insert(size_t *start*, const string &*strob*,
        size_t *InsertStart*=0, size_t *InsertNum*=NPOS);
string &remove(size_t *start*, size_t *num* = NPOS);
string &replace(size_t *OrgStart*, size_t *OrgNum*, const string &*strob*,
        size_t *ReplaceStart*=0, size_t *ReplaceNum*=NPOS);

The **insert( )** function inserts the string specified by *strob* into the invoking string at the index specified by *start*. If *InsertStart* and *InsertNum* are specified, then only *InsertNum* characters, beginning at *InsertStart*, of *strob* are copied.

The **remove( )** function removes *num* characters from the invoking string beginning at the index specified by *start*. If *num* is not specified, then all characters after *start* are removed.

The **replace( )** function replaces *OrgNum* characters from the invoking string, beginning at *OrgStart*, with the string specified by *strob*. If *ReplaceStart* and *ReplaceNum* are specified, then only *ReplaceNum* characters, beginning at *ReplaceStart*, of *strob* are copied.

The following program demonstrates these functions:

```
// Demonstrate insert(), remove(), and replace().
#define BORLAND

#ifdef BORLAND
#include <cstring.h>
#endif
#ifdef MICROSOFT
```

```
#include <bstring.h>
#endif
#include <iostream.h>

main()
{
  string str1("This is a test");
  string str2("ABCDEFG");

  cout << "Initial strings:\n";
  cout << "str1: " << str1 << endl;
  cout << "str2: " << str2 << "\n\n";

  // demonstrate insert()
  cout << "Insert str2 into str1:\n";
  str1.insert(5, str2);
  cout << str1 << "\n\n";

  // demonstrate remove()
  cout << "Remove 7 characters from str1:\n";
  str1.remove(5, 7);
  cout << str1 <<"\n\n";

  // demonstrate replace
  cout << "Replace 2 characters in str1 with str2:\n";
  str1.replace(5, 2, str2);
  cout << str1 << endl;

  return 0;
}
```

The output produced by this program is shown here:

```
Initial strings:
str1: This is a test
str2: ABCDEFG

Insert str2 into str1:
This ABCDEFGis a test

Remove 7 characters from str1:
This is a test

Replace 2 characters in str1 with str2:
This ABCDEFG a test
```

6

Searching for Substrings

The **string** class provides several member functions which search a string, including **find( )** and **rfind( )**. Here are the prototypes for the most common versions of these functions:

size_t find(const string &*strob*, size_t *start*=0);
size_t rfind(const string &*strob*, size_t *max*=NPOS);

Beginning at *start,* **find( )** searches the invoking string for the first occurrence of the string contained in *strob*. If found, **find( )** returns the index at which the match occurs within the invoking string. If no match is found, then **NPOS** is returned.

rfind( ) is the opposite of **find( )**. Ending at *max*, it searches the invoking string for the last occurrence of the string contained in *strob*. If *max* is not specified, the entire string is searched. If found, **rfind( )** returns the index at which the match occurs within the invoking string. If no match is found, **NPOS** is returned.

For both functions, if *start* is allowed to default, then the string is searched from its beginning.

The following program demonstrates **find( )** and **rfind( )**.

```
// Demonstrate find() and rfind().
#define BORLAND

#ifdef BORLAND
#include <cstring.h>
#endif
#ifdef MICROSOFT
#include <bstring.h>
#endif
#include <iostream.h>

main()
{
  string str1("This is a test");
  string str2("is");
  int i;

  i = str1.find(str2);
  cout << "using find(), substring found at: ";
  cout << i << endl;

  i = str1.rfind(str2);
```

```
    cout << "using rfind(), substring found at: ";
    cout << i << endl;

    return 0;
}
```

The output produced by this program is shown here:

    using find( ), substring found at: 2
    using rfind( ), substring found at: 5

As you might guess, it is quite easy to use **find( )** in conjunction with
replace( ) to perform a substring replacement. For example, the following
program replaces all instances of "is" with "XXX":

```
// Using find() and replace() together.
#define BORLAND

#ifdef BORLAND
#include <cstring.h>
#endif
#ifdef MICROSOFT
#include <bstring.h>
#endif
#include <iostream.h>

main()
{
  string str1("This is a test");
  string str2("is");
  size_t i;

  while ((i = str1.find(str2)) != NPOS) {
    str1.replace(i, 2, "XXX");
    cout << "Replacement at " << i << endl;
    cout << "str1 is now: " << str1 << endl;
  }

  return 0;
}
```

6

The output produced by this program is shown here:

    Replacement at 2
    str1 is now: ThXXX is a test
    Replacement at 6
    str1 is now: ThXXX XXX a test

Comparing Partial Strings

To compare the entire contents of one **string** object to another, you will normally use the overloaded relational operators described earlier. However, if you want to compare a portion of one string to another, then you will need to use the **compare( )** member function, shown here:

int compare(const string &*strob*, size_t *start=0*, size_t *num* = NPOS) const;

Here, *num* characters in *strob*, beginning at *start*, will be compared against the invoking string. If the invoking string is less than *strob*, **compare( )** will return less than zero. If the invoking string is greater than *strob*, it will return greater than zero. If *strob* is equal to the invoking string, **compare( )** will return zero. If *start* and *num* are allowed to default, then **compare( )** compares the entire string and functions much like the standard library function **strcmp( )**.

Here is a short example that uses **compare( )**:

```
// Using compare().

#define BORLAND

#ifdef BORLAND
#include <cstring.h>
#endif
#ifdef MICROSOFT
#include <bstring.h>
#endif
#include <iostream.h>

main()
{
  string str1("Demonstrating Strings");
  string str2("Demonstrating Strings, Again");

  // compare entire strings
  if(str1.compare(str2) < 0) cout << "str1 < str2\n";

  // compare only first 10 characters
  if(str1.compare(str2, 0, 10) < 0)
    cout << "First 10 characters in str1 < str2\n";
  if(str1.compare(str2, 0, 10) == 0)
    cout << "First 10 characters in str1 == str2\n";
  if(str1.compare(str2, 0, 10) > 0)
    cout << "First 10 characters in str1 > str2\n";
```

```
    return 0;
}
```

The output produced by this program is shown here:

```
str1 < str2
First 10 characters in str1 == str2
```

Obtaining the Length of a String

You can obtain the length of a string (that is, the number of characters contained within a string) by using the **length( )** member function, shown here:

```
size_t length( ) const;
```

It returns the length of the invoking string.

Obtaining a Null-Terminated String

Although **string** objects are useful in their own right, there will be times when you will need to obtain a null-terminated character array version of the string. For example, you might use a **string** object to construct a file name. However, when opening a file, you will need to specify a pointer to a standard, null-terminated string. To solve this problem, the member function **c_str( )** is provided. Its prototype is shown here:

```
const char *c_str( ) const;
```

This function returns a pointer to a null-terminated version of the string contained in the invoking **string** object. The null-terminated string must not be altered. It is also not guaranteed to be valid after any other operations have taken place on the **string** object.

To see the value of **c_str( )**, consider the following program. It determines if an executable version of a file exists in the current directory. Given the name of a file (which is specified on the command line), the program works by repeatedly trying different executable file extensions using that name. That is, to see if an executable version of a file exists, you specify only its filename (with no extension), and the program automatically attaches different executable file extensions. As the program is written, it works for a Windows/DOS environment in which the executable extensions are .EXE, .COM, and .BAT. Notice how easy the various string manipulations are made by the use of the **string** objects.

6

```
/* Using c_str().

   Given a name, this program determines
   if an executable file with that name exists.
*/
#define BORLAND

#ifdef BORLAND
#include <cstring.h>
#endif
#ifdef MICROSOFT
#include <bstring.h>
#endif

#include <iostream.h>
#include <fstream.h>

// executable file extensions
char ext[3][4] = {
  "EXE",
  "COM",
  "BAT"
};

main(int argc, char *argv[])
{
  string fname;
  int i;
  int len;

  if(argc != 2) {
    cout << "Usage: execfile filename\n";
    return 1;
  }

  fname = argv[1];

  fname = fname + ".";

  // save length of initial sequence
  len = fname.length();

  for(i=0; i<3; i++) {
    fname = fname + ext[i]; // add next extension

    // try to open file
    cout << "Trying " << fname << " ";
    ifstream f(fname.c_str()); // convert to char *
```

```
    if(f) { // file exists
      cout << "- Exists\n";
      f.close();
    }
    else cout << "- Not found\n";

    fname.remove(len); // remove extension
  }

  return 0;
}
```

Sample output from the program is shown here using the filename TEST (and assuming that TEST.EXE exists):

```
Trying TEST.EXE - Exists
Trying TEST.COM - Not found
Trying TEST.BAT - Not found
```

Looking at the program, you can see that each time through the **for** loop, a new extension is appended to the filename. Next, this file name is passed to the **ifstream** constructor. Since **ifstream** requires a **char *** argument, the **c_str( )** function is used to obtain a pointer to the start of the file name. If the file exists, then it can be successfully opened. In this case, the file is reported as existent and then closed. Otherwise, the file does not exist. In either case, the old extension is removed and the process repeats itself.

Using the String Class—A Simple Line-Oriented Editor

6

Now that you have seen some of the more common elements of the **string** class, it is time to see how it can be applied. One of the best ways to show off the power of strings is a text editor, because it must typically perform numerous string manipulations and comparisons. In this section a simple, yet functional, line-oriented editor is developed that uses the **string** class.

Although most editors today are screen oriented, line-oriented editors were once quite common. While screen editors are for the most part easier to use, line-oriented editors have two advantages over screen editors. First, they are much easier to create and require substantially less code than do screen editors. Second, line-oriented editors can operate in the most adverse environments. For example, a line-oriented editor can be used if the only available I/O device is an old teletype terminal! They are also useful in minimal environments, such as dedicated controls, in which only the most rudimentary editing capacity is needed. They also will work in low-memory situations. Having a simple line-oriented editor in your programmer's bag of tricks is a good idea. (You never know when one will come in handy.) However, the main reason that a line-oriented editor is developed here is that it readily shows off the **string** class without burying it within reams of other code!

Most likely, you have used line-oriented editors before. If you haven't, the following brief description will explain their basic operation. Line-oriented editors operate on lines (not screens) of text. They are command driven. To perform an editing operation, you issue a command. For example, in the editor shown in this section, to list your file, you enter the **L** command. To find a string, use the **F** command. No operations occur through the use of cursor keys, the mouse, or screen position. Line editors are simply command-drive text-manipulation engines.

Here is the entire line-oriented text editor:

```cpp
// A simple line-oriented text editor.

#define BORLAND

#ifdef BORLAND
#include <cstring.h>
#endif
#ifdef MICROSOFT
#include <bstring.h>
#endif

#include <iostream.h>
#include <fstream.h>
#include <ctype.h>

// line-oriented editor class
class ledit {
  string text; // holds the file being edited
  size_t loc; // current location
  size_t end; // end of file
public:
  ledit() { loc = end = 0; }
  void enter();
  void list(int numlines = 0);
  void findfirst(string what);
  void findnext(string what);
  void insert(string what);
  void del(string num);
```

```
    void exchange(string cmnd);
    void top() { loc = 0; }
    void bottom() { loc = end; }
    void where();
    void save(string fname);
    void load(string fname);
};

// Enter Text
void ledit::enter()
{
  char nstr[255];
  string temp;

  for(;;) {
    cout << "> ";
    cin.getline(nstr, 255); // get a line
    temp = nstr;
    if(temp == "*") break; // * ends entry mode
    temp += "\n";
    text.insert(loc, temp); // insert into file
    loc += temp.length();
    end = text.length();
  }
}

// List File
void ledit::list(int numlines)
{
  size_t i, j;
  int linenum = 1;
  string temp;
  char str[255];

  i = loc;
  do {
    j = text.find("\n", i);
    if(j != NPOS) {
      j++;
      temp.assign(text, i, j-i);
      i += temp.length();
      cout << temp; // display line of text
    }
    if(linenum==numlines) break;
    linenum++;
    if(!(linenum % 25)) {
      cout << "More? (Y/N)";
      cin.getline(str, 255);
```

6

```
      if(tolower(*str == 'n')) break;
    }
  } while(j != NPOS);
}

// Find
void ledit::findfirst(string what)
{
  size_t i;

  // find location of first match
  i = text.find(what, 0); // search from top of file

  if(i != NPOS) { // if found
    loc = i; // update current location
    list(1); // display text from that point
  }
  else cout << "Not Found\n";
}

// Find Next
void ledit::findnext(string what)
{
  size_t i;

  // find location of next match
  i = text.find(what, loc+1); // search from current location

  if(i != NPOS) {
    loc = i;
    list(1); // display text from that point
  }
  else cout << "Not Found\n";
}

// Insert
void ledit::insert(string what)
{
  size_t i;

  text.insert(loc, what); // insert text
  end = text.length();

  // display updated line
  i = loc;  // save location counter
  // find start of line
  while(text[loc]!='\n' && loc) loc--;
  if(loc) loc++; // move past \n
```

```
  list(1); // display line
  loc = i; // restore location counter
}

// Delete
void ledit::del(string num)
{
  size_t len;

  len = atoi(num.c_str()); // how many lines to delete
  text.remove(loc, len);
  end = text.length();
  list(1); // display line
}

// Exchange one string for another.
void ledit::exchange(string cmnd)
{
  string oldstr, newstr;
  size_t i;

  i = cmnd.find("|", 0); // vertical bar is separator
  oldstr.assign(cmnd, 0, i);
  newstr.assign(cmnd, i+1);

  // find location of next match
  i = text.find(oldstr, loc);

  if(i != NPOS) {
    loc = i;
    text.remove(i, oldstr.length());
    text.insert(i, newstr);
    end = text.length();
    list(1); // display text from that point
  }
  else cout << "Not Found\n";
}

// Show current location.
void ledit::where()
{
  list(1); // show one line
}

// Save File
void ledit::load(string fname)
{
  char ch;
```

6

```cpp
  if(fname == "") {
    cout << "Enter filename: ";
    cin >> fname;
  }

  ifstream in(fname.c_str());

  if(in) text = ""; // clear any preexisting text
  else {
    cout << "Cannot open file.\n";
    return ;
  }

  while(!in.eof()) {
    in.get(ch);
    if(!in.eof()) text += ch;
  }

  in.close();

  loc = 0;
  end = text.length();
}

// Load File
void ledit::save(string fname)
{
  if(fname == "") {
    cout << "Enter filename: ";
    cin >> fname;
  }

  ofstream out(fname.c_str());

  if(out)
    out.write(text.c_str(), text.length());
  else {
    cout << "Cannot open file.\n";
    return ;
  }

  out.close();
}

main()
{
  ledit EdOb;
```

```
string cmnd;
char nstr[255];
string temp;
char com;

do {
  do { // get user's next command
    cout << ": ";
    cin.getline(nstr, 255);
  } while(!*nstr);
  cmnd = nstr;
  com = cmnd[0]; // save first character
  cmnd.remove(0, 1); // remove first character

  switch(tolower(com)) {
    case 'f': // find
      EdOb.findfirst(cmnd);
      break;
    case 'n': // find next
      EdOb.findnext(cmnd);
      break;
    case 'i': // insert
      EdOb.insert(cmnd);
      break;
    case 'x': // exchange
      EdOb.exchange(cmnd);
      break;
    case 'd': // delete characters
      EdOb.del(cmnd);
      break;
    case 'e': // enter
      EdOb.enter();
      break;
    case 'l': // list
      EdOb.top();
      EdOb.list();
      break;
    case 'b': // bottom of file
      EdOb.bottom();
      break;
    case 't': // top of file
      EdOb.top();
      break;
    case 's': // save file
      EdOb.save(cmnd);
      break;
    case 'r': // load (i.e., read) file
      EdOb.load(cmnd);
```

6

```
      break;
   case 'w': // show current location in file
      EdOb.where();
      break;
   case 'q': // quit
      break;
   default:
      cout << "?\n"; // unknown command
   }
 } while (com != 'q');

 return 0;
}
```

The editor recognizes the following commands:

Command	Meaning
B	Move current location to bottom of file.
D*num*	Delete *num* characters beginning at the current location.
E	Enter lines of text at the current location. Begin entry mode.
F*text*	Find first occurrence of *text*.
N*text*	Find next occurrence of *text*.
I*text*	Insert *text* at current location.
L	List the file.
Q	Quit.
R*filename*	Load the file specified by *filename*.
S*filename*	Save current contents into the file specified by *filename*.
T	Move current location to top of file.
W	Show current location (i.e., Where am I?).
X*old\new*	Exchange *old* text with *new* text. The two strings must be separated by a vertical bar.
*	Terminate entry mode.

A short sample session using the editor is shown here:

```
: E
> This is a
> short test of
> the simple line-oriented editor
> that uses strings.
> *
: L
This is a
```

```
short test of
the simple line-oriented editor
that uses strings.
: Fis
is is a
: Nis
is a
: Xis|was
was a
: L
This was a
short test of
the simple line-oriented editor
that uses strings.
: T
: E
> This is on top line.
> *
: B
: E
> This is on the bottom line.
> *
: L
This is on top line.
This was a
short test of
the simple line-oriented editor
that uses strings.
This is on the bottom line.
: Q
```

6

A Closer Look at the Editor

The operation of the editor is straightforward and should be easy to understand. However, the following comments will be helpful. The line-oriented editor is encapsulated within the **ledit** class. The text currently being edited is held in the **text** object. The index of the current location is held in **loc**, and the index of the end of the file is stored in **end**. When an **ledit** object is created, these indexes are initialized to zero. They are changed appropriately by the actions of the various member functions.

Each editing command is handled by its own member function. For example, when you list the file, the **list( )** function is called. The operation of each function should be easy to follow. Pay special attention to the way the **string** class makes the various text manipulations easy and clear.

Some Things to Try

The best way to get familiar with the **string** class is to experiment with it. Try writing many short examples that exercise specific features, observing the results. Once you are comfortable with **string** objects, try using them to replace null-terminated (**char ***) strings in your own programs where appropriate. You will find that most of the time, the use of **string** objects simplifies the structure of the code that handles strings.

You might find it fun to enhance and expand the line-oriented editor. Here are some ideas. Add a range specification to the **L** command which causes it to list only the specified lines. As it stands, **L** causes the entire file to be displayed. Add **+** and **–** commands which cause the current location to move forward or backward one character. These will be useful in performing small alterations. Try adding line numbers, and then let the user go to a specific line of text by specifying its number. The editor is so straightforward in its operation that you should have little trouble expanding it in any way that you choose.

Chapter

7

Encryption and Data Compression

For some reason, there seems to be a high correlation between those people who like computers and programming and those who like to play with codes and ciphers. Perhaps it is because all codes involve algorithms—just as programs do. Or maybe it is just an affinity for cryptic things that most people cannot understand. Most programmers receive a great deal of satisfaction when a nonprogrammer looks at a program listing and says something like "Wow, that sure looks complicated!" After all, the act of writing a program is called "coding."

There are two main reasons that computer-based cryptography is important. The most obvious is the need to keep sensitive data on shared systems and networks secure. Although password protection is adequate for many situations, truly important, confidential files are routinely encrypted to provide a higher level of protection. The second need for computer-based codes is in data transmission. Sometimes, when information is transmitted, the information is not secret. However, the owner of the information wants to ensure that only those paying for the information actually receive it. For both reasons, digital coding techniques have come into their own.

Hand in hand with cryptography is data compression. Data compression is commonly used to increase the storage capacity of various storage devices. Although the cost of storage devices has fallen sharply in the past few years, there still can be the need to fit more information into smaller areas. In fact, there are several data compaction programs on the market for this purpose.

This chapter will look at several encryption algorithms and two data compression schemes. It is important to state at the outset that the purpose of this chapter (like all the chapters of this book) is to illustrate C++. As such, the encryption methods presented in this chapter are intentionally simplified and not for rigorous security needs. Instead, they are designed to demonstrate how C++ can be applied to problems of this type. They can also serve as starting points for the development of your own encryption algorithms. If you need break-proof encryption routines, you will need to use substantially more complex methods than those shown here. The data compression algorithms described in this chapter are also quite simple. However, they are effective when applied to text-only data.

A Short History of Cryptography

Although no one knows when secret writing began, one of the earliest known examples is found on a cuneiform tablet made around 1500 B.C. that contains a coded formula for making pottery glaze. The Greeks were known to use codes as early as 475 B.C., and simple ciphers were used frequently by the upper class in Rome during the reign of Julius Caesar. Like so many other intellectual pursuits, interest in cryptography waned during the Dark Ages except for occasional use by monks. With the birth of the Italian Renaissance, the art of cryptography once again began to flourish, and by the time of Louis the XIV of France, a code based on 587 randomly selected keys was used for government messages.

In the 1800s, two events helped move cryptography forward. The first was Edgar Allan Poe's stories (such as "The Gold Bug") featuring coded messages, which excited the imagination of many. The second was the invention of the telegraph and the Morse code. The Morse code was important because it was the first binary (dots and dashes) representation of the alphabet to be widely used. By World War I several nations had constructed "code machines," which permitted the easy encoding and decoding of text using sophisticated ciphers. These mechanical devices were able to utilize ciphers of significant complexity. At this point the story of cryptography changes slightly—to the story of code-breaking.

Prior to the use of mechanical devices to encode and decode messages, complex ciphers were used infrequently because of the time and effort required both for encoding and decoding. Hence, most codes could be broken in a relatively short time. However, the art of code-breaking became much more difficult when code machines were employed. Although the use of modern computers would have made breaking even those codes fairly easy, they do not dwarf the incredible talent of Herbert Yardley, still considered the grand master code-breaker of all time. He not only broke, in his spare time, the U.S. diplomatic code in 1915, but went on to his greatest accomplishment: the breaking of the Japanese diplomatic code in 1922— even though he did not know Japanese! He did this through the use of frequency tables of the Japanese language.

By World War II, encryption methods had grown in sophistication, and coded messages were often generated by use of code machines. Because of the complexity of the codes produced by these machines, a common method for "breaking codes" during this period was to steal the enemy's code machine. This meant that the tedious, but intellectually satisfying, process of code-breaking was bypassed. Of course, having in your possession an easy and reliable means of decoding the enemy's messages gives a substantial strategic advantage. For example, it is generally accepted that the Allies' possession of a German code machine (unbeknownst to the Germans) contributed greatly to the outcome of the war.

With the advent of computers and networks, the need for secure and unbreakable codes has become even more important. Not only do computer files occasionally need to be kept secret, but access to the computer itself must also be managed and regulated. Numerous methods of encrypting data files have been developed; the DES (Data Encryption Standard) algorithm has traditionally been considered to be secure from code-breaking efforts. (However, rumors have persisted that DES is breakable.) Other, public-domain encryption methods that provide a high level of security are also commonly available. This chapter will examine several less rigorous means of encoding messages.

The Three Basic Types of Ciphers

Of the more traditional coding methods, there are two basic types: *transposition* and *substitution*. Transposition ciphers essentially scramble the characters of a message according to some rule. A substitution cipher replaces one character with another, but leaves the message in the proper order. Both of these types of codes can be carried on to whatever level of complexity is desired, and can even be intermixed. The digital computer adds a third basic encryption technique, called *bit manipulation,* that alters the computerized representation of data by some algorithm.

All three methods may make use of a *key* if desired. A key is generally some string of characters that is needed to decode a message. Do not confuse the key with the encryption method, however, because the key is never sufficient to decode—the encryption algorithm must also be known. What the key does is "personalize" a coded message so that only the people that know the key can decode it—at least easily—even though the method used to encode the message may be generally accessible.

There are two terms with which you should become familiar: *plain-text* and *cipher-text.* The plain-text of a message is readable; the cipher-text is the encoded version.

This chapter will look at various computerized methods of coding text files using each of the three basic methods just described. It will explore several short programs that encode and decode text files. Keep in mind that all of these programs have both an **encode( )** and a **decode( )** function. The **decode( )** function always reverses the **encode( )** process used to create the cipher-text.

Substitution Ciphers

A *substitution cipher* is a method of encrypting a message by substituting, on a regular basis, one character for another. One of the simplest forms of substitution ciphers involves offsetting the alphabet by a specified amount. For example, if each letter is offset by three, then

abcdefghijklmnopqrstuvwxyz

becomes

defghijklmnopqrstuvwxyzabc

Therefore, an *a* becomes a *d,* a *b* becomes an *e,* and so on. Notice that the letters "abc" that were shifted off the front were added to the end. To encode a message using this method, you simply substitute the shifted alphabet for the real one. For example, the message:

meet me at sunset

becomes

phhw ph dw vxqvhw

The program shown here will enable you to code any text message using an offset by specifying which letter of the alphabet to begin with:

```cpp
// Simple substitution cipher.

#include <iostream.h>
#include <fstream.h>
#include <ctype.h>
#include <stdlib.h>

void encode(char *input, char *output, char start);
void decode(char *input, char *output, char start);

main(int argc, char *argv[])
{
  if(argc!=5) {
    cout << "Usage: input output encode/decode offset\n";
    exit(1);
  }

  if(!isalpha(*argv[4])){
    cout << "Start letter must be alphabetical character.\n";
    exit(1);
  }

  if(toupper(*argv[3])=='E')
    encode(argv[1], argv[2], *argv[4]);
  else
    decode(argv[1], argv[2], *argv[4]);

  return 0;
}

// Encode
void encode(char *input, char *output, char start)
{
  int ch;
  ifstream in(input, ios::in | ios::binary);
  ofstream out(output, ios::out | ios::binary);

  if(!in) {
    cout << "Cannot open input file.\n";
    exit(1);
```

7

```
    }

    if(!out) {
      cout << "Cannot open output file.\n";
      exit(1);
    }

    start = tolower(start);
    start = start-'a';
    do {
      ch = in.get();
      ch = tolower(ch);
      if(isalpha(ch)) {
        ch += start; // shift the letter
        if(ch > 'z') ch -= 26; // wrap around
      }
      if(!in.eof()) out.put((char) ch);
    } while(!in.eof());

    in.close();
    out.close();
}

// Decode
void decode(char *input, char *output, char start)
{
    int ch;
    ifstream in(input, ios::in | ios::binary);
    ofstream out(output, ios::out | ios::binary);

    if(!in) {
      cout << "Cannot open input file.\n";
      exit(1);
    }

    if(!out) {
      cout << "Cannot open output file.\n";
      exit(1);
    }

    start = tolower(start);
    start = start-'a';
    do {
      ch = in.get();
      ch = tolower(ch);
      if(isalpha(ch)) {
        ch -= start; // shift letter back to original
        if(ch < 'a') ch += 26;  // wrap around
```

```
      }
    if(!in.eof()) out.put((char) ch);
  } while(!in.eof());

  in.close();
  out.close();
}
```

To use this program to encode a file, specify the name of the file to encrypt, the name of the file that will hold the encoded version, the word "encode", and the letter of the alphabet at which the offset alphabet begins. For example, to encode a file called MESSAGE using an offset alphabet beginning with *c* and putting the output into a file called CODEMESS, use this command line:

>code message codemess encode c

To decode, you would type

>code codemess message decode c

Although a substitution cipher based on a constant offset, such as just described, will fool grade-schoolers, it is not suitable for much else, because it is too easy to crack. There are, after all, only 26 possible offsets, and it is possible to try all of them within a short time. A better version of the substitution cipher uses a scrambled alphabet instead of a simple offset. A second failing of the simple substitution cipher is that it preserves the spaces between words. This would made it doubly easy for a code-breaker to crack. A better version would require that spaces also be encoded. (Actually, all punctuation should be encoded, but for the simplicity of these examples, this will not be done.) For example, you could map the following string that contains a randomized alphabet onto the alphabet as shown here:

```
abcdefghijklmnopqrstuvwxyz<space>
qazwsxedcrfvtgbyhnujm ikolp
```

You may be wondering if there is a significant improvement in the security of a message encoded using a randomized version of the alphabet versus the simple offset version. The answer is *yes* because there are 26! (26 factorial) ways to arrange the alphabet—with the space, that number becomes 27! ways. You should recall that the factorial of a number is that number times every whole number smaller than it down to 1. That is, 6! is 6*5*4*3*2*1 = 720. Therefore 26! is a very large number.

The program shown next is an improved substitution cipher that uses the randomized alphabet just shown. If you encoded the message:

7

meet me at sunset

using the improved substitution cipher program, it would look like this:

tssjptspqjpumgusj

…a harder code to break.

```cpp
// Improved substitution cipher.

#include <iostream.h>
#include <fstream.h>
#include <ctype.h>
#include <stdlib.h>

const int SIZE = 28;

void encode(char *input, char *output);
void decode(char *input, char *output);
int find(char *s, char ch);

char sub[SIZE] =      "qazwsxedcrfvtgbyhnujm ikolp";
char alphabet[SIZE] = "abcdefghijklmnopqrstuvwxyz ";

main(int argc, char *argv[])
{
  if(argc!=4) {
    cout << "Usage: input output encode/decode\n";
    exit(1);
  }

  if(toupper(*argv[3])=='E')
    encode(argv[1], argv[2]);
  else
    decode(argv[1], argv[2]);

  return 0;
}

// Encode
void encode(char *input, char *output)
{
  int ch;
  ifstream in(input, ios::in | ios::binary);
  ofstream out(output, ios::out | ios::binary);

  if(!in) {
```

```
    cout << "Cannot open input file.\n";
    exit(1);
  }

  if(!out) {
    cout << "Cannot open output file.\n";
    exit(1);
  }

  do {
    ch = in.get();
    ch = tolower(ch);
    if(isalpha(ch) || ch==' ')
      ch = sub[find(alphabet, ch)];
    if(!in.eof()) out.put((char) ch);
  } while(!in.eof());

  in.close();
  out.close();
}

// Decode
void decode(char *input, char *output)
{
  int ch;
  ifstream in(input, ios::in | ios::binary);
  ofstream out(output, ios::out | ios::binary);

  if(!in) {
    cout << "Cannot open input file.\n";
    exit(1);
  }

  if(!out) {
    cout << "Cannot open output file.\n";
    exit(1);
  }

  do {
    ch = in.get();
    ch = tolower(ch);
    if(isalpha(ch) || ch==' ')
      ch = alphabet[find(sub, ch)];
    if(!in.eof()) out.put((char) ch);
  } while(!in.eof());

  in.close();
  out.close();
```

7

```
}

// Find the correct index.
find(char *s, char ch)
{
  register int t;

  for(t=0; t<SIZE; t++) if(ch==s[t]) return t;
  return -1;
}
```

It should be pointed out that even the improved substitution code can still be easily broken by using a frequency table of the English language in which the statistical information of the use of each letter of the alphabet is recorded. As you can readily see, by looking at the coded message, *s* almost certainly has to be *e*, the most common letter in the English language, and *p* must be a space. The rest of the message can be decoded if you try awhile. Furthermore, the larger the coded message is, the easier it is to crack with a frequency table. To impede the progress of a code-breaker applying frequency tables to a coded message, you can use a *multiple substitution cipher*. In this case, the same letter in the plain-text message will not necessarily translate into the same letter in the coded form. This can be accomplished by adding a second randomized alphabet and switching between it and the first alphabet using some predetermined method. The method that you will use next is to switch alphabets each time a space is encountered. (Hence, spaces will not be encoded.) For the second permutation of the alphabet, you can use the following:

poi uytrewqasdfghjklmnbvcxz

The program shown here implements this approach:

```
// Multiple substitution cipher.

#include <iostream.h>
#include <fstream.h>
#include <ctype.h>
#include <stdlib.h>

const int SIZE = 28;

void encode(char *input, char *output);
void decode(char *input, char *output);
int find(char *s, char ch);

char sub[SIZE] =        "qazwsxedcrfvtgbyhnujm ikolp";
```

```
char sub2[SIZE] =      "poi uytrewqasdfghjklmnbvcxz";
char alphabet[SIZE] = "abcdefghijklmnopqrstuvwxyz ";

main(int argc, char *argv[])
{
  if(argc!=4) {
    cout << "Usage: input output encode/decode\n";
    exit(1);
  }
  if(toupper(*argv[3])=='E')
    encode(argv[1],argv[2]);
  else
    decode(argv[1],argv[2]);

  return 0;
}

// Encode
void encode(char *input, char *output)
{
  int ch, change;
  ifstream in(input, ios::in | ios::binary);
  ofstream out(output, ios::out | ios::binary);

  if(!in) {
    cout << "Cannot open input file.\n";
    exit(1);
  }

  if(!out) {
    cout << "Cannot open output file.\n";
    exit(1);
  }

  change = 1;
  do {
    ch = in.get();
    ch = tolower(ch);
    if(isalpha(ch))
      if(change)
        ch = sub[find(alphabet, ch)];
      else
        ch = sub2[find(alphabet, ch)];
    if(!in.eof()) out.put((char) ch);
    if(ch==' ') change = !change;
  } while(!in.eof());

  in.close();
```

7

```
    out.close();
}

// Decode
void decode(char *input, char *output)
{
  int ch, change;
  ifstream in(input, ios::in | ios::binary);
  ofstream out(output, ios::out | ios::binary);

  if(!in) {
    cout << "Cannot open input file.\n";
    exit(1);
  }

  if(!out) {
    cout << "Cannot open output file.\n";
    exit(1);
  }

  change = 1;
  do {
    ch = in.get();
    ch = tolower(ch);
    if(isalpha(ch))
      if(change)
        ch = alphabet[find(sub, ch)];
      else
        ch = alphabet[find(sub2, ch)];
    if(!in.eof()) out.put((char) ch);
    if(ch==' ')  change = !change;
  } while(!in.eof());

  in.close();
  out.close();
}

// Find an element
find(char *s, char ch)
{
  register int t;

  for(t=0; t<SIZE; t++) if(ch==s[t]) return t;
  return -1;
}
```

Using the program to encode the message

meet me at sunset

produces the following coded form:

tssj su qj kmdkul

To see why, let's set up the ordered alphabet and the two randomized alphabets (called R1 and R2) over one another.

```
alphabet: abcdefghijklmnopqrstuvwxyz<space>
R1:       qazwsxedcrfvtgbyhnujm ikolp
R2:       poi uytrewqasdfghjklmnbvcxz
```

Here is how the program operates. At the start, the first random alphabet is selected. This randomized alphabet is used for the word "meet", producing the cipher-text "tssj". The space following "meet" causes the second randomized alphabet to be used for the word "me". This produces the cipher-text "su". The next space causes the first randomized alphabet to be reselected. This process of alternating alphabets continues until the message ends.

The use of multiple substitution ciphers makes it much harder to break a code using frequency tables because, at different times, different letters stand for the same thing! If you think about it, it would be possible to use several different randomized alphabets and a somewhat more complex means of switching between them. If properly designed, the cipher-text produced by such an approach will have all letters occur equally often. In this way a frequency table would be useless in breaking the code.

Transposition Ciphers

A *transposition cipher* is one in which the actual characters of the message are rearranged, according to some algorithm, in such a way as to conceal the content of the text. One of the earliest known uses of a transposition code was by the Spartans around 475 B.C., using a device call a "skytale." A skytale is basically a strap wrapped around a cylinder upon which a message is written crossways. The strap is then unwound and delivered to the recipient of the message, who also has a cylinder of equal size. Without the cylinder, it is impossible to read the strap because the letters are out of order. In actual practice, however, this method leaves something to be desired, because it is possible to construct many different-sized cylinders and keep trying them until the message begins to make sense.

7

You can create a computerized version of a skytale by placing your message into an array one way, and writing it out a different way. For example, if you have the following union:

```
union message {
   char s[100];
   char s2[20][5];
} skytale;
```

which is initialized to nulls, then, by placing the message

meet me at sunset

into **skytale.s** but viewing it as the two-dimensional array **skytale.s2**, it would look like

m	e	e	t	
m	e		a	t
	s	u	n	s
e	t	0	0	0
0	0	0	0	0

.
.
.

Then, if you wrote out the array a column at a time, the message would look like this:

mm e...eest...e u...tan... ts...

where the periods indicate the null padding. To decode the message, columns in **skytale.s2** are filled. Then the array **skytale.s** is displayed in normal order. **skytale.s** can be printed as a string because the message will be null terminated. The next program uses this method to code and decode messages.

.

```
// Skytale cipher

#include <iostream.h>
#include <fstream.h>
#include <ctype.h>
#include <stdlib.h>

union message {
  char s[100];
  char s2[20][5];
} skytale;

void encode(char *input, char *output);
void decode(char *input, char *output);

main(int argc, char *argv[])
{
  int t;

  // initialize array
  for(t=0; t<100; ++t) skytale.s[t] = '\0';

  if(argc!=4) {
    cout << "Usage: input output encode/decode\n";
    exit(1);
  }

  if(toupper(*argv[3])=='E')
    encode(argv[1], argv[2]);
  else
    decode(argv[1], argv[2]);

  return 0;
}

// Encode
void encode(char *input, char *output)
{
  int t, t2;
  ifstream in(input, ios::in | ios::binary);
  ofstream out(output, ios::out | ios::binary);

  if(!in) {
    cout << "Cannot open input file.\n";
    exit(1);
  }

  if(!out) {
```

```
      cout << "Cannot open output file.\n";
      exit(1);
    }

  for(t=0;  t<100;  ++t) {
    skytale.s[t] = in.get();
    if(in.eof())  break;
  }

  for(t=0; t<5; ++t)
    for(t2=0; t2<20; ++t2)
      out.put(skytale.s2[t2][t]);

  in.close();
  out.close();
}

// Decode
void decode(char *input, char *output)
{
  int t, t2;
  ifstream in(input, ios::in | ios::binary);
  ofstream out(output, ios::out | ios::binary);

  if(!in) {
    cout << "Cannot open input file.\n";
    exit(1);
  }

  if(!out) {
    cout << "Cannot open output file.\n";
    exit(1);
  }

  for(t=0; t<5 && !in.eof(); ++t)
    for(t2=0; t2<20 && !in.eof(); ++t2)
      skytale.s2[t2][t] = in.get();

  for(t=0;  t<100;  ++t)
    out.put(skytale.s[t]);

  in.close();
  out.close();
}
```

Of course, there are other methods of obtaining transposed messages. One method particularly suited for use by computer involves the swapping of letters within the message as defined by some algorithm. For example, the following program employs a method that transposes the letters that comprise a message, a packet at a time. (For the purposes of this program, a *packet* is simply a fixed unit of characters.) The user specifies the packet size on the command line. The program then transposes the characters within each packet, front to back, until the entire file is encoded.

```
// A transposition cipher.

#include <iostream.h>
#include <fstream.h>
#include <ctype.h>
#include <stdlib.h>

void encode(char *input, char *output, int packet_size);
void decode(char *input, char *output, int packet_size);

main(int argc, char *argv[])
{
  int packet_size;

  if(argc!=5) {
      cout << "Usage: input output encode/decode packet-size\n";
      exit(1);
  }

  packet_size = atoi(argv[4]);

  if(toupper(*argv[3])=='E')
    encode(argv[1], argv[2], packet_size);
  else
    decode(argv[1], argv[2], packet_size);

  return 0;
}

// Encode
void encode(char *input, char *output, int packet_size)
{
  char done, temp;
  int t;
  char s[256];
  ifstream in(input, ios::in | ios::binary);
  ofstream out(output, ios::out | ios::binary);

  if(!in) {
    cout << "Cannot open input file.\n";
    exit(1);
```

7

```
  }

  if(!out) {
    cout << "Cannot open output file.\n";
    exit(1);
  }

  done = 0;
  do {
    for(t=0; t<(packet_size*2); ++t) {
      s[t] = in.get();
      if(in.eof()) {
        s[t] = '\0';   // if eof then terminate
        done = 1;
      }
    }
    for(t=0; t<packet_size; t++) {
      temp = s[t];
      s[t] = s[t+packet_size];
      s[t+packet_size] = temp;
      t++;
      temp = s[t];
      s[t] = s[packet_size*2-t];
      s[packet_size*2-t] = temp;
    }
    for(t=0; t<packet_size*2; t++) out.put(s[t]);
  } while(!done);

  in.close();
  out.close();
}

// Decode
void decode(char *input, char *output, int packet_size)
{
  char done, temp;
  int t;
  char s[256];
  ifstream in(input, ios::in | ios::binary);
  ofstream out(output, ios::out | ios::binary);

  if(!in) {
    cout << "Cannot open input file.\n";
    exit(1);
  }

  if(!out) {
    cout << "Cannot open output file.\n";
```

```
       exit(1);
   }

   done=0;
   do {
     for(t=0; t<(packet_size*2); ++t) {
       s[t] = in.get();
       if(in.eof()) {
         s[t] = '\0';   // if eof then terminate
         done = 1;
       }
     }
     for(t=0; t<packet_size; t++) {
       t++;
       temp = s[t];
       s[t] = s[packet_size*2-t];
       s[packet_size*2-t] = temp;
       t--;
       temp = s[t];
       s[t] = s[t+packet_size];
       s[t+packet_size] = temp;
       t++;
     }
     for(t=0; t<packet_size*2; t++) out.put(s[t]);
   } while(!done);

   in.close();
   out.close();
}
```

Used by themselves, transposition ciphers suffer from the fact that often "clues" are accidentally created by the transposition process.

Bit-Manipulation Ciphers

The preceding methods of encoding a message are computerized versions of encryption previously done by hand. However, the computer has given rise to a new method of encoding messages through manipulation of the bits that comprise the actual characters of the plain-text. Computerized ciphers usually fall into the general class called *bit-manipulation* ciphers. Although the purist will argue that bit manipulation (or alteration, as it is sometimes called) is really just a variation on the substitution cipher, most will agree that the concepts, methods, and options differ so significantly that it must be considered as a distinct method in its own right.

There are two reasons for the popularity of bit-manipulation ciphers. First, they are well-suited for use on a computer, because they employ operations

7

easily performed by the system. The second reason is that the cipher-text tends to look completely unintelligible—that is, like complete garbage. This adds to the security of the message by making the data look like unused or crashed files—hence confusing anyone trying to gain access to the file.

Bit-manipulation ciphers are generally only applicable to computer-based files and cannot be used to create a "hard copy" message, because the bit manipulations tend to produce nonprinting characters. For this reason, let's assume that any file coded by bit-manipulation methods will remain in a computer file.

Bit-manipulation ciphers convert plain-text into cipher-text by altering the actual bit pattern of each character by use of one or more of the following logical operations:

AND OR NOT XOR

C++ is one of the best languages for creating bit-manipulation ciphers because it supports these operations on the bit level using the following bitwise operators:

Operator	Meaning
&	AND
|	OR
~	NOT (1's complement)
^	XOR

The simplest bit-manipulation cipher, and also the least secure, uses only the 1's complement, ~, operator. In case you have forgotten, the ~ operator causes each bit within a byte to be inverted. That is, a 1 becomes a 0, and a 0 becomes a 1. Therefore, a byte complemented twice is the same as the original. The following program demonstrates this approach to coding a file.

```
// 1's complement cipher
#include <iostream.h>
#include <fstream.h>
#include <stdlib.h>
#include <ctype.h>

void encode(char *input, char *output);
void decode(char *input, char *output);

main(int argc, char *argv[])
{
    if(argc!=4) {
```

```
      cout << "usage: input output encode/decode\n";
      exit(1);
    }

    if(toupper(*argv[3])=='E')
      encode(argv[1], argv[2]);
    else
      decode(argv[1], argv[2]);

    return 0;
}

// Encode
void encode(char *input, char *output)
{
  int ch;
  ifstream in(input, ios::in | ios::binary);
  ofstream out(output, ios::out | ios::binary);

  if(!in) {
    cout << "Cannot open input file.\n";
    exit(1);
  }

  if(!out) {
    cout << "Cannot open output file.\n";
    exit(1);
  }

  do {
    ch = in.get();
    ch = ~ch;
    if(!in.eof()) out.put((char) ch);
  } while(!in.eof());

  in.close();
  out.close();
}

// Decode
void decode(char *input, char *output)
{
  int ch;
  ifstream in(input, ios::in | ios::binary);
  ofstream out(output, ios::out | ios::binary);

  if(!in) {
    cout << "Cannot open input file.\n";
```

```
      exit(1);
   }

   if(!out) {
      cout << "Cannot open output file.\n";
      exit(1);
   }

   do {
      ch = in.get();
      ch = ~ch;
      if(!in.eof()) out.put((char) ch);
   } while(!in.eof());

   in.close();
   out.close();
}
```

It is not possible to show what the cipher-text of a message would look like because the bit manipulation used here generally creates nonprinting characters. Try it on your computer and examine the file—it will look quite cryptic, indeed!

There are really two problems with this simple coding scheme. First, the encryption program does not use a key to decode, so anyone with access to the program can decode an encoded file. Second, and perhaps more important, this method would be easily spotted by any experienced computer programmer!

An improved method of bit-manipulation coding uses the XOR operator. The XOR operator has the following truth table:

^	1	0
1	0	1
0	1	0

or, in words, the outcome of the XOR operation is true if and only if one operand is true and the other is false. This gives the XOR a unique property; if you XOR a byte with another byte, called the "key," and then take the outcome of that operation and XOR it again with the key, you will get the original byte back. For example:

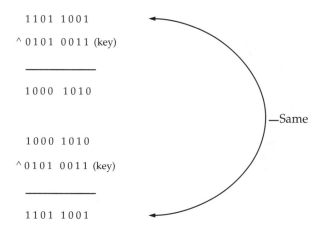

This process then could be used to code a file, and it solves the two problems with the simple 1's complement version. First, because it uses a key, the encryption program alone cannot decode a file. Second, the bit manipulation is not trivially easy to detect.

The key need not be just 1 byte long. In fact, you could use a key of several characters and alternate the characters through the file. However, for simplicity, the following program uses a single-character key to keep the program uncluttered.

```
// XOR cipher

#include <iostream.h>
#include <fstream.h>
#include <stdlib.h>
#include <ctype.h>

void encode(char *input, char *output, char key);
void decode(char *input, char *output, char key);

main(int argc, char *argv[])
{
  if(argc!=5) {
    cout << "Usage: input output decode/encode key\n";
    exit(1);
  }

  if(toupper(*argv[3])=='E')
    encode(argv[1], argv[2], *argv[4]);
  else
    decode(argv[1], argv[2], *argv[4]);

  return 0;
```

7

```
}

// Encode
void encode(char *input, char *output, char key)
{
  int ch;
  ifstream in(input, ios::in | ios::binary);
  ofstream out(output, ios::out | ios::binary);

  if(!in) {
    cout << "Cannot open input file.\n";
    exit(1);
  }

  if(!out) {
    cout << "Cannot open output file.\n";
    exit(1);
  }

  do {
    ch = in.get();
    ch = ch^key;
    if(!in.eof()) out.put((char) ch);
  } while(!in.eof());

  in.close();
  out.close();
}

// Decode
void decode(char *input, char *output, char key)
{
  int ch;
  ifstream in(input, ios::in | ios::binary);
  ofstream out(output, ios::out | ios::binary);

  if(!in) {
    cout << "Cannot open input file.\n";
    exit(1);
  }

  if(!out) {
    cout << "Cannot open output file.\n";
    exit(1);
  }

  do {
    ch = in.get();
```

```
    ch = ch^key;
    if(!in.eof()) out.put((char) ch);
  } while(!in.eof());

  in.close();
  out.close();
}
```

When you try this program, you will see that the coded version of the file is unintelligible and can only be decoded through the use of the key.

Data Compression

Data compression is essentially making the same amount of information fit into a smaller space. It is not limited to computers—consider microfilm, for example. However, it is often used in computer systems to effectively increase the storage of the system, to save transfer time (especially over phone lines), and to provide a level of security. There are many general-purpose data compression schemes available, such as Huffman coding and Lempel-Ziv. These techniques are rather sophisticated and are beyond the scope of this chapter. Instead, let's look at two easy but effective ways to compress textual data. The first compresses 8 bits into 7. The other compresses 4 bytes into 3. As you will see, even though these techniques are quite simple to implement, they provide significant compression when dealing with text-only files.

8 into 7

For most languages, it is possible to represent the entire character set by use of only 6 bits. For example, as you know, there are only 26 letters in the English alphabet. Thus, the uppercase and lowercase letters require only 52 distinct codes. Since 6 bits can hold the values 0 through 63, 6 bits are more than sufficient to represent the characters in the English language. In fact, for English, 6 bits could also hold several punctuation characters as well. However, most computers use an 8-bit byte. Therefore, if you are only storing textual information, the last two bits—25 percent of each byte—are wasted. Thus, you could, in theory, compact 4 characters into 3 if you were able to use the last two bits in each byte. The only problem is that there are more than 64 ASCII codes, and the uppercase and lowercase alphabet do not use the first 64 values. This means that the ASCII codes for several of the characters (specifically, the lowercase letters) require a 7th bit. It is possible to use a non-ASCII representation (which is the subject of the next section), but this is not always desirable. However, even using the standard ASCII character set, 1 bit is still wasted. Therefore, an alternative option is to compact 8 characters into 7, making use of the fact that no letter or common punctuation mark uses the 8th bit of a byte. This method will still save 12.5 percent. You should realize, however, that many computers, the PC included, do use 8-bit characters to represent special or graphics characters. Also, some word processors use the 8th bit to indicate text processing instructions. Therefore, the use of this type of data compaction will only work on standard ASCII files which do not use the 8th bit for anything.

There are various ways to compact 8 characters into 7 bytes. To understand the approach used by the example, consider the following eight characters represented using the standard 8-bit byte.

```
byte 1:  0 1 1 1   0 1 0 1
byte 2:  0 1 1 1   1 1 0 1
byte 3:  0 0 1 0   0 0 1 1
byte 4:  0 1 0 1   0 1 1 0
byte 5:  0 0 0 1   0 0 0 0
byte 6:  0 1 1 0   1 1 0 1
byte 7:  0 0 1 0   1 0 1 0
byte 8:  0 1 1 1   1 0 0 1
```

As you can see, the 8th bit is always zero. This will always be the case unless it is used for parity checking. The easiest way to compress eight characters into seven is to distribute the seven significant bits of byte 1 into the seven unused 8th bit positions of bytes 2 through 8. If this is done, the seven remaining bytes will look like this:

```
                 ┌──── byte 1—read down
byte 2:  1 1 1 1   1 1 0 1
byte 3:  1 0 1 0   0 0 1 1
byte 4:  1 1 0 1   0 1 1 0
byte 5:  0 0 0 1   0 0 0 0
byte 6:  1 1 1 0   1 1 0 1
byte 7:  0 0 1 0   1 0 1 0
byte 8:  1 1 1 1   1 0 0 1
```

To reconstruct byte 1, you only need to put it back together again by taking the 8th bit off of each of the 7 bytes.

The compression technique described here will compress any text file by one-eighth, or 12.5 percent. This is a fairly substantial savings. If you were, for example, transmitting the source code for your favorite program to a friend over long-distance phone lines, then you would be saving 12.5 percent of the expense of transmission.

The program shown here will compress a text file as described earlier. Be aware that in order for the algorithm to work correctly at the end of the file, up to 7 extra bytes may be appended to the output file. Thus, on extremely short files (fewer than 56 bytes), the compressed file may be longer than the noncompressed file. However, these extra bytes are insignificant in longer files. You might find it interesting to try to alter the algorithm so that these extra bytes are never needed.

```cpp
// Compressing 8 bytes into 7

#include <iostream.h>
#include <fstream.h>
#include <stdlib.h>
#include <ctype.h>

void compress(char *input, char *output);
void decompress(char *input, char *output);

main(int argc, char *argv[])
{
  if(argc!=4) {
    cout << "Usage: input output compress/decompress\n";
    exit(1);
  }

  if(toupper(*argv[3])=='C')
    compress(argv[1], argv[2]);
  else
    decompress(argv[1], argv[2]);

  return 0;
}

// Compress
void compress(char *input, char *output)
{
  char ch, ch2, done, t;
  ifstream in(input, ios::in | ios::binary);
  ofstream out(output, ios::out | ios::binary);

  if(!in) {
    cout << "Cannot open input file.\n";
    exit(1);
  }
```

```cpp
  if(!out) {
    cout << "Cannot open output file.\n";
    exit(1);
  }

  done = 0;
  do {
      /* Get the first byte.  This one will
         be distributed into the next 7 bytes. */
      ch = in.get();
      ch = ch << 1;   // shift off top bit

      // distribute remaining 7 bits into next 7 bytes
      for(t=0; t<7; ++t) {
        ch2 = in.get();
        if(in.eof()) {
          ch2 = 0;
          done = 1;
        }
        ch2 = ch2 & 127; // turn off top bit of next byte

        // now, OR in next bit from the first byte
        ch2 = ch2 | ((ch<<t) & 128);
        out.put((char) ch2);
      }
  } while(!done && !in.eof());

  in.close();
  out.close();
}

// Decompress
void decompress(char *input, char *output)
{
  unsigned char ch, ch2, t;
  char s[7];
  ifstream in(input, ios::in | ios::binary);
  ofstream out(output, ios::out | ios::binary);

  if(!in) {
    cout << "Cannot open input file.\n";
    exit(1);
  }

  if(!out) {
    cout << "Cannot open output file.\n";
    exit(1);
  }
```

```
do {
  ch = 0;
  // reconstruct the first byte */
  for(t=0;  t<7;  ++t) {
    ch2 = in.get();
    s[t] = ch2 & 127; // turn off top bit
    ch2 = ch2 & 128;  // turn off all but top bit
    ch2 = ch2 >> (t+1); // shift over existing bits
    ch = ch | ch2;      // OR in the next bit
  }

  out.put((char) ch); // write out the first byte

  // write out the remaining 7
  for(t=0; t<7; ++t) out.put(s[t]);

} while(!in.eof());

in.close();
out.close();
}
```

The bit-manipulation code is fairly complex, because bits that make the 8th byte must be shifted into their proper positions. Remember, in C++, the **>>** performs a right shift, and the **<<** performs a left shift. These operations are performed on a bitwise level. You should try to follow the operation of each until you are confident that you understand the **compress( )** and **decompress( )** functions.

4 into 3

As mentioned in the preceding section, the upper- and lowercase letters require only 52 characters, which can be represented by 6 bits. Thus, the entire upper- and lowercase alphabet plus the more common punctuation can be represented by a 6-bit word. But, as mentioned, the ASCII representations of the upper- and lowercase letters contain values that are greater than 63, thus requiring at least 7 bits. Despite this problem, it is still possible to compact characters into 6-bit words. To do this, the use of the ASCII codes must be abandoned. Instead, let's assign each character a new 6-bit value which is an index into a character table. The indexes will be stored when the file is compressed, with 4 index values compressed into a 3-byte packet. Thus a compression ratio of 25 percent will be achieved. When the file is expanded, the indexes will be used to obtain the standard ASCII representation of each character.

Here is the 4 into 3 compression program:

7

```
// Compress 4 characters into 3

#include <iostream.h>
#include <fstream.h>
#include <stdlib.h>
#include <ctype.h>

void compress(char *input, char *output);
void decompress(char *input, char *output);
char IndexToChar(char ch);
char CharToIndex(char i);

char letters[] =
  "abcdefghijklmnopqrstuvwxyz"
  "ABCDEFGHIJKLMNOPQRSTUVWXWY"
  " .,!:;\n\r\x1a";

union packet_type {
  char chrs[4];
  unsigned long bits;
} packet;

main(int argc, char *argv[])
{
  if(argc!=4) {
    cout << "Usage: input output compress/decompress\n";
    exit(1);
  }

  if(toupper(*argv[3])=='C')
    compress(argv[1], argv[2]);
  else
    decompress(argv[1], argv[2]);

  return 0;
}

// Compress
void compress(char *input, char *output)
{
  char ch;
  int i;
  ifstream in(input, ios::in | ios::binary);
  ofstream out(output, ios::out | ios::binary);

  if(!in) {
    cout << "Cannot open input file.\n";
    exit(1);
```

```
  }

  if(!out) {
    cout << "Cannot open output file.\n";
    exit(1);
  }

  do {
    packet.bits = 0L;

    ch = in.get(); // get first char
    if(in.eof()) break; // stop if end of file
    packet.bits = CharToIndex(ch); // convert to index
    packet.bits <<= 6; // make room for next char

    // now, get remaining three chars
    ch = in.get();
    if(in.eof()) ch = ' '; // pad uneven file with spaces
    packet.bits |= CharToIndex(ch);
    packet.bits <<= 6;

    ch = in.get();
    if(in.eof()) ch = ' '; // pad uneven file with spaces
    packet.bits |= CharToIndex(ch);
    packet.bits <<= 6;

    ch = in.get();
    if(in.eof()) ch = ' '; // pad uneven file with space
    packet.bits |= CharToIndex(ch);

    // output packet
    for(i=0; i<3; i++) out.put(packet.chrs[i]);

  } while(!in.eof());

  in.close();
  out.close();
}

// Decompress
void decompress(char *input, char *output)
{
  char ch, chrs[4];
  int i;
  ifstream in(input, ios::in | ios::binary);
  ofstream out(output, ios::out | ios::binary);

  if(!in) {
```

7

```
    cout << "Cannot open input file.\n";
    exit(1);
  }

  if(!out) {
    cout << "Cannot open output file.\n";
    exit(1);
  }

  do {
    packet.bits = 0L;

    for(i=0; i<3; i++) packet.chrs[i] = in.get();

    if(in.eof()) break;

    // mask off all but low-order 6 bits
    ch = packet.bits & 63;
    ch = IndexToChar(ch);
    chrs[3] = ch;

    packet.bits >>= 6; // shift down next 6 bits

    // mask off all but low-order 6 bits
    ch = packet.bits & 63;
    ch = IndexToChar(ch);
    chrs[2] = ch;

    packet.bits >>= 6; // shift down next 6 bits

    // mask off all but low-order 6 bits
    ch = packet.bits & 63;
    ch = IndexToChar(ch);
    chrs[1] = ch;

    packet.bits >>= 6; // shift down next 6 bits

    // mask off all but low-order 6 bits
    ch = packet.bits & 63;
    ch = IndexToChar(ch);
    chrs[0] = ch;

    for(i=0; i<4; i++) out.put(chrs[i]);
  } while(!in.eof());

  in.close();
  out.close();
}
```

```
// Find index given character
char CharToIndex(char ch)
{
  int i;
  for(i=0; i<63; i++)
    if(ch == letters[i]) return i;

  return -1;
}

// Find character given index
char IndexToChar(char i)
{
  return letters[i];
}
```

The program works like this. Each character of the plain-text file is converted into an index into the **letters** array by use of **CharToIndex( )**. Since no index will be greater than 63, only 6 bits are required to represent each index. After 4 characters have been read, the indexes are compacted into the low-order 3 bytes of an unsigned long integer. Since C++ operates on 8-bit bytes as its smallest unit of built-in data, several bit manipulations are required to accomplish this. In words, the algorithm can be stated as follows:

```
for(each four indexes) {
    Copy low-order 6 bits from the next index into the low-order
    word of an unsigned long integer.
    Shift all bits left 6 positions.
}
```

After each set of 4 bytes has been compacted into a 3-byte packet, the packet is written to the output file. To decode an encoded file, the process is reversed. Each packet is read, the indexes retrieved, and then converted into characters using **IndexToChar( )**.

7

Some Things to Try

It is possible to design your own highly secure encryption algorithms using bit manipulations. Here are some ideas.

♦ Use a variation on the XOR algorithm in which a longer key is used.

♦ Using a "traveling" XOR-based routine which codes a file a packet (a few bytes) at a time. Use the outcome of the preceding packet as a partial key to encode the next packet.

♦ Here is a very interesting idea: encode two different files into the same encrypted output file. When the file is decoded one way, the first file is produced. When decoded a second way, the other file is retrieved.

♦ Try "hiding" the file after it is encoded. To do this, distribute the contents of the encrypted file throughout several different files. One good way is to append pieces of the encoded file onto the end of the data areas of program files. This would make it very hard to reconstruct the file.

Data compression offers a nearly limitless challenge to the inventive mind. To begin, you might want to try implementing your own version of the Lempel-Ziv algorithm. A description of this compression technique can be found in numerous computer science textbooks and is often a topic of magazine articles. If you are particularly interested in data compression, you might find this book interesting: *The Data Compression Book* by Mark Nelson (1991, M&T Publishing, Inc., Redwood City, California). It provides an extensive presentation of the various data compression techniques, including Lempel-Ziv, Huffman coding, and lossy techniques.

Here is a compression idea you can try on your own. Think about a large text file. Most likely, it contains numerous repeated words, such as "the", "and", "which", "that", and the like. It is possible to build a table consisting of the different words in the file. Once this is done, the table, plus a stream of the indexes could be written to a new file, which will form the compressed version of the original. To reconstruct the file, simply use the indexes to index the table, and then write out the decompressed version.

Chapter 8

Interfacing to Assembly Language Functions

This chapter explains how to incorporate low-level assembly code into your C++ programs. If you're like most C++ programmers, then wringing the last bit of performance out of your programs is not something that you do from time to time, it is a way of life. While the first step to improving the performance of a program is to carefully examine the algorithms that underlie it, at some point you must turn to the actual machine instructions that implement those algorithms. It is at this juncture that assembly language interfacing comes into play. Through the judicious use of assembly language, you gain precise control over the execution of your program. As you will see, the way that you link assembly language routines with your C++ code will vary from compiler to compiler, but the general process described in this chapter applies to most compilers.

There are two ways to integrate assembly code modules into your C++ programs. You can code the assembler routine separately and link it with the rest of your program. Alternately, you can use the inline assembly code capabilities of C++. This chapter explores both methods.

A word of warning: This chapter does *not* teach you how to code in assembly language—it assumes that you already know how. If you do not, don't try the examples. It is extremely easy to do something slightly wrong and create a disaster—you could erase your hard disk, for example. However, if you are familiar with assembly language, then you will have no trouble using the examples or creating your own assembly language functions.

Why Use Assembly Language?

As powerful as C++ is, at times you will want to write a routine in assembly language. There are four main reasons for this:

◆   To gain speed and efficiency

◆   To perform some machine-specific function unavailable in C++

◆   To use third-party libraries

◆   To circumvent built-in safeguards provided by C++ or the operating system

Let's take a closer look at these now.

Although C++ compilers tend to produce extremely fast, compact object code, no compiler consistently creates code as good as that written by an excellent assembly language programmer. Most of the time, the small difference does not matter, nor does it warrant the extra time needed to write in assembly language. However, in selected cases it will make sense for an individual function to be coded in assembly language to improve its performance. For example, you might write a floating-point math package in assembly language because it is used frequently and greatly affects a program's execution speed. Another routine may be coded in assembly language to reduce its size. Also, special hardware devices may need exact timing, which means that you must code in assembly language to meet the strict timing requirement.

Many CPUs have certain instructions that most C++ compilers cannot execute. For example, when programming for one of the 8086-family processors, you cannot change data segments with any standard C++ instruction. Also, you cannot issue a software interrupt or control the contents of specific registers using a standard C++ statement.

Sometimes you will want to make use of a specialized library that is written in another language, such as FORTRAN (or even assembly language). For example, you might want to use a specialized library that controls a robot or draws special character fonts using a plotter. Occasionally, you can simply link these types of routines with code compiled by your compiler. At other times, you must write an interface module to correct any differences in the interface used by your compiler and the routines you are using.

The final reason to code in assembly language is a bit less benign than the preceding ones. While it is not usually a good idea to circumvent or defeat safeguards built into C++ or the operating system, it can occasionally be necessary. Using assembly language is one way that you can accomplish this. For example, relative to C++ source code, private members of a class can only be accessed by other members of that class. However, when using assembly language, private members are as easily accessible as public ones! Most of the time you would not want to tear down the wall of encapsulation, but in an emergency, you might. (One such case might occur after a system crash, when you're trying to recover valuable data.) Since the use of assembly language gives you access to the lowest-level instructions executed by the machine, you can (more or less) do any type of operation you choose.

Whatever the reason that you decide to include an assembly language module in your C++ program, the techniques described in this chapter will help you do it.

Assembly Language Interfacing Fundamentals

The interfacing of C++ and assembly language is affected by four things:

♦ The type of CPU

♦ The memory model being used

♦ The calling conventions of the compiler

♦ Whether 16-bit or 32-bit code is being generated

Let's look at each.

Each CPU defines its own assembly language. Thus, the target CPU has a profound effect on how you will write an assembly language module and link it to a C++ program.

For most CPUs, there are several ways in which memory may be organized. Each organization is called a *memory model*. The memory model determines such things as the size of a pointer (that is, address) and how large a single object may be. The memory models include tiny, small, compact, medium, large, huge, and flat. The specifics of these models are discussed in the next section.

8

Each C++ compiler is free to define its own calling convention, which determines how information is passed to and from a function. To interface an assembly code module to a C++ program, you must know the conventions used by your compiler.

As you probably know, older processors use 16-bit registers. Newer processors support both 16-bit registers (for compatibility) and 32-bit registers. Further complicating things is the fact that even though the newer processors can handle 32 bits, many operating systems, such as DOS and Windows 3.1, can't. (For the most part, they utilize only 16-bit values.) This would not matter except that, for various reasons, the assembly code instructions for 16-bit mode are often different from those for 32-bit mode. Also, when operating in 32-bit mode, integers are typically 32 bits wide, rather than 16.

Given the number of variables that affect the interfacing of assembly language with C++, there is no way to examine all possible variations. Instead, a specific environment must be assumed. Here are the assumptions used in this chapter. First, most of the examples use 16-bit code, the small memory model, and require at least an 80286 CPU. This means that these examples will work on most computers. However, one example of 32-bit code that uses the flat memory model is also included. (This program must be run under a 32-bit operating system, such as Windows 95.) The 32-bit example requires an 80386 or better CPU. Also, one 16-bit example is shown that is designed for the huge memory model. Since this chapter assumes an 8086-based CPU, 8086-based assembly language is used. The assembly language interfacing examples shown in this chapter assume the calling conventions used by both Borland C++ (version 4.5) and Microsoft Visual C++ (version 4), but you can generally apply the information to other C++ compilers. Even if you have a different CPU or compiler, the following discussion can serve as a guide. Remember, however, that interfacing to assembly language is an advanced technique.

The Calling Conventions of a C++ Compiler

A *calling convention* is the method that a particular C++ compiler uses to pass information into functions and to return values. Virtually all C++ compilers use the stack to pass arguments to functions. If the argument is one of the built-in data types or a structure, class, union, or enumeration, the actual value is passed on the stack. If the argument is an array, its address is placed on the stack. When a C++ function begins execution, it retrieves its parameter's value from the stack. When a C++ function terminates, it passes a return value back to the calling routine. Typically, this value is returned in a register, although some types of values (especially large ones) are returned on the stack or sometimes in an internally defined global variable.

The calling convention also determines exactly what registers must be preserved and which ones you can use freely. Often a compiler produces object code that needs only a portion of the available registers for a given CPU. You must preserve the contents of the registers used by your compiler, generally by pushing their contents on the stack before using them and then popping them when you are done. Any other registers are usually free for your use.

When you write an assembly language module that must interface to code compiled by your C++ compiler, you need to follow the conventions defined and used by your compiler. Only in this way can you hope to have assembly language routines interface correctly to your C++ code. The next section examines in detail the calling conventions of the Borland and Microsoft C++ compilers when operating in 16-bit mode. Remember, the calling conventions are sensitive to the memory model being used and to whether 16- or 32-bit code is being produced.

The Calling Conventions of Borland/Microsoft C++

Here is an overview of the calling conventions used by Borland C++ and Microsoft C++ when operating in 16-bit mode. As is the case with most C++ compilers, both Borland C++ and Microsoft Visual C++ pass arguments to functions on the stack. The arguments are pushed onto the stack from right to left. That is, given the call

    func(a, b, c);

c is pushed first, followed by **b**, and then **a**. Table 8-1 shows the number of bytes occupied on the stack by each type, assuming 16-bit code.

Upon entry into an assembly code function, the contents of the BP register must be saved on the stack, and the current value of the stack pointer (SP) is placed into BP. The only other registers that you must preserve are SI, DI, CS, SS, and DS (if your routine uses them). Before returning, your assembly language function must restore the values of BP, SI, DI, CS, SS, and DS and reset the stack pointer. (Since register conventions change over time, be sure to check your compiler's user manual for the list of registers that must be preserved.)

If your assembly language function returns an 8- or 16-bit value, it is placed into the AX register. Otherwise, it is returned according to Table 8-2.

The calling conventions for 32-bit mode will be similar to those for 16-bit mode, except that the extended, 32-bit registers must be saved.

8

Type	Number of Bytes
char	2
short	2
signed char	2
signed short	2
unsigned char	2
unsigned short	2
int	2
signed int	2
unsigned int	2
long	4
unsigned long	4
float	4
double	8
long double	10
(near) pointer	2 (offset only)
(far) pointer	4 (segment and offset)

One last point: A C++ program allocates space for local data on the stack. When you write your own assembly code functions, you must follow the same procedure for local variables.

Type	Register(s) and Meaning
char	AL
unsigned char	AL
short	AX
unsigned short	AX
int	AX
unsigned int	AX
long	Low-order word in AX High-order word in DX
unsigned long	Low-order word in AX High-order word in DX
float & double	Address to value returned; AX contains offset, DX contains segment
struct & union	Address to value returned; AX contains offset, DX contains segment
(near) pointer	AX
(far) pointer	Offset in AX, segment in DX

A Word About Memory Models

As mentioned, the memory model affects how an assembly code module will be written. Although it is beyond the scope of this book to go into detail about the various models and addressing modes supported by the 8086 family or processors, the following brief overview is sufficient for the purposes of this chapter.

When operating in segmented mode, the 8086 family of processors views memory as a collection of 64K chunks, each called a segment. Each byte of memory is defined by its segment address (held in a segment register of the CPU) and its offset (held in another register) within that segment. Both the segment and offset use 16-bit values. When a memory address is accessed that lies within the current segment, only the 16-bit offset need be loaded to access a specific byte of memory. However, if the memory address lies outside the current segment, both the 16-bit segment and the 16-bit offset need to be loaded. Thus, when accessing memory within the current segment, the C++ compiler can treat a pointer, call, or jump instruction as a 16-bit object. When accessing memory outside the current segment, the compiler must treat a pointer, call, or jump instruction as a 32-bit entity.

Given the segmented nature of the 8086 family, you can organize memory into one of these six models (shown in order of increasing execution time):

Tiny	All segment registers are set to the same value, and all addressing is done using 16 bits. This means that the code, data, and stack must all fit within the same 64K segment. Fastest program execution.
Small	All code must fit in one 64K segment, and all data must fit in a second 64K segment. All pointers are 16 bits. As fast as tiny model.
Medium	All data must fit in one 64K segment, but the code may use multiple segments. All pointers to data are 16 bits, but all jumps and calls require 32-bit addresses. Quick access to data, slower code execution.
Compact	All code must fit in one 64K segment, but the data may use multiple segments. However, no data item can exceed 64K. All pointers to data are 32 bits, but jumps and calls may use 16-bit addresses. Slow access to data, faster code execution.
Large	Both code and data may use multiple segments. All pointers are 32 bits. However, no single data item can exceed 64K. Slower program execution.
Huge	Both code and data may use multiple segments. All pointers are 32 bits. Single data items can exceed 64K. Slowest program execution.

8

As you might guess, it is much faster to access memory via 16-bit pointers than 32-bit pointers, because half as many bits need to be loaded into the CPU for each memory reference.

More modern CPUs, such as the 80486 and the Pentium, can also access memory as flat—that is, addresses are 32 bits wide and are not a combination of segments and offsets. The flat memory model is used when operating in 32-bit mode. Thus, in addition to the six segmented models, modern processors add a seventh, the flat model. The flat model is conceptually cleaner and easier to think about because it works in the same way that most people normally think about memory. Addresses are unique, single values that run consecutively from start to finish. However, because of the demand for downward compatibility, the 16-bit segmented models are still in wide use. While the future clearly belongs to the 32-bit, flat mode model, the 16-bit segmented modes will be around for a long time.

For most of the examples in this book, the small memory model is used because it is the lowest common denominator: anyone with an 8086-based computer and a C++ compiler can create a small-model program.

Creating an Assembly Code Function

The easiest way to learn to create assembly language functions that are compatible with your compiler's calling convention is to see how your compiler generates code. Virtually all C++ compilers have a compile-time option that causes the compiler to output an assembly language listing of the code that it generates. By examining this file, you can learn a great deal about not only how to interface to the compiler, but also how the compiler actually works.

To generate assembly code output using Borland C++, specify the **-S** option when using the command-line compiler. To produce an assembly language listing using the Microsoft Visual C++ compiler, either select the proper option within the Developer Studio, or specify the **-FA** option when using the command-line version. The assembly code contained in a file has the same filename as the original C++ program, but has the extension .ASM. This chapter uses the assembly code listings to show how a C++ compiler generates code for various types of operations.

Note: In some assembly code listings, lines containing debugging information have been deleted in the interest of clarity. Any such deletions have no effect on the operation of the assembly code.

Passing Arguments to a Function

Since most assembly language functions will operate on parameters and return values, let's begin with a simple example that passes two integer arguments to a function and returns a value using the short C++ program shown here:

```cpp
int sum;
int add(int a, int b);

main()
{
  sum = add(10, 12);

  return 0;
}

add(int a, int b)
{
  int t;

  t = a + b;
  return t;
}
```

The variable **sum** is intentionally declared as global so that you can see examples of both local and global data. If this program is called **test**, the following command line creates **test.asm** using Borland C++.

    bcc -S test.cpp

This causes the program to be compiled for the small memory model. The contents of **test.asm** are shown here:

```
          .286p
          ifndef  ??version
?debug    macro
          endm
publicdll macro name
          public  name
          endm
$comm     macro   name,dist,size,count
          comm    dist name:BYTE:count*size
          endm
          else
$comm     macro   name,dist,size,count
          comm    dist name[size]:BYTE:count
```

8

```
            endm
            endif
            ?debug  V 301h
            ?debug  S "test.cpp"
            ?debug  C E98FB09E1F08746573742E637070
_TEXT       segment byte public 'CODE'
_TEXT       ends
DGROUP      group   _DATA,_BSS
            assume  cs:_TEXT,ds:DGROUP
_DATA       segment word public 'DATA'
d@          label   byte
d@w         label   word
_DATA       ends
_BSS        segment word public 'BSS'
b@          label   byte
b@w         label   word
_sum        label   word
            db      2 dup (?)
_BSS        ends
_TEXT       segment byte public 'CODE'
    ;
    ;       main()
    ;
            assume  cs:_TEXT,ds:DGROUP
_main       proc    near
            push    bp
            mov     bp,sp
    ;
    ;       {
    ;         sum = add(10, 12);
    ;
            push    12
            push    10
            call    near ptr @add$qii
            add     sp,4
            mov     word ptr DGROUP:_sum,ax
    ;
    ;
    ;         return 0;
    ;
            xor     ax,ax
            pop     bp
            ret
    ;
    ;       }
    ;
            pop     bp
            ret
```

```
_main    endp
    ;
    ;       add(int a, int b)
    ;
         assume   cs:_TEXT,ds:DGROUP
@add$qii         proc     near
         enter    2,0
    ;
    ;       {
    ;          int t;
    ;
    ;          t = a + b;
    ;
         mov      ax,word ptr [bp+4]
         add      ax,word ptr [bp+6]
         mov      word ptr [bp-2],ax
    ;
    ;          return t;
    ;
         mov      ax,word ptr [bp-2]
         leave
         ret
    ;
    ;       }
    ;
         leave
         ret
@add$qii         endp
         ?debug   C E9
         ?debug   C FA00000000
_TEXT    ends
_DATA    segment word public 'DATA'
s@       label    byte
_DATA    ends
_TEXT    segment byte public 'CODE'
_TEXT    ends
_s@      equ      s@
         public   _sum
         public   @add$qii
         public   _main
         end
```

Let's look closely at this assembly code version of the program. One of the first things to notice is that the compiler automatically adds the underscore in front of **sum** and **main** to avoid confusion with any internal compiler names. In fact, the underscore is added to the front of all global variable names. (This is common practice and is used by most compilers.) Further,

8

notice that the name of the **add( )** function has been "mangled." Because C++ supports function overloading, the compiler must construct a unique function name for each overloaded version of a function. It does this through a process known as *name mangling,* in which information about the function's parameters is encoded into its internal name. Although this program does not overload **add( )**, the compiler will still apply the same name mangling conventions.

Look now at the code associated with **_main**. The first thing that it does is push BP and move SP into BP. Next, the two arguments to **add** are pushed on the stack and **add** is called. When **add** returns, the stack is reset (by use of **add sp,4**). Next, the return value, which is in AX, is moved into **_sum**. Finally, **_main** restores BP and returns zero.

The function **add** begins by executing an ENTER instruction, which constructs a standard stack frame. This instruction saves the contents of BP on the stack, moves the contents of SP into BP, and allocates space on the stack for local variables. After this has been accomplished, parameters can be accessed by use of positive offsets relative to BP. Local variables can be accessed by use of negative offsets relative to BP. The next three lines of code add the numbers and place their sum in **t**'s location on the stack. Notice how the parameters to **add** are accessed by indexing BP. After the addition has been performed, the return value (in this case **t**) is loaded into AX. Next, the LEAVE instruction is called, which undoes the operations performed by ENTER and then the function returns.

To use this assembly language file, you will need to assemble it and then link it with the run-time package provided by your C++ compiler. For example, if you are using Borland C++ and have TASM (the Borland assembler), then you can use the following command line to assemble the previous file and link it with Borland's C++ run-time package.

```
bcc test.asm
```

Here, Borland C++ automatically invokes TASM, which assembles the file. Next, Borland C++ automatically links it with its run-time library.

As mentioned, you must keep in mind that different compilers generate somewhat different code. Furthermore, differences between memory models, and whether 16-bit or 32-bit code is produced, have a substantial effect on the specific assembly code generated. To see an example, examine the following assembly language program. This program was produced by compiling the preceding C++ program using Microsoft Visual C++ 4, 32-bit version, using the flat (32-bit addressing) memory model. Notice the similarities (and differences) with the code produced by the Borland 16-bit compiler.

```
          TITLE    test.cpp
          .386P
include listing.inc
if @Version gt 510
.model FLAT
else
_TEXT    SEGMENT PARA USE32 PUBLIC 'CODE'
_TEXT    ENDS
_DATA    SEGMENT DWORD USE32 PUBLIC 'DATA'
_DATA    ENDS
CONST    SEGMENT DWORD USE32 PUBLIC 'CONST'
CONST    ENDS
_BSS     SEGMENT DWORD USE32 PUBLIC 'BSS'
_BSS     ENDS
_TLS     SEGMENT DWORD USE32 PUBLIC 'TLS'
_TLS     ENDS
FLAT     GROUP _DATA, CONST, _BSS
          ASSUME  CS: FLAT, DS: FLAT, SS: FLAT
endif
_BSS     SEGMENT
?sum@@3HA DD    01H DUP (?)                          ; sum
_BSS     ENDS
PUBLIC  ?add@@YAHHH@Z                        ; add
PUBLIC  _main
_TEXT    SEGMENT
; File test.cpp
_main   PROC NEAR
; Line 5
        push    ebp
        mov     ebp, esp
        push    ebx
        push    esi
        push    edi
; Line 6
        push    12                           ; 0000000cH
        push    10                           ; 0000000aH
        call    ?add@@YAHHH@Z                ; add
        add     esp, 8
        mov     DWORD PTR ?sum@@3HA, eax      ; sum
; Line 8
        xor     eax, eax
        jmp     $L173
; Line 9
$L173:
        pop     edi
        pop     esi
        pop     ebx
        leave
```

8

```
        ret     0
_main   ENDP
_a$ = 8
_b$ = 12
_t$ = -4
?add@@YAHHH@Z PROC NEAR                                   ; add
; Line 12
        push    ebp
        mov     ebp, esp
        sub     esp, 4
        push    ebx
        push    esi
        push    edi
; Line 15
        mov     eax, DWORD PTR _b$[ebp]
        add     eax, DWORD PTR _a$[ebp]
        mov     DWORD PTR _t$[ebp], eax
; Line 16
        mov     eax, DWORD PTR _t$[ebp]
        jmp     $L176
; Line 17
$L176:
        pop     edi
        pop     esi
        pop     ebx
        leave
        ret     0
?add@@YAHHH@Z ENDP                                        ; add
_TEXT   ENDS
END
```

The single most important difference between this version of the program
and the one produced by Borland C++ is that 32-bit instructions are used.
For example, instead of saving BP, which is a 16-bit register, the 32-bit
version saves EBP, which is the 32-bit version of BP. Further, all register
references are now to the extended, 32-bit registers. Notice that the
Microsoft version also creates the stack frame for **add** explicitly, rather than
using ENTER. (However, it does use LEAVE to clean up the stack prior to
returning.) As you can see, Microsoft applies name mangling to **add** for the
same reasons that the Borland compiler did. Keep in mind that all C++
compilers apply some form of name mangling to function names so that
overloaded versions of a function can be kept separate.

Calling Library Functions and Operators

Generally, standard library functions and operator functions (such as the
input and output operators) are called from assembly code in exactly the

same way that a function that you write is called. Any arguments are pushed on the stack, a CALL instruction is executed, and then the stack is cleaned up. Here is an example that calls the **ostream operator<<( )** function and the library functions **srand( )** and **rand( )**:

```
#include <iostream.h>
#include <stdlib.h>

int sum;
int randnum;

int add(int a, int b);

main()
{
  sum = add(10, 12);
  cout << sum;

  srand(1000);
  randnum = rand();
  cout << randnum;

  return 0;
}

add(int a, int b)
{
  int t;

  t = a + b;
  return t;
}
```

This program produces the following assembly code file. Pay special attention to the way that the output operator and the library functions are called.

```
          .286p
          ifndef   ??version
?debug    macro
          endm
publicdll macro name
          public   name
          endm
$comm     macro    name,dist,size,count
          comm     dist name:BYTE:count*size
          endm
```

8

```
            else
$comm      macro     name,dist,size,count
            comm      dist name[size]:BYTE:count
            endm
            endif
            ?debug    V 301h
            ?debug    S "test.cpp"
_TEXT      segment byte public 'CODE'
_TEXT      ends
DGROUP     group     _DATA,_BSS
            assume    cs:_TEXT,ds:DGROUP
_DATA      segment word public 'DATA'
d@         label     byte
d@w        label     word
_DATA      ends
_BSS       segment word public 'BSS'
b@         label     byte
b@w        label     word
_sum       label     word
            db        2 dup (?)
_randnum             label     word
            db        2 dup (?)
_BSS       ends
_TEXT      segment byte public 'CODE'
   ;
   ;       main()
   ;
            assume    cs:_TEXT,ds:DGROUP
_main      proc      near
            enter     4,0
   ;
   ;       {
   ;         sum = add(10, 12);
   ;
            push      12
            push      10
            call      near ptr @add$qii
            add       sp,4
            mov       word ptr DGROUP:_sum,ax
   ;
   ;         cout << sum;
   ;
            mov       ax,word ptr DGROUP:_sum
            mov       word ptr [bp-2],ax
            mov       ax,word ptr [bp-2]
            cwd
            push      dx
            push      ax
```

```
        push    offset DGROUP:_cout
        call    near ptr @ostream@$blsh$ql
        add     sp,6
;
;
;       srand(1000);
;
        push    1000
        call    near ptr _srand
        pop     cx
;
;       randnum = rand();
;
        call    near ptr _rand
        mov     word ptr DGROUP:_randnum,ax
;
;       cout << randnum;
;
        mov     ax,word ptr DGROUP:_randnum
        mov     word ptr [bp-4],ax
        mov     ax,word ptr [bp-4]
        cwd
        push    dx
        push    ax
        push    offset DGROUP:_cout
        call    near ptr @ostream@$blsh$ql
        add     sp,6
;
;
;       return 0;
;
        xor     ax,ax
        leave
        ret
;
;       }
;
        leave
        ret
_main   endp
;
;       add(int a, int b)
;
        assume  cs:_TEXT,ds:DGROUP
@add$qii        proc    near
        enter   2,0
;
;       {
```

8

```
;       int t;
;
;       t = a + b;
;
        mov     ax,word ptr [bp+4]
        add     ax,word ptr [bp+6]
        mov     word ptr [bp-2],ax
;
;       return t;
;
        mov     ax,word ptr [bp-2]
        leave
        ret
;
;       }
;
        leave
        ret
@add$qii        endp
        ?debug  C E9
        ?debug  C FA00000000
_TEXT   ends
_DATA   segment word public 'DATA'
s@      label   byte
_DATA   ends
_TEXT   segment byte public 'CODE'
_TEXT   ends
_s@     equ     s@
        extrn   @ostream@$blsh$ql:near
        extrn   _cout:word
_abs    equ     abs
_atoi   equ     atoi
        extrn   _rand:near
        extrn   _srand:near
        public  _sum
        public  _randnum
        public  @add$qii
        public  _main
        end
```

Notice that the calls to the **ostream operator<<( )** function have name mangling applied to them. This is to be expected because **ostream**'s output operator function is overloaded several times (once for each built-in data type). However, notice that calls to **rand( )** and **srand( )** do not have the same type of name mangling applied to them. In fact, aside from the addition of a leading underscore, their names are unchanged. The reason for this is easy to explain: **rand( )** and **srand( )** are part of the C standard library (which is also part of C++), and C does not support function overloading. This means that no part of the C standard library is overloaded. Thus, there is no need for name mangling. However, the compiler does add a leading underscore to both function names, which is standard practice when C functions are compiled.

In general, if your assembly language program must call a C-based library function, you must add a leading underscore to its name. To call an overloaded C++ function or operator, you must use the properly mangled name. The easiest way to obtain a mangled name is to write a short C++ program that calls the same function (in the same way) and then have the compiler produce an assembly code listing. The properly mangled name can then be easily found.

Accessing Structures and Classes

Although slightly more complex, members of structures and classes present no great difficulty when used to interface to assembly code. For example, here is a short program that uses a structure:

```
#include <iostream.h>

struct mystruct {
  int i;
  int j;
};

main()
{
  mystruct ob;

  ob.i = 10;
  ob.j = 99;

  cout << ob.i << " " << ob.j << endl;

  return 0;
}
```

When it is compiled to assembly code, the following assembly code file is produced:

```
        .286p
        ifndef  ??version
?debug  macro
        endm
```

8

```
publicdll macro name
        public  name
        endm
$comm   macro   name,dist,size,count
        comm    dist name:BYTE:count*size
        endm
        else
$comm   macro   name,dist,size,count
        comm    dist name[size]:BYTE:count
        endm
        endif
        ?debug  V 301h
        ?debug  S "test.cpp"
_TEXT   segment byte public 'CODE'
_TEXT   ends
DGROUP  group   _DATA,_BSS
        assume  cs:_TEXT,ds:DGROUP
_DATA   segment word public 'DATA'
d@      label   byte
d@w     label   word
_DATA   ends
_BSS    segment word public 'BSS'
b@      label   byte
b@w     label   word
_BSS    ends
_TEXT   segment byte public 'CODE'
    ;
    ;   main()
    ;
        assume  cs:_TEXT,ds:DGROUP
_main   proc    near
        enter   10,0
        push    si
    ;
    ;   {
    ;      mystruct ob;
    ;
    ;      ob.i = 10;
    ;
        mov     word ptr [bp-4],10
    ;
    ;      ob.j = 99;
    ;
        mov     word ptr [bp-2],99
    ;
    ;
    ;      cout << ob.i << " " << ob.j << endl;
    ;
```

```
        mov     ax,word ptr [bp-2]
        mov     word ptr [bp-6],ax
        mov     ax,word ptr [bp-4]
        mov     word ptr [bp-8],ax
        mov     ax,word ptr [bp-8]
        cwd
        push    dx
        push    ax
        push    offset DGROUP:_cout
        call    near ptr @ostream@$blsh$ql
        add     sp,6
        mov     si,ax
        push    0
        push    offset DGROUP:s@
        push    si
        call    near ptr @ostream@outstr$qpxct1
        add     sp,6
        mov     ax,word ptr [bp-6]
        cwd
        push    dx
        push    ax
        push    si
        call    near ptr @ostream@$blsh$ql
        add     sp,6
        mov     word ptr [bp-10],ax
        push    word ptr [bp-10]
        call    near ptr @endl$qr7ostream
        pop     cx
    ;
    ;
    ;       return 0;
    ;
        xor     ax,ax
        jmp     short @1@86
@1@86:
    ;
    ;       }
    ;
        pop     si
        leave
        ret
_main   endp
        ?debug  C E9
        ?debug  C FA00000000
_TEXT   ends
_DATA   segment word public 'DATA'
s@      label   byte
        db      ' '
```

8

```
        db       0
_DATA   ends
_TEXT   segment byte public 'CODE'
_TEXT   ends
_s@     equ      s@
        extrn    @ostream@$blsh$ql:near
        extrn    @ostream@outstr$qpxct1:near
        extrn    _cout:word
        extrn    @endl$qr7ostream:near
        public   _main
        end
```

As you can see, the members of the structure are accessed just like other types of variables. Remember, a structure is simply a logical grouping that applies to your high-level C++ source code. At the machine level, all data is the same. Therefore, within the assembly code version of the program, the member variables **i** and **j** are stored on the stack just like any other local variable.

Classes work just like structures. For example, consider this program:

```
#include <iostream.h>

class myclass {
  int i, j;
public:
  myclass(int x, int y) { i=x, j = y; }
  int geti() { return i*2; }
  int getj() { return j+3; }
};

main()
{
  myclass ob(10, 20);

  cout << ob.geti() << " " << ob.getj() << endl;

  return 0;
}
```

This program produces the following assembly language file:

```
        .286p
        ifndef  ??version
?debug  macro
        endm
publicdll macro name
```

```
            public  name
            endm
$comm       macro   name,dist,size,count
            comm    dist name:BYTE:count*size
            endm
            else
$comm       macro   name,dist,size,count
            comm    dist name[size]:BYTE:count
            endm
            endif
            ?debug  V 301h
            ?debug  S "test.cpp"
_TEXT       segment byte public 'CODE'
_TEXT       ends
DGROUP      group   _DATA,_BSS
            assume  cs:_TEXT,ds:DGROUP
_DATA       segment word public 'DATA'
d@          label   byte
d@w         label   word
_DATA       ends
_BSS        segment word public 'BSS'
b@          label   byte
b@w         label   word
_BSS        ends
_TEXT       segment byte public 'CODE'
    ;
    ;       main()
    ;
            assume  cs:_TEXT,ds:DGROUP
_main       proc    near
            enter   10,0
            push    si
    ;
    ;       {
    ;         myclass ob(10, 20);
    ;
            mov     word ptr [bp-4],10
            mov     word ptr [bp-2],20
    ;
    ;
    ;         cout << ob.geti() << " " << ob.getj() << endl;
    ;
            mov     ax,word ptr [bp-2]
            add     ax,3
            mov     word ptr [bp-6],ax
            mov     ax,word ptr [bp-4]
            add     ax,ax
            mov     word ptr [bp-8],ax
```

8

```
        mov     ax,word ptr [bp-8]
        cwd
        push    dx
        push    ax
        push    offset DGROUP:_cout
        call    near ptr @ostream@$blsh$ql
        add     sp,6
        mov     si,ax
        push    0
        push    offset DGROUP:s@
        push    si
        call    near ptr @ostream@outstr$qpxct1
        add     sp,6
        mov     ax,word ptr [bp-6]
        cwd
        push    dx
        push    ax
        push    si
        call    near ptr @ostream@$blsh$ql
        add     sp,6
        mov     word ptr [bp-10],ax
        push    word ptr [bp-10]
        call    near ptr @endl$qr7ostream
        pop     cx
    ;
    ;
    ;       return 0;
    ;
        xor     ax,ax
        jmp     short @1@86
@1@86:
    ;
    ;       }
    ;
        pop     si
        leave
        ret
_main   endp
        ?debug  C E9
        ?debug  C FA00000000
_TEXT   ends
_DATA   segment word public 'DATA'
s@      label   byte
        db      ' '
        db      0
_DATA   ends
_TEXT   segment byte public 'CODE'
_TEXT   ends
```

```
_s@        equ     s@
           extrn   @ostream@$blsh$ql:near
           extrn   @ostream@outstr$qpxct1:near
           extrn   _cout:word
           extrn   @endl$qr7ostream:near
           public  _main
           end
```

At first you may not notice anything unusual about this assembly code program. However, look again at the C++ program used to generate it. Specifically, notice that **i** and **j** are private members of **myclass**. It is important to understand that C++'s concepts of public and private do not translate into assembly code. Any member of a class (whether public or private) may be accessed by any other part of an assembly language program. For example, pay special attention to the two lines of code that initialize the private member variables **i** and **j** of **ob**. They are shown here:

```
mov     word ptr [bp-4],10
mov     word ptr [bp-2],20
```

As you can see, **ob.i** and **ob.j** are accessed just like any other type of variable. The fact that they are private members of **myclass** has no effect on the assembly code produced by the compiler. Put bluntly, encapsulation is a logical construct that has meaning only to your C++ source code. It is not relevant to assembly code functions.

The fact that private members of a class are not private at the assembly code level leads to an obvious conclusion: it is possible to bypass the encapsulation mechanism of C++. For example, in the program just shown, it is easy to give **ob.i** and **ob.j** new values by simply adding two new MOV instructions. Of course, bypassing encapsulation using assembly code defeats one of the most important (indeed, fundamental) features of C++. Therefore, you should not use assembly code functions for this purpose except in the most extraordinary of circumstances.

There is one other interesting thing to notice in this program. Look at the code produced by the calls to **geti( )** and **getj( )**. Since these member functions are defined inside **myclass**, they are automatically inlined, which causes their code to be expanded inline rather than called. This is why there are no call instructions to these functions in the assembly language version of the program.

8

Using Pointers and References

When pointers or references are used as function arguments, then addresses rather than values are passed to the function. To see how this affects the assembly code version of a function, consider the following program. In it, the function **get_val( )** is called using the address of **num** to illustrate the code produced when pointers are passed.

```cpp
#include <iostream.h>

void get_val(int *ptr);

main()
{
  int num;

  get_val(&num);
  cout << num;

  return 0;
}

void get_val(int *ptr)
{
  *ptr = 100;
}
```

The assembly language file is shown here:

```
          .286p
          ifndef  ??version
?debug    macro
          endm
publicdll macro name
          public  name
          endm
$comm     macro   name,dist,size,count
          comm    dist name:BYTE:count*size
          endm
          else
$comm     macro   name,dist,size,count
          comm    dist name[size]:BYTE:count
          endm
          endif
          ?debug  V 301h
          ?debug  S "test.cpp"
_TEXT     segment byte public 'CODE'
_TEXT     ends
DGROUP    group   _DATA,_BSS
          assume  cs:_TEXT,ds:DGROUP
_DATA     segment word public 'DATA'
```

```
d@        label    byte
d@w       label    word
_DATA     ends
_BSS      segment  word public 'BSS'
b@        label    byte
b@w       label    word
_BSS      ends
_TEXT     segment  byte public 'CODE'
    ;
    ;     main()
    ;
          assume   cs:_TEXT,ds:DGROUP
_main     proc     near
          enter    4,0
    ;
    ;     {
    ;       int num;
    ;
    ;       get_val(&num);
    ;
          lea      ax,word ptr [bp-2]
          push     ax
          call     near ptr @get_val$qpi
          pop      cx
    ;
    ;       cout << num;
    ;
          mov      ax,word ptr [bp-2]
          mov      word ptr [bp-4],ax
          mov      ax,word ptr [bp-4]
          cwd
          push     dx
          push     ax
          push     offset DGROUP:_cout
          call     near ptr @ostream@$blsh$ql
          add      sp,6
    ;
    ;
    ;       return 0;
    ;
          xor      ax,ax
          leave
          ret
    ;
    ;     }
    ;
          leave
          ret
```

8

```
_main     endp
   ;
   ;       void get_val(int *ptr)
   ;
          assume   cs:_TEXT,ds:DGROUP
@get_val$qpi   proc      near
          push     bp
          mov      bp,sp
          push     si
          mov      si,word ptr [bp+4]
   ;
   ;       {
   ;          *ptr = 100;
   ;
          mov      word ptr [si],100
   ;
   ;       }
   ;
          pop      si
          pop      bp
          ret
@get_val$qpi   endp
          ?debug   C E9
          ?debug   C FA00000000
_TEXT     ends
_DATA     segment word public 'DATA'
s@        label    byte
_DATA     ends
_TEXT     segment byte public 'CODE'
_TEXT     ends
_s@       equ      s@
          extrn    @ostream@$blsh$ql:near
          extrn    _cout:word
          public   @get_val$qpi
          public   _main
          end
```

As you can see, **get_val** is called with the address of **num**. The address of **num** is found by using the LEA (load effective address) assembly language instruction. Inside **get_val**, this address loads the value **100** into **num** by using the indirect addressing mode of the 8086 family.

Since reference parameters are (more or less) automated pointers in C++, you might expect that changing the preceding C++ program so that **get_val( )** uses a reference instead of a pointer would have little effect on the assembly code produced by the compiler. And, you would be right! For example, here is the reference parameter version of the preceding program:

```
#include <iostream.h>

void get_val(int &ref);

main()
{
  int num;

  get_val(num);
  cout << num;

  return 0;
}

void get_val(int &ref)
{
  ref = 100;
}
```

Here are the relevant parts of the assembly language file produced by this program:

```
_TEXT    segment byte public 'CODE'
    ;
    ;       main()
    ;
         assume   cs:_TEXT,ds:DGROUP
_main    proc     near
         enter    4,0
    ;
    ;       {
    ;         int num;
    ;
    ;         get_val(num);
    ;
         lea      ax,word ptr [bp-2]
         push     ax
         call     near ptr @get_val$qri
         pop      cx
    ;
    ;         cout << num;
    ;
         mov      ax,word ptr [bp-2]
         mov      word ptr [bp-4],ax
         mov      ax,word ptr [bp-4]
         cwd
         push     dx
         push     ax
```

8

```
        push    offset DGROUP:_cout
        call    near ptr @ostream@$blsh$ql
        add     sp,6
    ;
    ;
    ;       return 0;
    ;
        xor     ax,ax
        leave
        ret
    ;
    ;       }
    ;
        leave
        ret
_main   endp
    ;
    ;       void get_val(int &ref)
    ;
        assume  cs:_TEXT,ds:DGROUP
@get_val$qri    proc    near
        push    bp
        mov     bp,sp
        push    si
        mov     si,word ptr [bp+4]
    ;
    ;       {
    ;         ref = 100;
    ;
        mov     word ptr [si],100
    ;
    ;       }
    ;
        pop     si
        pop     bp
        ret
@get_val$qri    endp
        ?debug  C E9
        ?debug  C FA00000000
_TEXT   ends
_DATA   segment word public 'DATA'
s@      label   byte
_DATA   ends
_TEXT   segment byte public 'CODE'
_TEXT   ends
_s@     equ     s@
        extrn   @ostream@$blsh$ql:near
        extrn   _cout:word
```

```
          public  @get_val$qri
          public  _main
          end
```

As you can see, the code is virtually identical.

An Example That Uses the Huge Memory Model

As mentioned, when using 16-bit compilers, the memory model used to
compile a program has profound influence on the way that you must write
assembly language code that will interface with that produced by the
compiler. To illustrate this point, try compiling the C++ program shown in
the previous section using the huge memory model. This will cause calls to
library functions and global data to be FAR (that is, to require both a
segment and offset). To do this using the Borland compiler, specify the **-mh**
compiler option. The following assembly code module is produced:

```
          .286p
          ifndef  ??version
?debug    macro
          endm
publicdll macro name
          public  name
          endm
$comm     macro   name,dist,size,count
          comm    dist name:BYTE:count*size
          endm
          else
$comm     macro   name,dist,size,count
          comm    dist name[size]:BYTE:count
          endm
          endif
          ?debug  V 301h
          ?debug  S "test.cpp"
T2_TEXT   segment byte public 'CODE'
T2_TEXT   ends
          assume  cs:T2_TEXT,ds:T2_DATA
T2_DATA   segment word public 'FAR_DATA'
d@        label   byte
d@w       label   word
b@        label   byte
b@w       label   word
T2_DATA   ends
T2_TEXT   segment byte public 'CODE'
   ;
```

8

```
        ;     main()
        ;
              assume   cs:T2_TEXT,ds:T2_DATA
_main         proc     far
              enter    4,0
              push     ds
              mov      ax,T2_DATA
              mov      ds,ax
        ;
        ;       {
        ;         int num;
        ;
        ;         get_val(num);
        ;
              push     ss
              lea      ax,word ptr [bp-2]
              push     ax
              call     far ptr @get_val$qmi
              add      sp,4
        ;
        ;         cout << num;
        ;
              mov      ax,word ptr [bp-2]
              mov      word ptr [bp-4],ax
              mov      ax,word ptr [bp-4]
              cwd
              push     dx
              push     ax
              push     seg _cout
              push     offset _cout
              call     far ptr @ostream@0$blsh$ql
              add      sp,8
        ;
        ;
        ;         return 0;
        ;
              xor      ax,ax
              pop      ds
              leave
              ret
        ;
        ;       }
        ;
              pop      ds
              leave
              ret
```

```
_main      endp
   ;
   ;       void get_val(int &ref)
   ;
           assume   cs:T2_TEXT,ds:T2_DATA
@get_val$qmi    proc      far
           push     bp
           mov      bp,sp
   ;
   ;       {
   ;          ref = 100;
   ;
           les      bx,dword ptr [bp+6]
           mov      word ptr es:[bx],100
   ;
   ;       }
   ;
           pop      bp
           ret
@get_val$qmi    endp
           ?debug   C E9
           ?debug   C FA00000000
T2_TEXT ends
T2_DATA segment word public 'FAR_DATA'
s@         label    byte
T2_DATA ends
T2_TEXT segment byte public 'CODE'
T2_TEXT ends
_s@        equ      s@
           extrn    @ostream@0$blsh$ql:far
           extrn    _cout:word
           public   @get_val$qmi
           public   _main
           end
```

Notice two important differences between this version and the previous one. First, the address of **num** now requires 4 (not 2) bytes to be pushed onto the stack prior to the call to **get_val**. This allows both the segment (which is SS) and the offset of **num** to be passed. Inside **get_val**, **num** is accessed by use of its full 32-bit address. Second, the calls to **get_val** and the **ostream operator<<( )** function are now FAR. If you want to link your own assembly language functions with C++ code compiled for a large code and data model, you must generate compatible return code when returning from a FAR call. Confusing the two models will corrupt the stack and crash the program. Also, you must use FAR when referencing global data.

8

Hand Optimizing

One of the principal reasons for using assembly code is to enable hand optimization. As you might expect, no matter how good a compiler is, it will never be better than an accomplished assembly language programmer. One good way to improve the performance of a function is to use the assembly code listing of the file generated by the compiler as a starting point and hand-optimize the function yourself. Using this approach, you don't need to actually write the entire function from scratch. Instead, you can let the compiler do most of the work, allowing you to concentrate on improving its code.

At first you might think that hand optimizations would only apply to large or complicated functions, but this is not true. Most functions benefit from hand optimization because even optimizing compilers produce small inefficiencies in register usage. For example, consider this fragment from the assembly code for the reference parameter example shown earlier:

```
_main   proc    near
        enter   4,0
    ;
    ;       {
    ;         int num;
    ;
    ;         get_val(num);
    ;
        lea     ax,word ptr [bp-2]
        push    ax
        call    near ptr @get_val$qri
        pop     cx
    ;
    ;         cout << num;
    ;
        mov     ax,word ptr [bp-2]
        mov     word ptr [bp-4],ax
        mov     ax,word ptr [bp-4]
        cwd
        push    dx
        push    ax
        push    offset DGROUP:_cout
        call    near ptr @ostream@$blsh$ql
        add     sp,6
    ;
    ;
    ;         return 0;
    ;
        xor     ax,ax
        leave
```

```
        ret
;
;       }
;
        leave
        ret
_main   endp
```

Here, this sequence of lines is redundant:

```
mov     ax,word ptr [bp-2]
mov     word ptr [bp-4],ax
mov     ax,word ptr [bp-4]
```

As is clear, there is no reason to move AX into the location referred to by BP–4 and then to move it back to AX in the next line. The third MOV instruction could be eliminated, thus making the code smaller and faster. You might want to try this on your own.

There is another optimization that can be made to the function. Notice that when **main** returns, the sequence LEAVE followed by RET occurs twice. The second one is not required. Removing these lines will make the program smaller. As these examples show, even very small functions may benefit from hand optimizations.

Creating an Assembly Code Skeleton

The preceding examples may have suggested a useful technique which you can apply when writing your own assembly language functions: let the compiler generate an assembly language skeleton for you. Once you have the skeleton, you just have to fill in the details. For example, suppose that you need to create an assembly language routine that multiplies two integers. To have the compiler generate a skeleton for this function, first create a file that contains only this empty function:

```
mul(int a, int b)
{
}
```

Next, compile the file with the proper option to produce an assembly language file. If you use the Borland 16-bit compiler, this file is produced:

8

```
        .286p
        ifndef  ??version
?debug  macro
        endm
```

```
publicdll macro name
        public  name
        endm
$comm   macro   name,dist,size,count
        comm    dist name:BYTE:count*size
        endm
        else
$comm   macro   name,dist,size,count
        comm    dist name[size]:BYTE:count
        endm
        endif
        ?debug  V 301h
        ?debug  S "mul.cpp"
_TEXT   segment byte public 'CODE'
_TEXT   ends
DGROUP  group   _DATA,_BSS
        assume  cs:_TEXT,ds:DGROUP
_DATA   segment word public 'DATA'
d@      label   byte
d@w     label   word
_DATA   ends
_BSS    segment word public 'BSS'
b@      label   byte
b@w     label   word
_BSS    ends
_TEXT   segment byte public 'CODE'
    ;
    ;   mul(int a, int b)
    ;
        assume  cs:_TEXT,ds:DGROUP
@mul$qii        proc    near
        push    bp
        mov     bp,sp
    ;
    ;   {
    ;   }
    ;
        pop     bp
        ret
@mul$qii        endp
        ?debug  C E9
        ?debug  C FA00000000
_TEXT   ends
_DATA   segment word public 'DATA'
s@      label   byte
_DATA   ends
_TEXT   segment byte public 'CODE'
_TEXT   ends
```

```
_s@       equ     s@
          public  @mul$qii
          end
```

Given this skeleton, all you have to do is fill in the details. The finished **mul** function is shown here:

```
          .286p
          ifndef  ??version
?debug    macro
          endm
publicdll macro name
          public  name
          endm
$comm     macro   name,dist,size,count
          comm    dist name:BYTE:count*size
          endm
          else
$comm     macro   name,dist,size,count
          comm    dist name[size]:BYTE:count
          endm
          endif
          ?debug  V 301h
          ?debug  S "mul.cpp"
_TEXT     segment byte public 'CODE'
_TEXT     ends
DGROUP    group   _DATA,_BSS
          assume  cs:_TEXT,ds:DGROUP
_DATA     segment word public 'DATA'
d@        label   byte
d@w       label   word
_DATA     ends
_BSS      segment word public 'BSS'
b@        label   byte
b@w       label   word
_BSS      ends
_TEXT     segment byte public 'CODE'
    ;
    ;     mul(int a, int b)
    ;
          assume  cs:_TEXT,ds:DGROUP
@mul$qii          proc    near
          push    bp
          mov     bp,sp
          mov     ax, word ptr [bp+4]
          imul    word ptr [bp+6]
          pop     bp
          ret
```

8

```
@mul$qii      endp
        ?debug  C E9
        ?debug  C FA00000000
_TEXT   ends
_DATA   segment word public 'DATA'
s@      label   byte
_DATA   ends
_TEXT   segment byte public 'CODE'
_TEXT   ends
_s@     equ     s@
        public  @mul$qii
        end
```

As you can see, only the addition of two lines of code is required to complete the **mul** function. The rest of the work has been done for you by the compiler.

If your assembly language function uses local variables, then you will need to allocate space for them on the stack. To do this, subtract the required number of bytes from SP after it has been saved in BP. Then, to access a local variable, index the stack appropriately using negative offsets to BP. Also, be sure to save any registers that your function uses.

The best way to learn more about interfacing assembly language code with your C++ programs is to write short functions in C++ that do approximately what you want the assembly language version to do. Then, by using the assembly language compiler option, create an assembly language file. Most of the time, you will just need to hand-optimize this code instead of actually creating an assembly language routine from the ground up.

Using asm

In some cases there is an easier way to link assembly code with your C++ program. As you probably know, the C++ language allows inline assembly code to be part of a C++ program through the use of the **asm** keyword. The advantage to this is twofold. First, you don't need to write all of the interface code for each function. Second, all the code is in one place, which makes maintenance a little easier.

To insert assembly code into a program, precede the assembly code instruction with **asm**. That is, each line that contains assembly code must start with **asm**. The C++ compiler simply passes the assembly code instruction through, untouched, to the assembler phase of the compiler.

For example, the following short function called **init_port1( )** moves the value 88 into AX and outputs it to ports 20 and 21:

```
void init_port1()
{
   cout << "Initializing Port\n";
asm      mov AX, 88
asm      out 20, AX
asm      out 21, AX
}
```

Here, the compiler automatically provides the interface code to save registers and to return from the function. You just need to provide the code that runs inside the function.

You could use inline assembly code to create a function that multiplies two numbers, called **mul( )**, without actually creating a separate assembly language file. Using this approach, the code for **mul( )** is shown here:

```
mul(int a, int b)
{
asm      mov ax, word ptr [bp+4]
asm      imul word ptr [bp+6]
}
```

Remember, the C++ compiler provides all customary support for setting up and returning from a function call. You must simply provide the body of the function and follow the calling conventions to access the arguments.

Keep in mind that, whatever method you use, you are creating machine dependencies that will make your program difficult to port to another machine. However, for the demanding situations that require assembly code, it is usually worth the effort.

Things to Try

One of the first things that you will want to try is generating assembly code output using your compiler. Compare its output to that shown in this chapter. Does your compiler generate better code or worse code? Remember, even different versions of the same compiler will generate different assembly code. Next, try generating assembly code for each of the memory models supported by your compiler. Examine the differences.

If you feel confident in your assembly language abilities, try to hand-optimize one or two critical functions in one of your application programs. You might be surprised by the improvement.

8

Chapter

9

Creating and Integrating New Data Types

Using C++, you can define and fully integrate a new data type into your programming environment. This feature is called *type extensibility,* and it is one of C++'s most important, yet overlooked, features. Once you have fully defined a new type, it looks and acts just like one of C++'s built-in types. The ability to extend the C++ environment through the addition of new data types adds a dimension to programming that does not exist in other mainstream programming languages.

Although type extensibility involves object-oriented techniques, it is not what is usually thought of as object-oriented programming. For example, most of the time the term "object-oriented application" brings to mind large class hierarchies, virtual functions, and abstract classes. Type extensibility involves a simpler application of object-oriented principles. When adding a new data type, you are normally dealing with one class for which you must define various constructors, operators, and

269

conversions. The goal of type extension is the creation of a new, low-level data type which can then be used like any other built-in type. It is not the creation of a larger application. One of the best examples of type extension is the standard **string** class (discussed in Chapter 6) which adds a string type to C++.

In this chapter you will see how to add and fully integrate a new data type into C++. The data type that we will be adding is the *set*. As you may know, some computer languages, such as Modula-2, include a built-in set type. However, C++ does not. (The standard template library currently being defined for C++ does include a type called *set*, but it operates differently than the one developed in this chapter.) The set type that we will create can be used to store sets of items and perform various set operations upon them. For example, the set type implements the classical set operations, such as union, intersection, and symmetric difference.

While there is nothing fundamentally difficult in adding a new data type, several steps are required. For example, you must remember to define all operators that are applicable to the new data type, including such operators as input, output, and assignment. In fact, you will be surprised at how much code is required to add even a simple type such as sets to C++. However, once you have done the necessary work, you will have extended C++ relative to your own custom data type.

Set Theory

Before we begin implementing the set data type, it is important to understand precisely what that data type is. For the purposes of this chapter, a *set* is a collection of unique items. That is, no two items in a set have the same value. For example, this is a valid set:

{ A, B, C }

All of its elements are unique. However, the following is an invalid set because it contains duplicate members:

{ A, B, C, A }

Note: The traditional means of denoting a set in print is to enclose its members between curly braces, as the preceding example shows. Of course, these curly braces have no relationship to the curly braces used within a C++ program.

The ordering of the members is irrelevant. For example, the following sets are equivalent.

{ A, B, C }
{ C, B, A }

The standard exclusionary principle applies to sets. This means that an item is either a member of a set or it is not. It can't be both at the same time.

A set may be empty. An empty set is also called the *null set*.

One set is said to be a *subset* of another if all of its elements are also found in the other. For example, the set

{ A, B }

is a subset of

{ A, B, C }

Conversely, a set is a *superset* of another if the first contains all of the elements of the second.

An individual item is a member of a set if it is contained within the set. For example, A is a member of

{ A, B, C }

Set Operations

Sets can have various operations applied to them. The set type developed in this chapter implements the following operations:

♦ union
♦ intersection
♦ difference
♦ symmetric difference

The meaning of each operation is described here. For the sake of this discussion, assume the following sets:

Set S1: { A, B, C }
Set S2: { C, D, E }

The *union* of two sets produces a new set that contains all of the elements of both sets. For example, the union of S1 and S2 is

{ A, B, C, D, E }

Notice that C is included only once. Remember, duplicate items are not allowed in a set.

The *intersection* of two sets produces a new set that contains only those elements that both of the original sets have in common. For example, the intersection of S1 and S2 produces the following set:

{ C }

Since C is the only item that both S1 and S2 share, it is the only item in the resulting intersection.

The *difference* between two sets (sometimes called *set subtraction*) produces a new set that contains those elements of the first set that do not occur in the second set. For example, S1 – S2 produces the following set:

{ A, B }

Since C is found in S2, it is subtracted from S1 and is not found in the resulting set.

The *symmetric difference* between two sets is composed of those elements that occur in one set or the other, but not in both. For example, the symmetric difference of S1 and S2 is

{ A, B, D, E }

As you can see, C is not included because it is a member of both S1 and S2.

Defining the Set Type

The set type developed in this chapter will implement sets as just described. It uses the **Set** class shown here:

```
template <class Stype> class Set {
  Stype *SetPtr; // pointer to set members
  int MaxSize; // maximum size of set
  int NumMembers; // number of members in set
  void insert(Stype member); // insert a member
  void remove(Stype member); // remove a member
  int find(Stype member); // return index of a member
  int ismember(Stype member); // return true if member
```

```
public:
  Set();
  Set(int size);
  Set(const Set &ob); // copy constructor
  ~Set() { delete SetPtr; }

  Set<Stype> &operator=(Set<Stype> &ob); // assign sets

  // add member to set
  Set<Stype> operator+(Stype member);
  friend Set<Stype> operator+(Stype member, Set<Stype> ob);

  Set<Stype> operator+(Set<Stype> &ob); // create union

  Set<Stype> operator-(Stype member); // remove member
  Set<Stype> operator-(Set<Stype> &ob); // difference

  Set<Stype> operator&(Set<Stype> &ob); // intersection
  Set<Stype> operator^(Set<Stype> &ob); // sym-dif

  // relational ops
  int operator==(Set<Stype> &ob); // true if equal
  int operator!=(Set<Stype> &ob); // true if unequal
  int operator<(Set<Stype> &ob); // true if subset

  // true if member is part of ob
  friend int operator<(Stype member, Set<Stype> ob);

  // conversion to int returns number of members in set
  operator int() { return NumMembers; }

  // input and output members of set
  friend istream &operator<<(istream &stream,
                             Set<Stype> &ob);
  friend ostream &operator<<(ostream &stream,
                             Set<Stype> &ob);
};
```

As you can see, **Set** is a template class. This means that it can be used to create sets of any data type.

Set contains three data members: **SetPtr**, **MaxSize**, and **NumMembers**. Memory to hold a set is dynamically allocated, and a pointer to that memory is stored in **SetPtr**. The maximum number of members that a set may contain is stored in **MaxSize**. The number of members that the set currently holds is stored in **NumMembers**. These members are private and may not be altered by user-level code.

The next several sections detail the operation of the **Set** class.

Set Constructors and Destructor

Sets can be declared one of two ways. First, they can be created using the default set size. Second, they may be declared to be of a specific size. In this case, the size of the set is passed as a parameter to the constructor. Both **Set** constructors are shown here:

```
// Create default set.
template <class Stype> Set<Stype>::Set()
{
  SetPtr = new Stype[DEFSET];
  if(!SetPtr) {
    cout << "Allocation error.\n";
    exit(1);
  }
  NumMembers = 0;
  MaxSize = DEFSET;
}

// Create a set of known size.
template <class Stype> Set<Stype>::Set(int size)
{
  SetPtr = new Stype[size];
  if(!SetPtr) {
    cout << "Allocation error.\n";
    exit(1);
  }
  NumMembers = 0;
  MaxSize = size;
}
```

The value **DEFSET** is a **const int** that is defined by your program. For the example in this chapter, its value is 100. It is important to understand that the value contained in **MaxSize** only determines the maximum number of elements that it may hold. Sets are free to contain fewer.

The **Set** destructor is defined inline within the **Set** class. It simply frees the memory allocated when a set is created.

Inserting and Removing Members

All sets are initially empty. To add a member, the **Set** class uses the private member function **insert( )**, shown here:

```
// Insert a member.
template <class Stype>
void Set<Stype>::insert(Stype member)
{
  if(NumMembers == MaxSize) {
    cout << "Set is full.\n";
    exit(1);
  }

  if(!ismember(member)) {
    // not already in set
    SetPtr[NumMembers] = member; // add to set
    NumMembers++;
  }
}
```

The **insert( )** function is called with the new member specified in its parameter. If the set is full, then an error is reported. Otherwise, the new member is added to the set if it is not already part of the set. Remember, sets do not contain duplicate items. To determine whether an item is a member of a set, the **ismember( )** function is used. (This function will be described shortly.)

To remove an item from a set, the **Set** class uses the private member function **remove( )**, shown here:

```
// Remove a member
template <class Stype>
void Set<Stype>::remove(Stype member)
{
  int loc = find(member);

  if(loc != -1) {
    // found, now remove element by compressing set
    for(; loc<NumMembers-1; loc++)
      SetPtr[loc] = SetPtr[loc+1];
    NumMembers--;
  }
}
```

This function uses the **find( )** function to obtain the index of the item to remove. (**find( )** is described in the next section.) If the element exists, it is "removed" from the set by shifting the contents of the set down one position, overwriting the deleted element. Notice that **NumMembers** is also decremented.

As mentioned, both **insert( )** and **remove( )** are private members of **Set**. They implement the lowest level (that is, atomic) set operations. As such, they are for use by the **Set** class, not by users of **Set**. Instead, users of **Set** will employ operators to add or delete items.

Determining Membership

Internally, the **Set** class determines whether an item is a member of a set by calling either **find( )** or **ismember( )**. These private functions are shown here:

```
/* Find a member and return its index.
   Return -1 if not found.
*/
template <class Stype>
int Set<Stype>::find(Stype member)
{
  int i;

  for(i=0; i<NumMembers; i++)
    if(SetPtr[i] == member) return i;

  return -1;
}

// Return true if member of set.
template <class Stype>
int Set<Stype>::ismember(Stype member)
{
  if(find(member) != -1) return 1;
  else return 0;
}
```

The **find( )** function returns the index of a specified item if that item is a member of the set. Otherwise, it returns –1. This function primarily exists for use in the **remove( )** function, shown in the preceding section. Most of the time, it is not necessary to know the actual index of an item. In this case, the **ismember( )** function is used. It returns true if the specified item is a member of the set and false if it is not.

As was the case with **insert( )** and **remove( )**, **find( )** and **ismember( )** are for internal use by the **Set** class. Users of **Set** will employ operators to determine set membership.

The Copy Constructor

The **Set** class requires that a copy constructor be defined. As you probably know, a class' copy constructor is called whenever a copy of an object is made. Specifically, the copy constructor is called when an object is passed by value to a function, when a temporary object is constructed as the return value of a function, and when an object is used to initialize another object. If no copy constructor is explicitly defined for a class, then by default, a bitwise copy of an object is made when one of these three situations occurs. However, a bitwise copy is not always adequate. When it isn't, you will need to define your own copy constructor.

The reason that the **Set** class requires its own copy constructor is easy to understand. Recall that memory for each set is allocated using **new**, and a pointer to this memory is stored in **SetPtr**. Using the default copy constructor, when a copy of a set is made, a bitwise copy takes place. This means that **SetPtr** in the copy will point to the same piece of memory as does **SetPtr** in the original. Thus, both objects will be using the same memory to hold their sets. This means that changes to one object will affect the other. Also, when one of the objects is destroyed, it will free its memory. But, this same memory will still be in use by the other object! This, as you might expect, usually leads to a program crash. Fortunately, by defining a copy constructor for **Set** objects, it is possible to prevent such problems. To accomplish this, the copy constructor for the **Set** class must make sure that **SetPtr** in each object points to its own piece of memory. To ensure this, the copy constructor will allocate new memory to hold the set when it makes a copy of an object. The **Set** copy constructor is shown here:

```
// Copy constructor.
template <class Stype>
Set<Stype>::Set(const Set<Stype> &ob)
{
  int i;

  MaxSize = ob.MaxSize;

  SetPtr = new Stype[MaxSize];
  if(!SetPtr) {
    cout << "Allocation error.\n";
    exit(1);
  }

  NumMembers = 0;

  for(i=0; i<ob.NumMembers; i++)
    insert(ob.SetPtr[i]);
}
```

9

As you can see, the copy constructor allocates memory for the copy and then copies each item in the original set into the copy. In this way, the memory pointed to by **SetPtr** in the original is separate from that pointed to by **SetPtr** in the copy.

Assigning Sets

As you know, when the assignment operator is not overloaded relative to a class, then a default, bitwise copy occurs when one object is assigned to another. However, for the **Set** class (and most other real world classes), the bitwise copy is not acceptable. Instead, it is necessary to create a custom assignment operation for **Set** by overloading the assignment operator. The reason for this is the same as that given for creating a copy constructor. If a bitwise copy occurs, then you will have two objects using the same piece of memory to hold their sets. To avoid this, the assignment operation must simply copy the members of one set into the other, but not change what the **SetPtr** member of either set is pointing to. The **operator=( )** function, shown here, does precisely that.

```cpp
// Overload assignment for sets.
template <class Stype>
Set<Stype> &Set<Stype>::operator=(Set<Stype> &ob)
{
  int i;

  // handle s = s case.
  if(SetPtr == ob.SetPtr) return *this;

  // make sure that target is large enough
  if(ob.NumMembers > MaxSize ) {
    delete SetPtr;
    SetPtr = new Stype[ob.NumMembers];
    if(!SetPtr) {
      cout << "Allocation error.\n";
      exit(1);
    }
    MaxSize = ob.NumMembers;
  }
  NumMembers = 0; // remove old set

  for(i=0; i<ob.NumMembers; i++)
    insert(ob.SetPtr[i]);

  return *this;
}
```

Let's look closely at this function. First, notice that if the **SetPtr** members of both objects point to the same memory, then no action takes place. The reason for this is to handle the special case of an object being assigned to itself. While this act is pointless in its most direct form (that is, setob = setob), it could occur indirectly. In any event, because of the way that **operator=( )** is implemented, this situation must be handled as a special case.

Next, if the target object is not large enough to hold the source object, the memory associated with the target is freed and more memory is allocated. Then, the **NumMembers** variable is reset to 0. This effectively removes all previous elements in the target set. Next, the contents of the source set are inserted into the target set. Finally, the function returns ***this**. This is necessary to allow the assignment operator to be used inside a larger expression.

Overloading the + Operator

The **Set** class overloads the + for two types of operations. The first operation uses the + to add an element to a set. The second operation creates a set union. Both uses are described here.

Adding Elements to a Set

Using the + to add an element to a set requires two slightly different versions of the **operator+( )** function. The first handles *set + item,* the other handles *item + set.* Both versions are shown here:

```
/* Overload addition for set members.  This adds
   a member to a set using this form:

      set = set + item;

*/
template <class Stype>
Set<Stype> Set<Stype>::operator+(Stype member)
{
  int i;
  Set<Stype> temp(NumMembers + 1);

  // copy existing members into temporary set
  for(i=0; i<NumMembers; i++)
    temp.insert(SetPtr[i]);

  // insert new member
  temp.insert(member);
```

9

```
  // return new set
  return temp;
}

/* Overload addition for set members.  This adds
   a member to a set using this form:

     set = item + set;

*/
template <class Stype>
Set<Stype> operator+(Stype member, Set<Stype> ob)
{
  int i;
  Set<Stype> temp(ob.NumMembers + 1);

  // copy existing members into temporary set
  for(i=0; i<ob.NumMembers; i++)
    temp.insert(ob.SetPtr[i]);

  // insert new member
  temp.insert(member);

  // return new set
  return temp;
}
```

The operation of these functions is straightforward. Each first creates a temporary set, called **temp**, that is large enough to hold the original set plus one additional element. Next, the original set is copied into **temp**. Then, the new item is inserted. Finally, **temp** is returned.

The first version of **operator+( )** allows the following type of expression to be used to add items.

    set = set + item;

Here, the left operand of the + is a set, and the right operand is the item being inserted.

The second version of **operator+( )**, which is a **friend** rather than a member function, handles the case in which the left operand is the item being inserted into the set on the right. That is, it handles statements like this:

    set = item + set;

Since an item may be of a built-in type, it is necessary to use a **friend** function to allow this second form. Remember, when a member operator function is used, the left operand is passed implicitly through **this**. This means that the left operand of a member operator function must be an object of the class for which the operator function is defined. Thus, to allow an item (which is not a **Set** object) to be on the left side of the **+** requires the use of a **friend**, rather than a member, function. Using a **friend** makes it possible to define the left operand to be of some type other than **Set**.

Creating a Set Union

The second operation for which the **+** is overloaded creates a union of two sets. That is, it "adds" two sets together. This form is shown here:

```
// Overload addition for sets.  This creates a union.
template <class Stype>
Set<Stype> Set<Stype>::operator+(Set<Stype> &ob)
{
  int i;
  Set<Stype> temp(NumMembers + ob.NumMembers);

  for(i=0; i<NumMembers; i++)
    temp.insert(SetPtr[i]);
  for(i=0; i<ob.NumMembers; i++)
    temp.insert(ob.SetPtr[i]);

  return temp;
}
```

This function can be used for the following type of operation:

    set1 = set2 + set3;

After this statement executes, *set1* will contain the union of *set2* and *set3*. The function works by first creating a temporary set, **temp**, that is large enough to hold all of the elements contained in the two sets being operated upon. Although the result of a union will contain this many elements only if the sets have no common elements, the function must allow for this possibility. Next, the function inserts the contents of both sets into **temp**. Remember, the **insert( )** function will not insert duplicate elements, so there is no need for the **operator+( )** function to check for this manually.

Overloading the – Operator

The – operator is also overloaded for two slightly different operations. The first operation removes (that is, subtracts) an item from a set. The second creates a set difference. Both uses are examined here.

Removing an Element from a Set

To remove an element from a set, this form of the **operator–( )** function is used.

```
/* Overload subtraction for set members.  This
   removes a member from a set.
*/
template <class Stype>
Set<Stype> Set<Stype>::operator-(Stype member)
{
  int i;
  Set<Stype> temp = *this;

  temp.remove(member);

  return temp;
}
```

This function allows the following type of statement.

```
    set1 = set2 – item;
```

After the operation, *set1* will contain all of the members of *set2* except for the one specified by *item*.

Set Difference

The second form of **operator–( )** performs a set difference. That is, it subtracts the contents of one set from another. This version is shown here:

```
/* Overload subtraction for sets.  This
   yields set difference.
*/
template <class Stype>
Set<Stype> Set<Stype>::operator-(Set<Stype> &ob)
{
  int i;
  Set<Stype> temp = *this;

  // remove members that *this has in common with ob
```

```
for(i=0; i<NumMembers; i++) {
  if(ob.ismember(SetPtr[i]))
    temp.remove(SetPtr[i]);
}

return temp;
}
```

This version allows operations such as

    set1 = set2 – set3;

After the operation, *set1* will contain those members of *set2* that are not part of *set3*. The function works by initializing **temp** to ***this** (which is the set on the left side of the –). Then, it removes any members of this set that also occur in the set on the right side.

Set Intersection

The intersection of two sets is implemented by use of the **&** operator. This function is shown here:

```
// Intersection of two sets.
template <class Stype>
Set<Stype> Set<Stype>::operator&(Set<Stype> &ob)
{
  int i, j;
  Set<Stype> temp(NumMembers);

  for(i=0; i<NumMembers; i++) {
    if(ob.ismember(SetPtr[i]))
      temp.insert(SetPtr[i]);
  }

  return temp;
}
```

This function works by first creating a temporary object which is large enough to hold the largest possible intersection. It then copies into that set those members common to both of the original two sets.

The **&** operator can be used in the following type of statement:

    set1 = set2 & set3;

After the statement executes, *set1* will contain the intersection of sets *set2* and *set3*.

Symmetric Difference

The symmetric difference (that is, the union of two sets minus the intersection of those sets) is implemented by use of the ^ operator. It is shown here:

```
/* Symmetric difference of two sets.  This is the
   union of the sets minus their intersection.
*/
template <class Stype>
Set<Stype> Set<Stype>::operator^(Set<Stype> &ob)
{
  int i, j;
  Set<Stype> temp1, temp2;

  temp1 = *this + ob;
  temp2 = *this & ob;
  temp1 = temp1 - temp2;

  return temp1;
}
```

This function is easy to understand. First, it creates a temporary set consisting of the union of the original two sets. Next, it creates a second temporary set that contains the intersection of the two sets. Finally, it subtracts the intersection from the union.

The ^ operator can be used in the following type of statement:

    set1 = set2 ^ set3;

After the statement executes, *set1* will contain the symmetric difference of sets *set2* and *set3*.

Determining Set Equality, Inequality, and Subset

The **Set** class provides operators that determine if two sets are equal or unequal and if one set is a subset of another. Set equality and inequality are implemented by overloading the == and != operators, respectively. Subset status is determined by the < operator. These operator functions are shown here:

```
// Return true if sets are equal.
template <class Stype>
int Set<Stype>::operator==(Set<Stype> &ob)
```

```
{
  // number of members must be the same
  if(NumMembers != ob.NumMembers) return 0;

  return *this < ob;
}

// Return true if sets are unequal.
template <class Stype>
int Set<Stype>::operator!=(Set<Stype> &ob)
{
  return !(*this == ob);
}

// Return true if *this is subset of ob.
template <class Stype>
int Set<Stype>::operator<(Set<Stype> &ob)
{
  int i;

  for(i=0; i<NumMembers; i++)
    if(!ob.ismember(SetPtr[i])) return 0;

  return 1;
}
```

The operation of these functions should be clear. However, notice in
operator==( ), that equality is determined by first confirming that the two
sets contain the same number of members. If they do, then the subset
operator is used to determine if one is a subset of the other. Given two sets of
equal size, if one is a subset of the other, then they must be equivalent.

These functions allow statements such as those shown here:

```
if(set1 == set2) cout << "Sets equal.";
if(set1 != set2)  cout << "Sets differ.";
if(set1 < set2)  cout << "set1 is a subset of set2.";
```

Determining Membership

Sometimes it is useful to know if an element is a member of a set. To do this,
Set overloads the **<** a second way, as shown here:

```
// Return true if member is part of ob.
template <class Stype>
int operator<(Stype member, Set<Stype> ob)
{
```

```
    return ob.ismember(member);
}
```

This function allows the following type of statement:

    if(item < set) cout << "Item is in set.";

It uses the private **ismember( )** function to determine membership.

A Conversion to Integer

The **Set** class includes one conversion function which provides a conversion to integer. As defined here, the conversion of a **Set** object to integer returns the number of members currently contained in the set. If the set is empty, zero is returned. As you probably know from your previous C++ experience, a conversion function is used to define an automatic conversion from a class type to another type (which is usually a built-in type). A conversion function allows objects of a class to be used in expressions involving other types of data. In the case of the **Set** class, only a conversion to **int** is needed. However, for other types of classes that you create, various conversion functions may be valuable.

The integer conversion function is quite short and is defined inline within the **Set** class. It is shown here for your convenience:

```
operator int() { return NumMembers; }
```

This conversion function is quite useful. For example, it allows statements like the following:

    if(set) cout << "set has members";
    cout << "set1 has " << (int) set1 << " members\n";

In the first statement, the conversion to integer causes the condition controlling the **if** to succeed only if *set* contains members. In the second statement, the explicit cast to **int** causes the number of members in **set1** to be displayed.

Overloading the I/O Operators

The last operators overloaded by **Set** are the I/O operators. They are shown here:

```
// Input member.
template <class Stype>
```

```
istream &operator>>(istream &stream, Set<Stype> &ob)
{
  Stype member;

  stream >> member;
  ob = ob + member;

  return stream;
}

// Output contents of set.
template <class Stype>
ostream &operator<<(ostream &stream, Set<Stype> &ob)
{
  int i;

  for(i=0; i<ob.NumMembers; i++)
    stream << ob.SetPtr[i] << " ";

  stream << endl;

  return stream;
}
```

Keep in mind that these functions are very simple. If you will be creating
complex set types, then you will probably need to provide custom versions
to handle I/O on those types.

A Set Demonstration Program

The following program contains the entire **Set** class and includes a **main( )**
function that demonstrates the various set operations.

```
// A set class

#include <iostream.h>
#include <stdlib.h>

const int DEFSET = 100;

template <class Stype> class Set {
  Stype *SetPtr; // pointer to set members
  int MaxSize; // maximum size of set
  int NumMembers; // number of members in set
  void insert(Stype member); // insert a member
  void remove(Stype member); // remove a member
  int find(Stype member); // return index of a member
```

9

```
    int ismember(Stype member); // return true if member
public:
  Set();
  Set(int size);
  Set(const Set &ob); // copy constructor
  ~Set() { delete SetPtr; }

  Set<Stype> &operator=(Set<Stype> &ob); // assign sets

  // add member to set
  Set<Stype> operator+(Stype member);
  friend Set<Stype> operator+(Stype member, Set<Stype> ob);

  Set<Stype> operator+(Set<Stype> &ob); // create union

  Set<Stype> operator-(Stype member); // remove member
  Set<Stype> operator-(Set<Stype> &ob); // difference

  Set<Stype> operator&(Set<Stype> &ob); // intersection
  Set<Stype> operator^(Set<Stype> &ob); // sym-dif

  // relational ops
  int operator==(Set<Stype> &ob); // true if equal
  int operator!=(Set<Stype> &ob); // true if unequal
  int operator<(Set<Stype> &ob); // true if subset

  // true if member is part of ob
  friend int operator<(Stype member, Set<Stype> ob);

  // conversion to int returns number of members in set
  operator int() { return NumMembers; }

  // input and output members of set
  friend istream &operator<<(istream &stream,
                             Set<Stype> &ob);
  friend ostream &operator<<(ostream &stream,
                             Set<Stype> &ob);
};

// Create default set.
template <class Stype> Set<Stype>::Set()
{
  SetPtr = new Stype[DEFSET];
  if(!SetPtr) {
    cout << "Allocation error.\n";
    exit(1);
  }
  NumMembers = 0;
```

```
    MaxSize = DEFSET;
  }

  // Create a set of known size.
  template <class Stype> Set<Stype>::Set(int size)
  {
    SetPtr = new Stype[size];
    if(!SetPtr) {
      cout << "Allocation error.\n";
      exit(1);
    }
    NumMembers = 0;
    MaxSize = size;
  }

  // Copy constructor.
  template <class Stype>
  Set<Stype>::Set(const Set<Stype> &ob)
  {
    int i;

    MaxSize = ob.MaxSize;

    SetPtr = new Stype[MaxSize];
    if(!SetPtr) {
      cout << "Allocation error.\n";
      exit(1);
    }

    NumMembers = 0;

    for(i=0; i<ob.NumMembers; i++)
      insert(ob.SetPtr[i]);
  }

  // Insert a member.
  template <class Stype>
  void Set<Stype>::insert(Stype member)
  {
    if(NumMembers == MaxSize) {
      cout << "Set is full.\n";
      exit(1);
    }

    if(!ismember(member)) {
      // not already in set
      SetPtr[NumMembers] = member; // add to set
      NumMembers++;
```

```
  }
}

// Remove a member
template <class Stype>
void Set<Stype>::remove(Stype member)
{
  int loc = find(member);

  if(loc != -1) {
    // found, now remove element by compressing set
    for(; loc<NumMembers-1; loc++)
      SetPtr[loc] = SetPtr[loc+1];
    NumMembers--;
  }
}


// Return true if member of set.
template <class Stype>
int Set<Stype>::ismember(Stype member)
{
  if(find(member) != -1) return 1;
  else return 0;
}

/* Find a member and return its index.
   Return -1 if not found.
*/
template <class Stype>
int Set<Stype>::find(Stype member)
{
  int i;

  for(i=0; i<NumMembers; i++)
    if(SetPtr[i] == member) return i;

  return -1;
}

// Overload assignment for sets.
template <class Stype>
Set<Stype> &Set<Stype>::operator=(Set<Stype> &ob)
{
  int i;

  // handle s = s case.
  if(SetPtr == ob.SetPtr) return *this;
```

```
    // make sure that target is large enough
    if(ob.NumMembers > MaxSize ) {
      delete SetPtr;
      SetPtr = new Stype[ob.NumMembers];
      if(!SetPtr) {
        cout << "Allocation error.\n";
        exit(1);
      }
      MaxSize = ob.NumMembers;
    }
    NumMembers = 0; // remove old set

    for(i=0; i<ob.NumMembers; i++)
      insert(ob.SetPtr[i]);

    return *this;
}

/* Overload addition for set members.  This adds
   a member to a set using this form:

   set = set + item;
*/
template <class Stype>
Set<Stype> Set<Stype>::operator+(Stype member)
{
  int i;
  Set<Stype> temp(NumMembers + 1);

  // copy existing members into temporary set
  for(i=0; i<NumMembers; i++)
    temp.insert(SetPtr[i]);

  // insert new member
  temp.insert(member);

  // return new set
  return temp;
}

/* Overload addition for set members.  This adds
   a member to a set using this form:

   set = item + set;
*/
template <class Stype>
Set<Stype> operator+(Stype member, Set<Stype> ob)
```

9

```
{
  int i;
  Set<Stype> temp(ob.NumMembers + 1);

  // copy existing members into temporary set
  for(i=0; i<ob.NumMembers; i++)
    temp.insert(ob.SetPtr[i]);

  // insert new member
  temp.insert(member);

  // return new set
  return temp;
}

// Overload addition for sets.  This creates a union.
template <class Stype>
Set<Stype> Set<Stype>::operator+(Set<Stype> &ob)
{
  int i;
  Set<Stype> temp(NumMembers + ob.NumMembers);

  for(i=0; i<NumMembers; i++)
    temp.insert(SetPtr[i]);
  for(i=0; i<ob.NumMembers; i++)
    temp.insert(ob.SetPtr[i]);

  return temp;
}

/* Overload subtraction for sets.  This
   yields set difference.
*/
template <class Stype>
Set<Stype> Set<Stype>::operator-(Set<Stype> &ob)
{
  int i;
  Set<Stype> temp = *this;

  // remove members that *this has in common with ob
  for(i=0; i<NumMembers; i++) {
    if(ob.ismember(SetPtr[i]))
      temp.remove(SetPtr[i]);
  }

  return temp;
}
```

```
/* Overload subtraction for set members.  This
   removes a member from a set.
*/
template <class Stype>
Set<Stype> Set<Stype>::operator-(Stype member)
{
  int i;
  Set<Stype> temp = *this;

  temp.remove(member);

  return temp;
}


// Intersection of two sets.
template <class Stype>
Set<Stype> Set<Stype>::operator&(Set<Stype> &ob)
{
  int i, j;
  Set<Stype> temp(NumMembers);

  for(i=0; i<NumMembers; i++) {
    if(ob.ismember(SetPtr[i]))
      temp.insert(SetPtr[i]);
  }

  return temp;
}


/* Symmetric difference of two sets.  This is the
   union of the sets minus their intersection.
*/
template <class Stype>
Set<Stype> Set<Stype>::operator^(Set<Stype> &ob)
{
  int i, j;
  Set<Stype> temp1, temp2;

  temp1 = *this + ob;
  temp2 = *this & ob;
  temp1 = temp1 - temp2;

  return temp1;
}

// Return true if sets are equal.
template <class Stype>
```

```
int Set<Stype>::operator==(Set<Stype> &ob)
{
  // number of members must be the same
  if(NumMembers != ob.NumMembers) return 0;

  return *this < ob;
}

// Return true if sets are unequal.
template <class Stype>
int Set<Stype>::operator!=(Set<Stype> &ob)
{
  return !(*this == ob);
}

// Return true if *this is subset of ob.
template <class Stype>
int Set<Stype>::operator<(Set<Stype> &ob)
{
  int i;

  for(i=0; i<NumMembers; i++)
    if(!ob.ismember(SetPtr[i])) return 0;

  return 1;
}

// Return true if member is part of ob.
template <class Stype>
int operator<(Stype member, Set<Stype> ob)
{
  return ob.ismember(member);
}

// Input member.
template <class Stype>
istream &operator>>(istream &stream, Set<Stype> &ob)
{
  Stype member;

  stream >> member;
  ob = ob + member;

  return stream;
}

// Output contents of set.
template <class Stype>
```

```cpp
ostream &operator<<(ostream &stream, Set<Stype> &ob)
{
  int i;

  for(i=0; i<ob.NumMembers; i++)
    stream << ob.SetPtr[i] << " ";

  stream << endl;

  return stream;
}

main()
{
  // sets of integers
  Set<int> set1(10), set2(10), set3(10);

  if(set1)
    cout << "set1 contains members.\n";
  else
    cout << "set1 is empty.\n";

  set1 = set1 + 1; // set + member
  set1 = 2 + set1; // member + set
  set1 = set1 + 3; // set + member
  set1 = 4 + set1; // member + set

  set2 = set2 + 1;
  set2 = set2 + 3;
  set2 = set2 + 5;
  set2 = set2 + 6;

  if(set1)
    cout << "set1 contains members.\n";
  else
    cout << "set1 is empty.\n";

  cout << "Set in set1: ";
  cout << set1;
  cout << "Set in set2: ";
  cout << set2;

  cout << "Union of set1 and set2: ";
  set3 = set1 + set2;
  cout << set3;

  cout << "Intersection of set1 and set2: ";
  set3 = set1 & set2;
```

```
cout << set3;

cout << "Difference of set1 - set2: ";
set3 = set1 - set2;
cout << set3;

cout << "Symmetric difference of set1 and set2: ";
set3 = set1 ^ set2;
cout << set3;
cout << endl;

set3 = set1 + set2;
cout << "set3 now contains set1 + set2: ";
cout << set3;

if(1 < set3)
  cout << "1 is a member of set3.\n";
if(0 < set3)
  cout << "0 is a member of set3.\n";
else
  cout << "0 is not a member of set3.\n";

if(set1 < set3)
  cout << "set1 is a subset of set3.\n";
if(set3 < set1)
  cout << "This will not be printed.\n";
else
  cout << "set3 is not a subset of set1.\n";

set1 = set1 + 99;
cout << "set1 now contains: ";
cout << set1;
if(set1 < set3)
  cout << "This will not be printed\n";
else
  cout << "Now, set1 is not a subset of set3.\n";

cout << "Enter an integer: ";
cin >> set3;
cout << "set3 now contains: " << set3;

cout << "set3 after removing 1: ";
set3 = set3 - 1;
cout << set3;
cout << "set3 after removing 3: ";
set3 = set3 - 3;
cout << set3;
cout << endl;
```

```
Set<int> set4 = set1, set5 = set1;
cout << "Here is set4: ";
cout << set4;
cout << "Here is set5: ";
cout << set5;

if(set4 == set5)
  cout << "Sets in set4 and set5 are equal.\n";

set4 = set4 + 30;
cout << "Now, here is set4: ";
cout << set4;
if(set4 != set5)
  cout << "Now, set4 and set5 are not equal.\n";

cout << endl;
// set of char * pointers
Set<char *> strset(4);
strset = strset + "one";
strset = strset + "two";

cout << "Set of char *: ";
cout << strset << endl;

// set of characters
Set<char> chset1, chset2;

chset1 = chset1 + 'a';
chset1 = chset1 + 'b';
chset1 = chset1 + 'c';

chset2 = chset1 + 'z';

cout << "chset1 and chset2:\n";
cout << chset1 << chset2;
cout << "Intersection of chset1 and chset2: ";
cout << (chset1 & chset2);
cout << "Symmetric difference of chset1 and chset2: ";
cout << (chset1 ^ chset2);

return 0;
}
```

As you can see by looking at the code inside **main( )**, the **Set** type can be used like any other data type. It is fully integrated into the C++ environment. Specifically, expressions involving the **Set** class look just like expressions using the built-in types. This illustrates the power of C++'s type extension capabilities.

Sample output from the program is shown here:

```
set1 is empty.
set1 contains members.
Set in set1: 1 2 3 4
Set in set2: 1 3 5 6
Union of set1 and set2: 1 2 3 4 5 6
Intersection of set1 and set2: 1 3
Difference of set1 – set2: 2 4
Symmetric difference of set1 and set2: 2 4 5 6

set3 now contains set1 + set2: 1 2 3 4 5 6
1 is a member of set3.
0 is not a member of set3.
set1 is a subset of set3.
set3 is not a subset of set1.
set1 now contains: 1 2 3 4 99
Now, set1 is not a subset of set3.
Enter an integer: 2500
set3 now contains: 1 2 3 4 5 6 2500
set3 after removing 1: 2 3 4 5 6 2500
set3 after removing 3: 2 4 5 6 2500

Here is set4: 1 2 3 4 99
Here is set5: 1 2 3 4 99
Sets in set4 and set5 are equal.
Now, here is set4: 1 2 3 4 99 30
Now, set4 and set5 are not equal.

Set of char *: one two

chset1 and chset2:
a b c
a b c z
Intersection of chset1 and chset2: a b c
Symmetric difference of chset1 and chset2: z
```

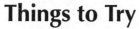

Things to Try

Here are three things that you might want to try adding to the **Set** class. First, let sets grow dynamically instead of being of fixed size. Second, add a superset operator function by defining **operator>( )**. Have it return true if the set on the left is a superset of the set on the right. Third, create an iterator function for the **Set** class. Have it return the next item in the set each time it is called.

On your own, try defining your own new data type and fully integrating it into C++. As you have seen, it really doesn't require all that much work.

Chapter

10

Implementing Language
Interpreters in C++

Have you ever wanted to create your own computer language? If you're like most programmers, you probably have. Most programmers find the idea of being able to create, control, enhance, and modify their own computer language very appealing. However, few programmers realize how easy and enjoyable the creation of a computer language can be. Be assured that the development of a full-featured compiler is a major undertaking, but the creation of a *language interpreter* is a much simpler task. In this chapter, you will learn the secrets of language interpretation and see a working, practical example.

Interpreters are important for four widely different reasons. First, they can provide a truly interactive environment. Many applications, such as robotics, require an interactive rather than a compiled environment. Second, because of the nature of language interpreters, they are especially well-suited for interactive debugging. Third, interpreters make excellent query languages for database management programs. In fact, most database query languages were initially designed as interpreters. The fourth reason that interpreters are important is that they allow the same program to run on a variety of platforms. Only the interpreter's run-time package must be implemented for each new environment. The source for the program remains the same. For example, Java, the Internet's applet language, is an interpreter for this reason.

Although compilers will always be at the front line of programming, interpreters are becoming increasingly important. It is quite likely that you will need to write one or more interpreters during your career as a C++ programmer. Fortunately, C++ is an ideal language for creating interpreters.

To illustrate how an interpreter is designed, it is necessary to actually interpret some language. Although C++ would seem an obvious choice, it is far too large and complicated a language to easily create an interpreter for. (Also, the source code of an interpreter for even a small subset of the C++ language would never fit into a chapter of a book!) Instead, let's use a subset of standard BASIC, hereafter referred to as *Small BASIC,* to illustrate interpreter techniques. BASIC is chosen for three reasons. First, it was designed to be an interpreter. As such it is relatively easy to implement an interpreter for it. For example, standard BASIC does not support local variables, recursive functions, blocks, classes, overloading, templates, and so on—all of which increase the complexity of an interpreter. (This is why C++ is a much more difficult language to interpret than is BASIC.) However, the same principles used to interpret BASIC will also apply to any other language, and you can use the routines developed here as a starting point. The second reason for selecting BASIC is that a reasonable subset can be implemented in a relatively small amount of code. Finally, BASIC is chosen because most programmers have at least a passing acquaintance with it. If you don't know BASIC, don't worry. The commands used in Small BASIC are trivially easy to understand.

Note: If you are particularly interested in interpreters, you will find the C interpreter described in my book, *C: The Complete Reference, 3rd Edition* (Osborne/McGraw-Hill, 1995), particularly interesting. If you think that you might like to try your hand at a C++ interpreter, then the C interpreter described there will be a good starting point.

The Small Basic Expression Parser

The single most important part of a language interpreter is the expression parser. As you know from Chapter 3, an expression parser is used to transform numeric expressions such as (10–X)/23 into a form that the computer can understand and evaluate. Since expression parsing is fully described in Chapter 3, that discussion need not be repeated here. However, the parser used here is not exactly like the one shown in Chapter 3. Although its fundamental operation is unchanged, the parser used for Small BASIC is sufficiently different from the one shown in Chapter 3 that a specialized version of it is required. For example, the parser must be able to recognize the keywords of the BASIC language, it must not treat the = sign as an operator, and it must evaluate relational operators and compute integer exponentiation. Also, the **get_token( )** function is substantially altered to handle the expanded demands placed upon it.

Since the Small BASIC expression parser uses the same techniques as described earlier, you will have no trouble following what is occurring. However, a brief description of how it has been modified to work with BASIC will still be helpful. Let's begin with defining precisely what an expression is as it relates to Small BASIC.

Small BASIC Expressions

As they apply to the Small BASIC interpreter developed in this chapter, expressions are comprised of the following items:

♦   Numbers
♦   The operators +, –, /, *, ^, =, ( ), <, >, >=, <=, <>
♦   Variables

In BASIC, the ^ indicates exponentiation. The = is used both for assignments and for equality. However, relative to BASIC expressions, it is only an operator when used in a relational expression. (In standard BASIC, assignment is a statement and not an operation.) Not equal is denoted as < >. These items can be combined in expressions according to the rules of algebra. Here are some examples:

```
7 – 8
(100–5) * 14/6
a + b – c
10 ^ 5
```

The precedence of the operators is shown here:

highest:	( )
	unary + −
	^
	* /
	+ −
lowest	< > <= >= <> =

Operators of equal precedence evaluate from left to right.

Small BASIC makes the following assumptions:

♦ All variables are single letters; this means that 26 variables, the letters *A* through *Z,* are available for use. Although standard BASIC supports more variable names by allowing a number to follow a letter, such as X27, the Small BASIC interpreter developed here does not, in the interest of simplicity.

♦ The variables will not be case sensitive; *a* and *A* will be treated as the same variable.

♦ All numbers are integers, although you could easily write the routines to handle other types of values, such as floating-point numbers.

♦ Finally, no string variables will be supported, although quoted string constants can be used for writing messages to the screen.

These assumptions will be built into the parser.

Small BASIC Tokens

At the core of the Small BASIC parser is the **get_token( )** function. This function is an expanded version of the one shown in Chapter 3. The changes allow it to tokenize not just expressions, but also other elements of the BASIC language, such as keywords and strings.

In Small BASIC, each token has two formats: external and internal. The external format is the string form that you use when writing a program. For example, "PRINT" is the external form of the PRINT command. Although it is possible for an interpreter to be designed in such a way that each token is used in its external string format, this is seldom (if ever) done because it is horribly inefficient. Instead, the internal format of a token, which is simply an integer, is used. For example, the PRINT command might be represented by a 1, the INPUT command by a 2, and so on. The advantage of the internal representation is that much faster routines can be written using integers rather than strings. It is the job of **get_token( )** to convert the token from its external format into its internal format. Keep in mind that not all tokens will have different formats. For example, there is no advantage to converting most of the operators, because they are already single characters in their external form.

It is important to know what type of token is being returned. For example, the expression parser needs to know whether the next token is a number, an operator, or a variable. The importance of the token type will become evident as the interpreter is developed.

In Small BASIC, the program being interpreted is stored as one long, null-terminated string. The **get_token( )** function progresses through the program a character at a time. The next character to be read is pointed to by a global character pointer. In the version of **get_token( )** shown here this pointer is called **prog**. The reason that **prog** is global is that it must maintain its value between calls to **get_token( )** and allow other functions access to it. The parser developed in this chapter uses six types: **DELIMITER**, **VARIABLE**, **NUMBER**, **COMMAND**, **STRING**, and **QUOTE**. (These types are enumerated values declared elsewhere in the program.) **DELIMITER** is used for both operators and parentheses. **VARIABLE** is used when a variable is encountered. **NUMBER** is for numbers. The **COMMAND** type is assigned when a BASIC command is found. **STRING** is a temporary type used inside **get_token( )** until a determination is made about a token. Type **QUOTE** is for quoted strings. The global variable **token_type** holds the token type. The internal representation of the token is placed into the global **tok**. Here is the version of **get_token( )** used by Small BASIC:

```
// Get a token.
get_token()
{
  register char *temp;

  token_type = 0;
  tok = 0;
  temp = token;

  if(*prog=='\0') { // end of file
    *token = 0;
    tok = FINISHED;
    return(token_type=DELIMITER);
  }

  while(is_sp_tab(*prog)) ++prog;  // skip over white space

  if(*prog=='\r') { // crlf
    ++prog; ++prog;
```

```
      tok = EOL; *token='\r';
      token[1]='\n'; token[2]=0;
      return (token_type = DELIMITER);
    }

  if(strchr("<>", *prog)) { // check for double op
    switch(*prog) {
      case '<':
        if(*(prog+1)=='>') {
          prog++; prog++;
          *temp = NE;
        }
        else if(*(prog+1)=='=') {
          prog++; prog++;
          *temp = LE;
        }
        else {
          prog++;
          *temp = '<';
        }
        temp++;
        *temp = '\0';
        break;
      case '>':
        if(*(prog+1)=='=') {
          prog++; prog++;
          *temp = GE;
        }
        else {
          prog++;
          *temp = '>';
        }
        temp++;
        *temp = '\0';
        break;
    }
    return(token_type = DELIMITER);
  }

  if(strchr("+-*^/=;(),", *prog)){ // delimiter
    *temp = *prog;
    prog++; // advance to next position
    temp++;
    *temp = 0;
    return (token_type=DELIMITER);
  }
```

```
if(*prog=='"') { // quoted string
  prog++;
  while(*prog!='"'&& *prog!='\r') *temp++ = *prog++;
  if(*prog=='\r') serror(MISS_QUOTE);
  prog++;*temp = 0;
  return(token_type=QUOTE);
}

if(isdigit(*prog)) { // number
  while(!isdelim(*prog)) *temp++ = *prog++;
  *temp = '\0';
  return(token_type = NUMBER);
}

if(isalpha(*prog)) { // var or command
  while(!isdelim(*prog)) *temp++ = *prog++;
  token_type = STRING;
}

*temp = '\0';

// see if a string is a command or a variable
if(token_type==STRING) {
  tok = look_up(token); // convert to internal rep
  if(!tok) token_type = VARIABLE;
  else token_type = COMMAND; // is a command
}
return token_type;
}
```

Look closely at **get_token( )**. Because people like to put spaces into expressions to add clarity, leading spaces are skipped over using the function **is_sp_tab( )**, which returns true if its argument is a space or tab. Once the spaces have been skipped, **prog** will be pointing to either a number, a variable, a command, a carriage return/line feed, an operator, a quoted string, or a null, if trailing spaces end the program. If a carriage return is next, **tok** is set equal to **EOL**, a carriage return/line feed sequence is stored in **token**, and **DELIMITER** is put into **token_type**. Otherwise, double operators (such as **<=**) are checked for. **get_token( )** converts double operators into their internal representation. The values **NE**, **GE**, and **LE** are defined by an enumeration outside of **get_token( )**. If the next character is a single operator or other type of delimiter, it is returned as a string in the global variable **token**, and the type of **DELIMITER** is placed in **token_type**. Otherwise, a quoted string is checked for. If that is not the case, **get_token( )** checks if the next token is a number by seeing if the next character is a digit. If instead the next character is a letter, then it will be either a variable or a command (such as **PRINT**). The function **look_up( )** compares the token against commands in a table and, if it finds a match, returns the appropriate internal representation of the command. (The **look_up( )** function will be discussed later.) If a match is not found, then the token is assumed to be a variable. Finally, if the next character is none of the preceding, then it is assumed that the end of the expression has been reached and **token** is null, signaling the end of the expression.

To better understand how this version of **get_token( )** works, study what it returns for each token and type for the following expression:

PRINT A + 100 – (B * C) / 2

Token	Token Type
PRINT	COMMAND
A	VARIABLE
+	DELIMITER
100	NUMBER
–	DELIMITER
(	DELIMITER
B	VARIABLE
*	DELIMITER
C	VARIABLE
)	DELIMITER
/	DELIMITER
2	NUMBER

Remember that **token** will always hold a null-terminated string, even if it contains just a single character.

The Small BASIC Expression Parser

Here is the entire expression parser modified for use in the Small BASIC interpreter. You should put this code into its own file. (When added together, the code to the parser and the interpreter make a fairly large file, so two separately compiled files are recommended.) The meaning and use of the external variables will be described shortly, when the interpreter is discussed.

```
/* The Small BASIC Expression Parser

   This parser is a specialized version of
   the parser described in Chapter 3.  It is
```

```
                designed to support simple language
                interpreters, such as Small BASIC.
*/

#include <iostream.h>
#include <ctype.h>
#include <stdlib.h>
#include <string.h>

enum tok_types {DELIMITER, VARIABLE, NUMBER, COMMAND,
                STRING, QUOTE};

enum tokens {PRINT=1, INPUT, IF, THEN, FOR, NEXT, TO,
             GOTO, GOSUB, RETURN, EOL, FINISHED, END};

enum double_ops {LE=1, GE, NE};

extern char *prog;  // points into the program
extern char *p_buf; // points to start of program

extern int variables[26]; // variables

extern struct commands {
  char command[20];
  char tok;
} table[];

extern char token[80]; // holds string representation of token
extern char token_type; // contains type of token
extern char tok; // holds the internal representation of token

void eval_exp(int &result);
void eval_exp1(int &result);
void eval_exp2(int &result);
void eval_exp3(int &result);
void eval_exp4(int &result);
void eval_exp5(int &result);
void eval_exp6(int &result);
void atom(int &result);
void putback();
void serror(int error);
int get_token();
int look_up(char *s);
int isdelim(char c);
int is_sp_tab(char c);
int find_var(char *s);
```

```
/* These are the constants used to call serror() when
   a syntax error occurs.  Add more if you like.
   NOTE: SYNTAX is a generic error message used when
   nothing else seems appropriate.
*/
enum error_msg
     {SYNTAX, UNBAL_PARENS, NO_EXP, EQUAL_EXP,
      NOT_VAR, LAB_TAB_FULL, DUP_LAB, UNDEF_LAB,
      THEN_EXP, TO_EXP, TOO_MNY_FOR, NEXT_WO_FOR,
      TOO_MNY_GOSUB, RET_WO_GOSUB, MISS_QUOTE};

// Entry point into parser.
void eval_exp(int &result)
{
  get_token();
  if(!*token) {
    serror(NO_EXP);
    return;
  }
  eval_exp1(result);
  putback(); // return last token read to input stream
}

// Process relational operators.
void eval_exp1(int &result)
{
  // Relational operators.
  char relops[] = {
    GE, NE, LE, '<', '>', '=', 0
  };

  int temp;
  register char op;

  eval_exp2(result);
  op = *token;
  if(strchr(relops, op)) {
    get_token();
    eval_exp1(temp);
    switch(op) { // perform the relational operation
      case '<':
        result = result < temp;
        break;
      case LE:
        result = result <= temp;
        break;
      case '>':
        result = result > temp;
        break;
```

```
        case GE:
          result = result >= temp;
          break;
        case '=':
          result = result == temp;
          break;
        case NE:
          result = result != temp;
          break;
      }
    }
  }

//   Add or subtract two terms.
void eval_exp2(int &result)
{
  register char op;
  int temp;

  eval_exp3(result);
  while((op = *token) == '+' || op == '-') {
    get_token();
    eval_exp3(temp);
    switch(op) {
      case '-' :
        result = result - temp;
        break;
      case '+':
        result = result + temp;
        break;
    }
  }
}

// Multiply or divide two factors.
void eval_exp3(int &result)
{
  register char op;
  int temp;

  eval_exp4(result);
  while((op = *token) == '*' || op == '/') {
    get_token();
    eval_exp4(temp);
    switch(op) {
      case '*' :
        result = result * temp;
        break;
```

```
      case '/':
        result = result / temp;
        break;
    }
  }
}

// Process integer exponent.
void eval_exp4(int &result)
{
  int temp, ex;
  register int t;

  eval_exp5(result);
  if(*token== '^') {
    get_token();
    eval_exp4(temp);
    if(!temp) {
      result = 1;
      return;
    }
    ex = result;
    for(t=temp-1; t>0;   t--) result = result * ex;
  }
}

// Is a unary + or -.
void eval_exp5(int &result)
{
  register char op;

 op = 0;
  if((token_type==DELIMITER) &&
      *token=='+' || *token=='-')
  {
    op = *token;
    get_token();
  }
  eval_exp6(result);
  if(op=='-') result = -result;
}

// Process parenthesized expression.
void eval_exp6(int &result)
{
  if(*token == '(') {
    get_token();
    eval_exp2(result);
```

```cpp
      if(*token != ')')
        serror(UNBAL_PARENS);
      get_token();
    }
    else
      atom(result);
}

// Find value of number or variable.
void atom(int &result)
{
  switch(token_type) {
    case VARIABLE:
      result = find_var(token);
      get_token();
      return;
    case NUMBER:
      result = atoi(token);
      get_token();
      return;
    default:
      serror(SYNTAX);
    }
}

// Find the value of a variable.
int find_var(char *s)
{
  if(!isalpha(*s)){
    serror(NOT_VAR); // not a variable
    return 0;
  }
  return variables[toupper(*token)-'A'];
}

// Display an error message.
void serror(int error)
{
  char *p, *temp;
  int linecount = 0;
  register int i;

  static char *e[]= {
    "Syntax error",
    "Unbalanced parentheses",
    "No expression present",
    "Equal sign expected",
    "Not a variable",
```

```
    "Label table full",
    "Duplicate label",
    "Undefined label",
    "THEN expected",
    "TO expected",
    "Too many nested FOR loops",
    "NEXT without FOR",
    "Too many nested GOSUBs",
    "RETURN without GOSUB",
    "Double quotes needed"
  };
  cout << e[error];

  p = p_buf;
  while(p != prog) {  // find line number of error
    p++;
    if(*p == '\r') {
      linecount++;
    }
  }
  cout << " in line " << linecount << ".\n";

 temp = p;  // display line with error
  for(i=0; i<20 && p>p_buf && *p!='\n'; i++, p--);
  for(; p<=temp; p++) cout << *p;

  throw(1); // throw an exception
}

// Get a token.
get_token()
{
  register char *temp;

  token_type = 0;
  tok = 0;
  temp = token;

  if(*prog=='\0') { // end of file
    *token = 0;
    tok = FINISHED;
    return(token_type=DELIMITER);
  }

  while(is_sp_tab(*prog)) ++prog;  // skip over white space

  if(*prog=='\r') { // crlf
    ++prog; ++prog;
```

```cpp
    tok = EOL; *token='\r';
    token[1]='\n'; token[2]=0;
    return (token_type = DELIMITER);
  }


if(strchr("<>", *prog)) { // check for double op
   switch(*prog) {
     case '<':
       if(*(prog+1)=='>') {
         prog++; prog++;
         *temp = NE;
       }
       else if(*(prog+1)=='=') {
         prog++; prog++;
         *temp = LE;
       }
       else {
         prog++;
         *temp = '<';
       }
       temp++;
       *temp = '\0';
       break;
     case '>':
       if(*(prog+1)=='=') {
         prog++; prog++;
         *temp = GE;
       }
       else {
         prog++;
         *temp = '>';
       }
       temp++;
       *temp = '\0';
       break;
   }
   return(token_type = DELIMITER);
 }


if(strchr("+-*^/=;(),", *prog)){ // delimiter
   *temp = *prog;
   prog++; // advance to next position
   temp++;
   *temp = 0;
   return (token_type=DELIMITER);
 }
```

```
  if(*prog=='"') { // quoted string
    prog++;
    while(*prog!='"'&& *prog!='\r') *temp++ = *prog++;
    if(*prog=='\r') serror(MISS_QUOTE);
    prog++;*temp = 0;
    return(token_type=QUOTE);
  }

  if(isdigit(*prog)) { // number
    while(!isdelim(*prog)) *temp++ = *prog++;
    *temp = '\0';
    return(token_type = NUMBER);
  }

  if(isalpha(*prog)) { // var or command
    while(!isdelim(*prog)) *temp++ = *prog++;
    token_type = STRING;
  }

  *temp = '\0';

  // see if a string is a command or a variable
  if(token_type==STRING) {
    tok = look_up(token); // convert to internal rep
    if(!tok) token_type = VARIABLE;
    else token_type = COMMAND; // is a command
  }
  return token_type;
}

// Return a token to input stream.
void putback()
{

  char *t;

  t = token;
  for(; *t; t++) prog--;
}

/* Look up a token's internal representation in the
   token table.
*/
look_up(char *s)
{
  register int i;
  char *p;
```

```
    // convert to lowercase
    p = s;
    while(*p){
      *p = tolower(*p);
      p++;
    }

    // see if token is in table
    for(i=0; *table[i].command; i++)
      if(!strcmp(table[i].command, s))
        return table[i].tok;
    return 0; // unknown command
}

// Return true if c is a delimiter.
isdelim(char c)
{
  if(strchr(" ;,+-<>/*%^=()", c) ||
         c==9 || c=='\r' || c==0)
           return 1;
  return 0;
}

// Return 1 if c is space or tab.
is_sp_tab(char c)
{
  if(c==' ' || c=='\t') return 1;
  else return 0;
}
```

The parser as it is shown can handle the following operators: +, –, *, /, integer exponentiation (^), and the unary minus. It will also deal with parentheses correctly. You should notice that it has six levels as well as the **atom( )** function, which returns the value of a number. Also included are various support routines as well as the **get_token( )** code.

To evaluate an expression, set **prog** to point to the beginning of the string that holds the expression, and call **eval_exp( )** with the variable you want to hold the result. Notice that **eval_exp1( )** is different from the one shown in Chapter 3. As you might recall from Chapter 3, **eval_exp1( )** was used to handle the assignment operator. However, in BASIC, assignment is a statement, not an operation. Therefore, **eval_exp1( )** is not used for this purpose when parsing expressions found in BASIC programs. Instead, it is used to evaluate the relational operators. However, if you use the interpreter to experiment with other types of languages, then you may need to add a function called **eval_exp0( )**, which would be used to handle assignment as an operator.

You should pay special attention to the **serror( )** function, which is used to report errors. When a syntax error is detected, **serror( )** is called with the number of the error that occurred. It then displays the appropriate error message, the line number in which the error occurred, and part of the line that contains the error. It is easiest to call **serror( )** using the enumerated values defined by **error_msg** near the start of the parser code instead of trying to remember the actual number of each error message. As the comments preceding the **error_msg** enumeration indicate, the "syntax error" message is used when nothing else applies. Otherwise, a specific error is reported. Notice that **serror( )** ends by throwing an exception using a **throw** statement. This exception must be caught by a **catch** statement that takes some reasonable action. For the purposes of the Small BASIC interpreter, the **catch** statement is found in **main( )** and simply causes program execution to stop.

Note: If your compiler does not support the C++ exception-handling keywords (**try**, **catch**, and **throw**), you will need to use the C-based functions **setjmp( )** and **longjmp( )** for this purpose.

How the Parser Handles Variables

A short explanation of how the parser handles variables is in order. As stated earlier, the Small BASIC interpreter will only recognize the variables A through Z. Each variable will use one array location in a 26-element array of integers called **variables**. This array is defined in the interpreter code as shown here, with each variable initialized to 0:

```
int variables[26]= { // 26 user variables,  A-Z
  0, 0, 0, 0, 0, 0, 0, 0, 0,
  0, 0, 0, 0, 0, 0, 0, 0, 0,
  0, 0, 0, 0, 0, 0, 0, 0
};
```

Because the variable names are the letters *A* through *Z*, they can easily be used to index the array **variables** by subtracting the ASCII value for *A* from the variable name. The function **find_var( )** finds a variable's value. This function is contained in the full parser listing and is shown here for your convenience:

```
// Find the value of a variable.
int find_var(char *s)
{
```

```
if(!isalpha(*s)){
  serror(NOT_VAR); // not a variable
  return 0;
}
return variables[toupper(*token)-'A'];
}
```

Notice that as it is currently written, **find_var( )** will actually accept long variable names, but only the first letter is significant. You can modify it to enforce single-letter variable names if you like.

The Small BASIC Interpreter

Interpreters consist of two basic pieces: the *parser,* which evaluates expressions, and the *interpreter,* proper, which actually executes the program. In this section the interpreter module is examined.

The Keywords

As stated at the start of this chapter, Small BASIC interprets a small subset of the BASIC language. Here are keywords that it recognizes:

PRINT
INPUT
IF
THEN
FOR
NEXT
TO
GOTO
GOSUB
RETURN
END

The internal representation of these commands plus **EOL**, for end-of-line, and **FINISHED**, which signals the end of the program, are enumerated as shown here:

```
enum tokens {PRINT=1, INPUT, IF, THEN, FOR, NEXT, TO,
            GOTO, GOSUB, RETURN, EOL, FINISHED, END};
```

The reason that the **tokens** enumeration begins with 1 is that the value 0 is used by the **look_up( )** function (discussed shortly) to indicate an unknown command.

For the external representation of a token to be converted into the internal representation, both the external and internal formats are held in an array of structures called **table**, shown here:

```
// keyword lookup table
struct commands {
  char command[20]; // string form
  char tok; // internal representation
} table[] = { // commands must be entered lowercase
  "print", PRINT, // in this table.
  "input", INPUT,
  "if", IF,
  "then", THEN,
  "goto", GOTO,
  "for", FOR,
  "next", NEXT,
  "to", TO,
  "gosub", GOSUB,
  "return", RETURN,
  "end", END,
  "", END  // mark end of table
};
```

Notice that a null string marks the end of the table. The function **look_up( )**, shown here, uses **table** to return either a token's internal representation or a null if no match is found. (This function is part of the parser file, shown earlier.)

```
/* Look up a token's internal representation in the
   token table.
*/
look_up(char *s)
{
  register int i;
  char *p;

  // convert to lowercase
  p = s;
  while(*p){
    *p = tolower(*p);
    p++;
  }

  // see if token is in table
  for(i=0; *table[i].command; i++)
    if(!strcmp(table[i].command, s))
```

```
        return table[i].tok;
    return 0; // unknown command
}
```

Loading the Program

No integral editor is included in the Small BASIC interpreter. Instead, you must create a BASIC program using a standard text editor. When Small BASIC begins, the program is read in and then executed by the interpreter. The function that loads the program is called **load_program( )** and is shown here:

```
// Load a program.
load_program(char *p, char *fname)
{
  ifstream in(fname, ios::in | ios::binary);
  int i=0;

  if(!in) {
    cout << "File not found ";
    cout << "-- be sure to specify .BAS extension.\n";
    return 0;
  }

  i = 0;
  do {
    *p = in.get();
    p++; i++;
  } while(!in.eof() && i<PROG_SIZE);

  // null terminate the program
  if(*(p-2)==0x1a) *(p-2) = '\0'; // discard eof marker
  else *(p-1) = '\0';

  in.close();
  return 1;
}
```

As the comments indicate, this function will discard any trailing EOF marker found in the text file. As you may know, some editors append an end-of-file marker. Others do not. **load_program( )** handles both cases.

The Main Loop

All interpreters are driven by a top-level loop that operates by reading the next token from the program and then selecting the appropriate action to process it. The Small BASIC interpreter is no exception. The main loop for the Small BASIC interpreter looks like this:

```
do {
  token_type = get_token();
  // check for assignment statement
  if(token_type==VARIABLE) {
    putback(); // return the var to the input stream
    assignment(); // must be assignment statement
  }
  else // is command
    switch(tok) {
      case PRINT:
        print();
        break;
      case GOTO:
        exec_goto();
        break;
      case IF:
        exec_if();
        break;
      case FOR:
        exec_for();
        break;
      case NEXT:
        next();
        break;
      case INPUT:
        input();
        break;
      case GOSUB:
        gosub();
        break;
      case RETURN:
        greturn();
        break;
      case END:
        return 0;
    }
} while (tok != FINISHED);
```

First, a token is read from the program. In BASIC, the first token on each line determines what kind of statement occurs on that line. (No look-ahead is required for this step.) Assuming no syntax errors have been made, if the token is a variable, then an assignment statement is occurring. Otherwise,

10

the token must be a command, and the appropriate **case** statement is selected based on the value of **tok**. Let's see how each of these commands works.

The Assignment Function

As mentioned earlier, in BASIC, assignment is a statement, not an operation. The general form of a BASIC assignment statement is

   var-name = expression

The assignment statement is interpreted using the **assignment( )** function shown here:

```
// Assign a variable a value.
void assignment()
{
  int var, value;

  // get the variable name
  get_token();
  if(!isalpha(*token)) {
    serror(NOT_VAR);
    return;
  }

  // convert to index into variable table
  var = toupper(*token)-'A';

  // get the equal sign
  get_token();
  if(*token != '=') {
    serror(EQUAL_EXP);
    return;
  }

  // get the value to assign
  eval_exp(value);

  // assign the value
  variables[var] = value;
}
```

The first thing that **assignment( )** does is to read a token from the program. This will be the variable that will have its value assigned. If it is not a valid variable, an error will be reported. Next, the equal sign is read. Then, **eval_exp( )** is called so that the value to assign to the variable can be computed. Finally, the value is assigned to the variable. The function is surprisingly simple and uncluttered because the expression parser and the **get_token( )** function do much of the "messy" work.

The PRINT Command

In BASIC, the PRINT command is actually quite powerful and flexible. While it is beyond the scope of this chapter to create a function that supports all the functionality of the PRINT command, the one developed here embodies its most important essential features. The general form of the Small BASIC print command is

PRINT *arg-list*

where *arg-list* is a comma- or semicolon-separated list of expressions or quoted strings. The function **print( )**, shown here, interprets the PRINT command:

```
// Execute a simple version of the BASIC PRINT statement.
void print()
{
  int result;
  int len=0, spaces;
  char last_delim, str[80];

  do {
    get_token(); // get next list item
    if(tok==EOL || tok==FINISHED) break;
    if(token_type==QUOTE) { // is string
      cout << token;
      len += strlen(token);
      get_token();
    }
    else { // is expression
      putback();
      eval_exp(result);
      get_token();
      cout << result;
      itoa(result, str, 10);
      len += strlen(str); // save length
    }
    last_delim = *token;
```

```
      // if comma, move to next tab stop
      if(*token == ',') {
        // compute number of spaces to move to next tab
        spaces = 8 - (len % 8);
        len += spaces; // add in the tabbing position
        while(spaces) {
          cout << " ";
          spaces--;
        }
      }
      else if(*token==';') {
        cout << " ";
        len++;
      }
      else if(tok!=EOL && tok!=FINISHED) serror(SYNTAX);
    } while (*token==';' || *token==',');

    if(tok==EOL || tok==FINISHED) {
      if(last_delim != ';' && last_delim != ',')
        cout << endl;
    }
    else serror(SYNTAX);

}
```

The PRINT command can be used to print a list of variables and quoted strings on the screen. If one item is separated from the next by a semicolon, then one space is printed between them. If two items are separated by a comma, then the second item will be displayed beginning with the next tab position. If the list ends in a comma or semicolon, then no newline is issued. Here are some examples of valid PRINT statements:

```
PRINT X; Y; "THIS IS A STRING"
PRINT 10 / 4
PRINT
```

The last example simply prints a newline.

Notice that **print( )** makes use of the **putback( )** function to return a token to the input stream. The reason is that **print( )** must look ahead to see whether the next item to be printed is a quoted string or a numeric expression. If it is an expression, then the first term in the expression must be returned to the input stream so that the expression parser can correctly compute the value of the expression.

The INPUT Command

In BASIC, the INPUT command is used to read information from the keyboard into a variable. It has two general forms. The first is

INPUT *var-name*

which displays a question mark and waits for input. The second is

INPUT "*prompt-string*", *var-name*

which displays a prompting message and waits for input. The function **input( )**, shown here, implements the INPUT command:

```cpp
// Execute a simple form of the BASIC INPUT command.
void input()
{
  char var;
  int i;

  get_token(); // see if prompt string is present
  if(token_type==QUOTE) {
    cout << token; // if so, print it and check for comma
    get_token();
    if(*token != ',') serror(SYNTAX);
    get_token();
  }
  else cout << "? "; // otherwise, prompt with ?
  var = toupper(*token)-'A'; // get the input var

  cin >> i; // read input

  variables[var] = i; // store it
}
```

The operation of this function is straightforward and should be clear from its comments.

The GOTO Command

Now that you have seen the way a few simple commands work, it is time to develop a somewhat more difficult command. In BASIC, the most important form of program control is the lowly GOTO. In standard BASIC, the object of a GOTO must be a line number. In Small BASIC, this traditional approach is preserved. However, Small BASIC does not require a line number for each line; one is needed only if that line will be the target of a GOTO. The general form of the GOTO is

GOTO *line-number*

The main complexity associated with the GOTO is that both forward and backward jumps must be allowed. To satisfy this constraint in an efficient manner requires that the entire program be scanned prior to execution and the location of each label be placed in a table. Then, each time a GOTO is executed, the location of the target line can be looked up, and program control transferred to that point. The table that holds the labels is declared like this:

```
// label lookup table
struct label {
  char name[LAB_LEN]; // label
  char *p; // points to label's location in source file
} label_table[NUM_LAB];
```

The routine that scans the program and puts each label's location in the table is called **scan_labels( )** and is shown here along with several of its support functions:

```
// Find all labels.
void scan_labels()
{
  int addr;
  char *temp;

  label_init(); // zero all labels
  temp = prog;   // save pointer to top of program

  // if the first token in the file is a label
  get_token();
  if(token_type==NUMBER) {
    strcpy(label_table[0].name, token);
    label_table[0].p = prog;
  }

  find_eol();
  do {
    get_token();
    if(token_type==NUMBER) {
      addr = get_next_label(token);
      if(addr == -1 || addr == -2) {
```

```
         (addr == -1) ? serror(LAB_TAB_FULL):serror(DUP_LAB);
      }
      strcpy(label_table[addr].name, token);

      // save current location in program
      label_table[addr].p = prog;
    }

  // if not on a blank line, find next line
   if(tok!=EOL) find_eol();
  } while(tok!=FINISHED);
  prog = temp; // restore original location
}

// Find the start of the next line.
void find_eol()
{
  while(*prog!='\n'  && *prog!='\0') ++prog;
  if(*prog) prog++;
}

/* Return index of next free position in label array.
   -1 is returned if the array is full.
   -2 is returned when duplicate label is found.
*/
get_next_label(char *s)
{
  register int i;

  for(i=0; i<NUM_LAB; ++i) {
    if(label_table[i].name[0]==0) return i;
    if(!strcmp(label_table[i].name, s)) return -2;
  }

  return -1;
}

/* Find location of given label.  A null is returned
   if label is not found; otherwise a pointer to the
   position of the label is returned.
*/
char *find_label(char *s)
{
  register int i;

  for(i=0; i<NUM_LAB; ++i)
    if(!strcmp(label_table[i].name, s))
```

```
        return label_table[i].p;
  return '\0'; // error condition
}


/* Initialize the array that holds the labels.
   By convention, a null label name indicates that
   the array position is unused.
*/
void label_init()
{
  register int i;

  for(i=0; i<NUM_LAB; ++i)
    label_table[i].name[0] = '\0';
}
```

Two types of errors are reported by **scan_labels( )**. The first is duplicate labels. In BASIC (and most other languages) no two labels can be the same. Second, a full label table is reported. The table's size is defined by **NUM_LAB**, which you can set to any size you desire.

Once the label table has been built, it is quite easy to execute a GOTO instruction, as is shown in **exec_goto( )**, here:

```
// Execute a GOTO statement.
void exec_goto()
{
  char *loc;

  get_token(); // get label to go to

  // find the location of the label
  loc = find_label(token);
  if(loc==NULL)
    serror(UNDEF_LAB); // label not defined

  else prog = loc;  // start program running at that loc
}
```

The support function **find_label( )** looks up a label in the label table and returns a pointer to it. If the label is not found, a null—which can never be a valid pointer—is returned. If the address is not null, it is assigned to **prog** causing execution to resume at the location of the label. (Remember, **prog** is a pointer to the place at which the program is currently being executed.) If the label is not found, an undefined label message is issued.

The IF Statement

The Small BASIC interpreter executes a subset of the standard BASIC's IF statement. In Small BASIC, no ELSE is allowed. (However, you will find it easy to add the ELSE once you understand the operation of the IF.) The IF statement takes this general form:

IF *expression rel-op expression* THEN *statement*

The statement that follows the THEN is executed only if the relational expression is true. The following function, called **exec_if( )**, executes the IF statement:

```
// Execute an IF statement.
void exec_if()
{
  int result;
  char op;

  eval_exp(result); // get value of expression

  if(result) { // is true so process target of IF
    get_token();
    if(tok!=THEN) {
      serror(THEN_EXP);
      return;
    } // else, target statement will be executed
  }
  else find_eol(); // find start of next line
}
```

The **exec_if( )** function operates as follows. First, the value of the relational expression is computed. If the expression is true, the target of the THEN is executed; otherwise, **find_eol( )** finds the start of the next line. Notice that if the expression is true, the **exec_if( )** simply returns. This causes the main loop to iterate, and the next token is read. Since the target of an IF is a statement, returning to the main loop simply causes the target statement to be executed as if it were on its own line. If the expression is false, then the start of the next line is found before execution returns to the main loop.

The FOR Loop

The implementation of the BASIC FOR loop presents a challenging problem that lends itself to a rather elegant solution. The general form of the FOR loop is

FOR *control-var* = *initial-value* TO *target-value*

.

.

.

NEXT

The Small BASIC version of the FOR allows only positively running loops that increment the control variable by one each iteration. The STEP command is not supported.

In BASIC, as in C++, loops may be nested to several levels. The main challenge presented by this is keeping the information associated with each loop straight. (That is, each NEXT must be associated with the proper FOR.) The solution to this problem is to implement the FOR loop using a stack-based mechanism. At the top of the loop, information about the status of the control variable, the target value, and the location of the top of the loop in the program is pushed onto a stack. Each time the NEXT is encountered, this information is popped, the control variable updated, and its value checked against the target value. If the control value exceeds the target, the loop stops and execution continues with the next line following the NEXT statement. Otherwise, the updated information is pushed back onto the stack, and execution resumes at the top of the loop. Implementing a FOR loop in this way works not only for a single loop, but also for nested loops, because the innermost NEXT will always be associated with the innermost FOR. (The last information pushed on the stack will be the first information popped.) Once an inner loop terminates, its information is popped from the stack and, if it exists, an outer loop's information comes to the top of the stack. Thus, each NEXT is automatically associated with its corresponding FOR.

To support the FOR loop, a stack must be created that holds the loop information, as shown here:

```
// support for FOR loops
struct for_stack {
  int var; // counter variable
  int target; // target value
  char *loc; // place in source code to loop to
} fstack[FOR_NEST]; // stack for FOR/NEXT loop
```

The value of **FOR_NEST** defines how deeply nested the FOR loops may be. (Twenty-five is generally more than adequate.)

The FOR stack is managed by two stack functions called **fpush( )** and **fpop( )**, which are shown here:

```
// Push the FOR stack.
void fpush(struct for_stack stckvar)
{
  if(ftos==FOR_NEST)
    serror(TOO_MNY_FOR);

  fstack[ftos] = stckvar;
  ftos++;
}

// Pop the FOR stack.
struct for_stack fpop()
{
  if(ftos==0)
    serror(NEXT_WO_FOR);

  ftos--;
  return(fstack[ftos]);
}
```

Now that the necessary support is in place, the functions that execute the FOR and NEXT statements can be developed as shown here:

```
// Execute a FOR loop.
void exec_for()
{
  struct for_stack stckvar;
  int value;

  get_token(); // read the control variable
  if(!isalpha(*token)) {
    serror(NOT_VAR);
    return;
  }
  // save index of control var
  stckvar.var = toupper(*token)-'A';

  get_token(); // read the equal sign
  if(*token != '=') {
    serror(EQUAL_EXP);
    return;
  }

  eval_exp(value); // get initial value

  variables[stckvar.var] = value;

  get_token();
```

```
    if(tok!=TO) serror(TO_EXP); // read and discard the TO

    eval_exp(stckvar.target); // get target value

    /* if loop can execute at least once,
       push info on stack */
    if(value >= variables[stckvar.var]) {
      stckvar.loc = prog;
      fpush(stckvar);
    }
    else // otherwise, skip loop code altogether
      while(tok!=NEXT) get_token();
}

// Execute a NEXT statement.
void next()
{
  struct for_stack stckvar;

  stckvar = fpop(); // read the loop info

  variables[stckvar.var]++; // increment control var

  // if done, return
  if(variables[stckvar.var] > stckvar.target) return;

  fpush(stckvar);  // otherwise, restore the info
  prog = stckvar.loc;  // loop
}
```

You should be able to follow the operation of these routines by reading the comments. As the code stands, it does not prevent a GOTO out of a FOR loop. However, jumping out of a FOR loop will corrupt the FOR stack and should be avoided.

The stack-based solution to the FOR loop problem can be generalized to all loops. Although Small BASIC does not implement any other loop statements, you can apply the same sort of procedure to any type of loop, including the WHILE and DO/WHILE loops. Also, as you will see in the next section, the stack-based solution can be applied to any language element that may be nested, including calling subroutines.

The GOSUB

Although standard BASIC does not support true stand-alone subroutines, it does allow portions of a program to be called and returned from using the GOSUB and RETURN statements. The general form of a GOSUB/RETURN is

GOSUB *line-num*

.

.

.

line-num
subroutine code
RETURN

Calling a subroutine, even the limited subroutines as implemented in BASIC, requires the use of a stack. The reason for this is similar to that given for the FOR statement. It is to allow nested subroutine calls. Because it is possible to have one subroutine call another, a stack is necessary to ensure that a RETURN statement is associated with its proper GOSUB. The GOSUB stack is defined as

```
char *gstack[SUB_NEST]; // stack for gosub
```

As you can see, the **gstack** is simply an array of character pointers. It holds the location in the program to return to once a subroutine has finished.

The function **gosub( )** and its support routines are shown here:

```
// Execute a GOSUB command.
void gosub()
{
  char *loc;

  get_token();

  // find the label to call
  loc = find_label(token);
  if(loc==NULL)
    serror(UNDEF_LAB); // label not defined
  else {
    gpush(prog); // save place to return to
    prog = loc;  // start program running at that loc
  }
}

// Return from GOSUB.
void greturn()
{
   prog = gpop();
}

// Push GOSUB stack.
```

```
void gpush(char *s)
{
  if(gtos==SUB_NEST)
    serror(TOO_MNY_GOSUB);

  gstack[gtos] = s;
  gtos++;
}

// Pop GOSUB stack.
char *gpop()
{
  if(gtos==0)
    serror(RET_WO_GOSUB);

  gtos--;
  return(gstack[gtos]);
}
```

The GOSUB command works like this. When a GOSUB is encountered, the current value of **prog** is pushed on the GOSUB stack. (This is the point in the program that the subroutine will return to once it is finished.) The target line number is looked up, and the address associated with it is assigned to **prog**. This causes program execution to resume at the start of the subroutine. When a RETURN is encountered, the GOSUB stack is popped, and this value is assigned to **prog**, causing execution to continue on the next line after the GOSUB statement. Because the return address is pushed on the GOSUB stack, subroutines may be nested. In each case, the most recently called subroutine will be the one returned from when its RETURN statement is encountered. (That is, the return address of the most recently called subroutine will be on the top of the **gstack** stack.) This process allows GOSUBs to be nested to any depth.

The Entire Interpreter File

All the code for the Small BASIC interpreter, except those routines found in the expression parser file, is shown here. Once you have entered it into your computer, you should compile both the interpreter and the parser files and link them together. Call the executable version SBASIC.

```
/* A Small BASIC interpreter

   You can easily expand this interpreter or
   use it as a starting point for developing
   your own computer language.
*/
```

```cpp
#include <iostream.h>
#include <fstream.h>
#include <ctype.h>
#include <stdlib.h>
#include <string.h>

const int NUM_LAB = 100;
const int LAB_LEN = 10;
const int FOR_NEST = 25;
const int SUB_NEST = 25;
const int PROG_SIZE = 10000;

enum tok_types {DELIMITER, VARIABLE, NUMBER, COMMAND,
                STRING, QUOTE};

enum tokens {PRINT=1, INPUT, IF, THEN, FOR, NEXT, TO,
             GOTO, GOSUB, RETURN, EOL, FINISHED, END};

char *prog; // points into the program
char *p_buf; // points to start of program

int variables[26]= { // 26 user variables,  A-Z
  0, 0, 0, 0, 0, 0, 0, 0, 0,
  0, 0, 0, 0, 0, 0, 0, 0, 0,
  0, 0, 0, 0, 0, 0, 0, 0
};

// keyword lookup table
struct commands {
  char command[20]; // string form
  char tok; // internal representation
} table[] = { // commands must be entered lowercase
  "print", PRINT, // in this table.
  "input", INPUT,
  "if", IF,
  "then", THEN,
  "goto", GOTO,
  "for", FOR,
  "next", NEXT,
  "to", TO,
  "gosub", GOSUB,
  "return", RETURN,
  "end", END,
  "", END  // mark end of table
};
```

```cpp
char token[80];
char token_type, tok;

// label lookup table
struct label {
  char name[LAB_LEN]; // label
  char *p; // points to label's location in source file
} label_table[NUM_LAB];

// support for FOR loops
struct for_stack {
  int var; // counter variable
  int target; // target value
  char *loc; // place in source code to loop to
} fstack[FOR_NEST]; // stack for FOR/NEXT loop

char *gstack[SUB_NEST]; // stack for gosub

int ftos;  // index to top of FOR stack
int gtos;  // index to top of GOSUB stack

void print();
void scan_labels();
void find_eol();
void exec_goto();
void exec_if();
void exec_for();
void next();
void fpush(struct for_stack i);
void input();
void gosub();
void greturn();
void gpush(char *s);
void label_init();
void assignment();
char *find_label(char *s);
char *gpop();
struct for_stack fpop();
int load_program(char *p, char *fname);
int get_next_label(char *s);

// prototypes for functions in the parser file
void eval_exp(int &result);
int get_token();
void serror(int error), putback();
```

```
/* These are the constants used to call serror() when
   a syntax error occurs.  Add more if you like.
   NOTE: SYNTAX is a generic error message used when
   nothing else seems appropriate.
*/
enum error_msg
     {SYNTAX, UNBAL_PARENS, NO_EXP, EQUAL_EXP,
      NOT_VAR, LAB_TAB_FULL, DUP_LAB, UNDEF_LAB,
      THEN_EXP, TO_EXP, TOO_MNY_FOR, NEXT_WO_FOR,
      TOO_MNY_GOSUB, RET_WO_GOSUB, MISS_QUOTE};

main(int argc, char *argv[])
{
  if(argc!=2) {
    cout << "Usage: sbasic <filename>\n";
    exit(1);
  }

  // allocate memory for the program
  prog = new char [PROG_SIZE];
  if(!prog) {
    cout << "Allocation Failure";
    exit(1);
  }
  p_buf = prog;

  // load the program to execute
  if(!load_program(prog, argv[1])) exit(1);

  // begin try block
  try {
    scan_labels(); // find the labels in the program
    ftos = 0; // initialize the FOR stack index
    gtos = 0; // initialize the GOSUB stack index/
    do {
      token_type = get_token();
      // check for assignment statement
      if(token_type==VARIABLE) {
        putback(); // return the var to the input stream
        assignment(); // must be assignment statement
      }
      else // is command
        switch(tok) {
          case PRINT:
            print();
            break;
          case GOTO:
            exec_goto();
```

10

```
            break;
          case IF:
            exec_if();
            break;
          case FOR:
            exec_for();
            break;
          case NEXT:
            next();
            break;
          case INPUT:
            input();
            break;
          case GOSUB:
            gosub();
            break;
          case RETURN:
            greturn();
             break;
          case END:
            return 0;
      }
    } while (tok != FINISHED);
  } // end of try block

  /* catch throws here.  As implemented, only
     serror() throws an exception.  However,
     when creating your own languages, you can
     throw a variety of different exceptions.
  */
  catch(int) {
    return 0; // fatal error
  }
  return 0;
}


// Load a program.
load_program(char *p, char *fname)
{
  ifstream in(fname, ios::in | ios::binary);
  int i=0;

  if(!in) {
    cout << "File not found ";
    cout << "-- be sure to specify .BAS extension.\n";
    return 0;
  }
```

```
  i = 0;
  do {
    *p = in.get();
    p++; i++;
  } while(!in.eof() && i<PROG_SIZE);

  // null terminate the program
  if(*(p-2)==0x1a) *(p-2) = '\0'; // discard eof marker
  else *(p-1) = '\0';

  in.close();
  return 1;
}

// Find all labels.
void scan_labels()
{
  int addr;
  char *temp;

  label_init(); // zero all labels
  temp = prog;  // save pointer to top of program

  // if the first token in the file is a label
  get_token();
  if(token_type==NUMBER) {
    strcpy(label_table[0].name, token);
    label_table[0].p = prog;
  }

  find_eol();
  do {
    get_token();
    if(token_type==NUMBER) {
      addr = get_next_label(token);
      if(addr == -1 || addr == -2) {
        (addr == -1) ? serror(LAB_TAB_FULL):serror(DUP_LAB);
      }
      strcpy(label_table[addr].name, token);

      // save current location in program
      label_table[addr].p = prog;
    }
```

```
      // if not on a blank line, find next line
      if(tok!=EOL) find_eol();
   } while(tok!=FINISHED);
   prog = temp; // restore original location
}


// Find the start of the next line.
void find_eol()
{
  while(*prog!='\n'  && *prog!='\0') ++prog;
  if(*prog) prog++;
}


/* Return index of next free position in label array.
    -1 is returned if the array is full.
    -2 is returned when duplicate label is found.
*/
get_next_label(char *s)
{
  register int i;

  for(i=0; i<NUM_LAB; ++i) {
    if(label_table[i].name[0]==0) return i;
    if(!strcmp(label_table[i].name, s)) return -2;
  }

  return -1;
}


/* Find location of given label.  A null is returned
   if label is not found; otherwise a pointer to the
   position of the label is returned.
*/
char *find_label(char *s)
{
  register int i;

  for(i=0; i<NUM_LAB; ++i)
    if(!strcmp(label_table[i].name, s))
      return label_table[i].p;
  return '\0'; // error condition
}
```

```
/* Initialize the array that holds the labels.
   By convention, a null label name indicates that
   the array position is unused.
*/
void label_init()
{
  register int i;

  for(i=0; i<NUM_LAB; ++i)
    label_table[i].name[0] = '\0';
}

// Assign a variable a value.
void assignment()
{
  int var, value;

  // get the variable name
  get_token();
  if(!isalpha(*token)) {
    serror(NOT_VAR);
    return;
  }

  // convert to index into variable table
  var = toupper(*token)-'A';

  // get the equal sign
  get_token();
  if(*token != '=') {
    serror(EQUAL_EXP);
    return;
  }

  // get the value to assign
  eval_exp(value);

  // assign the value
  variables[var] = value;
}

// Execute a simple version of the BASIC PRINT statement.
void print()
{
  int result;
  int len=0, spaces;
  char last_delim, str[80];
```

```
      do {
        get_token(); // get next list item
        if(tok==EOL || tok==FINISHED) break;
        if(token_type==QUOTE) { // is string
          cout << token;
          len += strlen(token);
          get_token();
        }
        else { // is expression
          putback();
          eval_exp(result);
          get_token();
          cout << result;
          itoa(result, str, 10);
          len += strlen(str); // save length
        }
        last_delim = *token;

        // if comma, move to next tab stop
        if(*token == ',') {
          // compute number of spaces to move to next tab
          spaces = 8 - (len % 8);
          len += spaces; // add in the tabbing position
          while(spaces) {
            cout << " ";
            spaces--;
          }
        }
        else if(*token==';') {
          cout << " ";
          len++;
        }
        else if(tok!=EOL && tok!=FINISHED) serror(SYNTAX);
      } while (*token==';' || *token==',');

    if(tok==EOL || tok==FINISHED) {
        if(last_delim != ';' && last_delim != ',')
          cout << endl;
    }
    else serror(SYNTAX);

}

// Execute a GOTO statement.
void exec_goto()
{
  char *loc;
```

```
  get_token(); // get label to go to

  // find the location of the label
  loc = find_label(token);
  if(loc==NULL)
    serror(UNDEF_LAB); // label not defined

  else prog = loc;  // start program running at that loc
}

// Execute an IF statement.
void exec_if()
{
  int result;
  char op;

  eval_exp(result); // get value of expression

  if(result) { // is true so process target of IF
    get_token();
    if(tok!=THEN) {
      serror(THEN_EXP);
      return;
    } // else, target statement will be executed
  }
  else find_eol(); // find start of next line
}

// Execute a FOR loop.
void exec_for()
{
  struct for_stack stckvar;
  int value;

  get_token(); // read the control variable
  if(!isalpha(*token)) {
    serror(NOT_VAR);
    return;
  }
  // save index of control var
  stckvar.var = toupper(*token)-'A';

  get_token(); // read the equal sign
  if(*token != '=') {
    serror(EQUAL_EXP);
    return;
  }
}
```

```
    eval_exp(value); // get initial value

    variables[stckvar.var] = value;

    get_token();
    if(tok!=TO) serror(TO_EXP); // read and discard the TO

    eval_exp(stckvar.target); // get target value

    /* if loop can execute at least once,
       push info on stack */
    if(value >= variables[stckvar.var]) {
      stckvar.loc = prog;
      fpush(stckvar);
    }
    else // otherwise, skip loop code altogether
      while(tok!=NEXT) get_token();
}

// Execute a NEXT statement.
void next()
{
  struct for_stack stckvar;

  stckvar = fpop(); // read the loop info

  variables[stckvar.var]++; // increment control var

  // if done, return
  if(variables[stckvar.var] > stckvar.target) return;

  fpush(stckvar);  // otherwise, restore the info
  prog = stckvar.loc;  // loop
}

// Push the FOR stack.
void fpush(struct for_stack stckvar)
{
  if(ftos==FOR_NEST)
    serror(TOO_MNY_FOR);

  fstack[ftos] = stckvar;
  ftos++;
}

// Pop the FOR stack.
struct for_stack fpop()
{
```

```
    if(ftos==0)
      serror(NEXT_WO_FOR);

    ftos--;
    return(fstack[ftos]);
}


// Execute a simple form of the BASIC INPUT command.
void input()
{
    char var;
    int i;

    get_token(); // see if prompt string is present
    if(token_type==QUOTE) {
      cout << token; // if so, print it and check for comma
      get_token();
      if(*token != ',') serror(SYNTAX);
      get_token();
    }
    else cout << "? "; // otherwise, prompt with ?
    var = toupper(*token)-'A'; // get the input var

    cin >> i; // read input

    variables[var] = i; // store it
}

// Execute a GOSUB command.
void gosub()
{
    char *loc;

    get_token();

    // find the label to call
    loc = find_label(token);
    if(loc==NULL)
      serror(UNDEF_LAB); // label not defined
    else {
      gpush(prog); // save place to return to
      prog = loc;  // start program running at that loc
    }
}


// Return from GOSUB.
void greturn()
```

```
{
    prog = gpop();
}

// Push GOSUB stack.
void gpush(char *s)
{
  if(gtos==SUB_NEST)
    serror(TOO_MNY_GOSUB);

  gstack[gtos] = s;
  gtos++;
}

// Pop GOSUB stack.
char *gpop()
{
  if(gtos==0)
    serror(RET_WO_GOSUB);

  gtos--;
  return(gstack[gtos]);
}
```

Using Small BASIC

Here is a sampling of programs that Small BASIC will execute. Notice that both upper- and lowercase are supported. You will want to write several of your own programs, too. Also, try writing programs that have syntax errors, and observe the way Small BASIC reports them.

The following program exercises all of the commands supported by Small BASIC. Call this program TEST.BAS.

```
PRINT "This program demonstrates all commands."
FOR X = 1 TO 100
PRINT X; X/2, X; X*X
NEXT
GOSUB 300
PRINT "hello"
INPUT H
IF H<11 THEN GOTO 200
PRINT 12-4/2
PRINT 100
200 A = 100/2
IF A>10 THEN PRINT "this is ok"
PRINT A
```

```
PRINT A+34
INPUT H
PRINT H
INPUT "this is a test ",y
PRINT H+Y
END
300 PRINT "this is a subroutine"
    RETURN
```

Assuming that you called the Small BASIC interpreter SBASIC, then to run this program you will use the following command line:

SBASIC TEST.BAS

Small BASIC will automatically load the program and begin execution.

The next program demonstrates nested subroutines.

```
PRINT "This program demonstrates nested GOSUBs."
INPUT "enter a number: ", I
GOSUB 100

END

100 FOR T = 1 TO I
  X = X + I
  GOSUB 150
NEXT
RETURN

150 PRINT X;
    RETURN
```

This program illustrates the INPUT command:

```
print "This program computes the volume of a box."
input "Enter length of first side ", l
input "Enter length of second side ", w
input "Enter length of third side ", d
t = l * w * d
print "Volume is ", t
```

The next program illustrates nested FOR loops.

```
PRINT "This program demonstrates nested FOR loops."
FOR X = 1 TO 100
  FOR Y = 1 TO 10
```

```
    PRINT X; Y; X*Y
  NEXT
NEXT
```

10

Enhancing and Expanding the Interpreter

It is quite easy to add commands to the Small BASIC interpreter. Just follow the general format taken by the ones presented in the chapter. To add different variable types, you will need to use an array of structures to hold the variables, with one member in the structure indicating the type of the variable and the other member holding the value. To add strings, you will need to establish a string table. You might want to use the new C++ **string** class to support strings in Small BASIC. This would allow a one-to-one translation between BASIC string operations and C++ **string** operations.

One other point. As written, the various enumerations and constants used by the interpreter and the parser are simply duplicated in each file. This is appropriate for its presentation in a book because it prevents things from being overlooked by the reader. However, as you enhance and expand the interpreter, you will want to move these types of declarations into a header file that is included in all the files that comprise the interpreter. This not only makes things easier as your project grows in size, but it also prevents one file from being out-of-sync with another.

Creating Your Own Computer Language

While enhancing or expanding Small BASIC is a good way to become more familiar with its operation and with the way that language interpreters function, you are not limited to the BASIC language. You can use the same techniques described in this chapter to write an interpreter for just about any computer language. You can even invent your own language which reflects your own programming style and personality. In fact, the interpreter skeleton used by Small BASIC is a perfect "test bench" for any type of special language feature that you might want to try. For example, to add a REPEAT/UNTIL loop to the interpreter, you need to follow these four steps:

1. Add REPEAT and UNTIL to the **tokens** enumeration.
2. Add REPEAT and UNTIL to the **commands** table.
3. Add REPEAT and UNTIL to the main loop **switch** statement.
4. Define **repeat( )** and **until( )** functions that process the REPEAT and UNTIL commands. (Use the **exec_for( )** and **next( )** as starting points.)

One final thought: the types of statements that you can interpret are bounded only by your imagination. Don't be afraid to experiment.

Chapter

11

Exploring the C++ Frontier: Java

When the chronicle of computer languages is written, the following will be said: B spawned C, C evolved into C++, and C++ transmuted into Java. This final chapter of the book takes a brief look at the frontier of C++: Java.

As anyone involved with computers knows, the World Wide Web and the Internet have become part and parcel of the computing universe. The Internet has moved from being simply an information distribution system into what amounts to a vast, distributed computing environment. And this change has prompted the invention of the latest evolution of C++: Java. Here is why.

As you know, in a network there are two very broad categories of objects that are transmitted between the server and your personal computer: passive information and dynamic, active programs. For example, when you read your e-mail, you are viewing passive data. Even when you download a program, the program's code is still only passive data until you execute it. However, there is a second type of object that can be transmitted to your computer: a dynamic program. For example, such a program might be provided by a server to properly display the data that it is sending to you. While their appeal is great, dynamic, networked programs have also been greeted with concern because of the security and portability problems involved. As you will see, Java is an attempt to answer those concerns.

This chapter gives a brief overview of the Java language. Keep in mind that Java is a rich programming environment. Full coverage of the Java language and its libraries would require a large book. The purpose of this overview is only to whet your interest.

Note: At the time of this writing, Java is still undergoing development. Although the information presented here is accurate at this time, it is obviously subject to change.

What Is Java?

Java is the language of the Internet. It was conceived by James Gosling, Patrick Naughton, and Mike Sheridan at Sun Microsystems, Inc. in 1990 and took five years to develop. To understand the importance of Java, consider the following analogy: Java is to Internet programming what C/C++ is to systems programming. Java is that fundamental.

Java relates to C++ in two important ways. First, it uses a syntax similar to C++. For example, the general forms of the **for**, **while**, and **do** loops are the same. Second, it supports object-oriented programming in much the same way as C++. Because of the surface similarities between Java and C++, it is easy to simply think of Java as the Internet version of C++. However, this statement is not quite true, because Java also has significant differences from C++ which fundamentally alter its character. But don't worry. As a C++ programmer, you will feel right at home with Java.

Java can be used to create two types of programs: applications and *applets*. An application is a program that runs on your computer, under the operating system of that computer. That is, an application created by Java is (more or less) like one created using C++. An applet is an application which is designed to be transmitted over the Internet and must be executed by a

Java-compatible web browser. The sample code in this chapter creates stand-alone applications. However, most of the techniques can be generalized to applets, as well.

Why Java?

Since C and C++ are powerful, well-defined, professional programming languages, you might be wondering why another computer language is needed. The answer to this question can be summarized in two words: safety and portability. Let's look at each.

11

Safety

As you are almost certainly aware, every time you download a "normal" program, you are risking a viral infection. Prior to Java, most users did not download executable programs frequently and those that did, scanned them for viruses prior to execution. Even so, most users still worried about the possibility of infecting their systems with a virus or allowing a malicious program to run wild in their systems. Java answers these concerns by providing a "fire wall" between a networked application and your computer.

When using a Java-compatible web browser, it is possible to safely download Java applets without fear of viral infection. The way that Java achieves this is by confining a Java applet to the Java execution environment and not allowing it access to other parts of the computer. (You will see how this is accomplished, shortly.) The ability to download applets with confidence that no harm will be done to the client computer is the single most important aspect of Java.

Portability

There are many different types of computers and operating systems in use throughout the world—and many are connected to the Internet. For programs to be dynamically downloaded to all of the various types of platforms connected to the web, some means of generating portable executable code is needed. As you will see, the means by which Java achieves portability is both elegant and efficient.

Java's Magic Solution: Java Bytecode

The key that allows Java to solve both the security and the portability problems just described is the fact that the output of a Java compiler is not executable code. Rather it is *bytecode*. Bytecode is a highly optimized set of instructions that are designed to be executed by a virtual machine which the Java run-time system emulates. That is, the Java run-time system is an *interpreter for bytecode*. Thus, the Java bytecode is simply a highly efficient means of encoding a program for interpretation.

The fact that Java is an interpreted language may come as a bit of a surprise. As you know, programs written for C++ (and most other contemporary languages) are compiled to executable object code. In reality, few languages are designed to be interpreted—mostly because of performance concerns. However, the fact that a Java program is interpreted helps solve the major problems associated with downloading programs over the Internet. Here is why.

Since Java was designed to be an interpreted language, it is much easier to allow Java programs to run in a wide variety of environments. The reason for this is straightforward: only the Java run-time system needs to be implemented for each platform. Once the run-time package exists for a given system, the bytecode version of any Java program can run on it. Remember, although the details of the Java run-time system will differ from platform to platform, they will all interpret the same Java bytecode. If Java programs were compiled to executable object code, then different versions of the same program would have to exist for each type of CPU connected to the Internet. This is, of course, not a feasible solution. Thus, using bytecode to represent programs is the easiest way to create truly portable programs.

The fact that Java is interpreted also helps make safety possible. Because the execution of every Java program is under the control of the run-time system, the run-time system can contain the program and not allow it to generate side effects outside the system. As you will see, safety is also enhanced by certain restrictions that exist in the Java language.

As you may know, when a program is interpreted, it generally runs substantially slower than the same program would run if compiled. However, with Java, the differential between the two is not so great. The use of bytecode makes it possible for the Java run-time system to execute programs much faster than one would ordinarily expect.

One final point. Although Java was designed to be interpreted, there is nothing about Java that technically prevents "on the fly" compilation of bytecode into native code by the Java run-time system. However, even if dynamic compilation is applied to bytecode, the portability and safety features will still apply because the run-time system will still be in charge of the execution environment.

Differences Between Java and C++

Although the Java language is modeled on C++, it has several differences. Some of these differences are simply that—just slight alterations. Others are major design decisions that profoundly affect how you write programs. While all of the differences won't be enumerated, several are highlighted here. Before beginning, keep in mind one important fact: Java was designed to allow portable applications to be safely downloaded over a network. It was not designed to replace C or C++ as a systems programming language. With this firmly in mind, let's take a look at some of the differences between C++ and Java.

What Java Doesn't Have

11

Although Java is similar to C++, there are a number of C++ features which Java does not support. In some cases, a specific C++ feature simply didn't relate to the Java environment. In other cases, the designers of Java eliminated some of the duplication of features that exist in C++. In still other instances, a feature of C++ is not supported by Java because it was deemed too dangerous for Internet applets. Here are a few of the most important "deletions."

Perhaps the single biggest difference between Java and C++ is that Java does not support pointers! As a C++ programmer, you know that the pointer is one of C++'s most powerful and important language features. It is also one of its most dangerous when used improperly. Pointers don't exist in Java for two reasons. First, pointers are inherently insecure. For example, using a C++-style pointer, it is possible to gain access to memory addresses outside a program's code and data. A malicious program could make use of this fact to damage the system, perform unauthorized accesses (such as obtaining passwords), or otherwise violate security restrictions. Second, even if pointers could be restricted to the confines of the Java run-time system (which is theoretically possible since Java programs are interpreted), the designers of Java believed that pointers were inherently troublesome. Since pointers don't exist in Java, neither does the –> operator.

Here are some other C++ features not found in Java.

♦ Java does not include structures or unions. These were felt to be redundant since the class encompasses these other forms.

♦ Java does not support operator overloading. The designers simply did not see this as an important feature.

♦ Java does not include a preprocessor or support the preprocessor directives. As you may know, the preprocessor plays a less important role in C++ than it does in C. The designers of Java felt that it was time to eliminate it entirely.

♦ Java does not perform any automatic type conversions that result in a loss of precision. For example, a conversion from long integer to integer must be explicitly cast.

♦ All the code in a Java program is encapsulated within one or more classes. Therefore, Java does not have what you normally think of as global variables or global functions.

♦ Java does not support multiple inheritance.

♦ Although Java supports constructors, it does not support destructors. It does, however, add the **finalize( )** function.

♦ Java does not support **typedef**.

♦ It is not possible to declare unsigned integers.

♦ Java does not allow the **goto**.

♦ It does not have the **delete** operator.

♦ The **<<** and **>>** are not overloaded for I/O operations.

♦ Java does not support templates.

What Java Adds

In addition to the elements of C++ that it does not support, Java also differs from C++ by adding new features of its own. Perhaps the most important is multithreaded programming. As you probably know, multithreading allows two or more pieces of the same program to execute concurrently. Another important new feature is Java's approach to memory allocation. Like C++, it supports the **new** keyword. However, it does not have **delete**. Instead, when the last reference to an object is destroyed, the object, itself, is deleted. Also, Java includes automatic garbage collection, which eliminates the need for you to manually perform such tasks. Here are some additional, new features.

♦ The **break** and **continue** statements have been enhanced to accept labels as targets.

♦ The **char** type declares 16-bit-wide Unicode characters. This makes them similar to C++'s **wchar_t** type. The use of Unicode helps ensure portability.

♦ Java adds the **>>>** operator, which performs an unsigned right shift.

♦ In addition to supporting single-line and multiline comments, Java adds a third comment form: the *documentation comment*. Documentation comments begin with a **/**** and end with a ***/**.

♦ Java contains a built-in string type called **String**. **String** is somewhat similar to the standard **string** class type provided by C++. Of course, in

C++ **string** is only available if you include its class declarations in your program. It is not a built-in type.

A Sample Java Program

Before discussing any more theory, let's see an actual example of a Java program. Here is a simple one that declares three variables, assigns them values, and then displays those values:

```java
/* This is a simple Java Program.
   Notice that Java supports multiline
   comments.
*/
// It also supports single-line comments

class JavaTest {
  public static void main(String strargs[])
  {
    // Java declares built-in variables just like C++
    int x;
    double y;
    char ch;

    // Assignments are just like C++, too.
    x = 10;
    y = 10.23;
    ch = 'X';

    // However, console output is performed using functions
    System.out.print("This is x: ");
    System.out.print(x);
    System.out.println();
    System.out.println("This is y: " + y);
    System.out.println("This is ch: " + ch);
  }
}
```

The output from this program is shown here:

```
This is x: 10
This is y: 10.23
This is ch: X
```

Let's take a close look at this program. At first glance, it appears to be a normal C++ program. However, even with this simple program, several differences are apparent upon closer examination. First, notice that the **main( )** function is declared *within* the class **JavaTest**. As mentioned, all Java code occurs within a class definition—even **main( )**. Notice that **main( )** is declared as **public** and **static**. Here is why. As it is in C++, **main( )** is the first function called when a Java program begins execution. Since it is called from outside its class, it must be **public**. It must be **static** because it is called prior to the creation of any instances of the class. In this case, **static** works the same in Java as it does in C++: it allows the declaration of a classwide member that exists before any objects of its class have been created. This allows **main( )** to be called before any objects of type **JavaTest** have been created.

Notice that the parameter to **main( )** is of type **String**. This parameter receives any command-line arguments associated with the program when it is executed. The first argument is **String[0]**, the second is **String[1]**, and so on. This differs from C++, where the first command-line argument is the name of the program.

As the comments indicate, variables are declared and assigned values in Java in just the same way that they are in C++. As mentioned earlier, Java utilizes the C++ syntax, so most basic statements look the same in Java as they do in C++. However, notice that the contents of these variables are output by use of calls to the **print( )** and **println( )** functions instead of using the standard C++ I/O operators. In Java, console I/O is performed by use of calls to I/O functions. The **print( )** function prints its argument to the screen. The **println( )** function does the same thing, except that it also appends a newline. As you might expect, several overloaded forms of these functions exist, making them able to output any built-in type. Pay special attention to this line:

```
System.out.println("This is y: " + y);
```

Notice that it causes the string "This is y: " and the value of **y** to be output. As you can easily guess, in Java, the **+** operator has been defined for string operations. In this case, it causes the value of **y** to be obtained, automatically converted into its string equivalent, and then concatenated with the preceding string.

Methods Versus Functions

In the language of Java, the word *function* is seldom used. Instead, what a C++ programmer normally calls a "member function," a Java programmer calls a "method." The reason for these different terms is to emphasize the fact that Java does not support global functions. All functions are members of a class. However, since this book is for C++ programmers, it will continue to refer to functions as *functions*. Be aware, however, that Java programmers often prefer the term *method!*

Compiling a Java Program

Now that you have seen a Java program, you need to understand how to compile it and then run it. These operations are not quite as trivial as you may think. First, all Java programs use the **.java** extension. Second, you must name the file that contains the program the same as the class that it contains. Further, the filename must use the same capitalization as the class name. For the preceding example, this means that the file name that holds the program must be **JavaTest.java**.

Once you have entered the program using the proper file name, you will use the Java compiler, called **javac**, to compile your program into bytecode. The bytecode file will be given the file extension **.class**. To interpret the bytecode, you will use the Java interpreter, called **java**. (Again, capitalization counts.) For example, the following sequence compiles and then runs the preceding program:

```
javac JavaTest.java
java JavaTest
```

When your program begins, Java will look for the specified class and begin interpreting it from the **main( )** function.

A Second Example

Before moving on to a few of Java's more advanced features, let's look at one more simple program. The following example demonstrates the expanded features of **break** in Java and performs simple console input:

```
/* Here is an example that illustrates the expanded
   capabilities of break and performs simple input.
*/
class JavaTest {
  public static void main(String strargs[])
        throws java.io.IOException
  {
    int i, j, k;

    System.out.println("Display ASCII codes.");

lab1: for(;;) {
      System.out.println("Enter a character: ");
      do {
```

```
        k = System.in.read();
      } while((char) k == '\n');
      i = k;
      j = 1;
lab2:
      while(i>0) {
        while(i>0) {
          j++;
          if((j%20)==0) break;
          if((char) k == 'q') break lab1;
          if((char) k == '\n') break lab2;
          System.out.print(i+" ");
          i--;
        }
        System.out.println();
        j = 1;
      }
    }
  }
}
```

This program prompts for a character to be entered by the user. It then displays all the ASCII codes beginning with that character and counting down to zero. Sample output is shown here:

```
Display ASCII codes.
Enter a character:
1
49 48 47 46 45 44 43 42 41 40 39 38 37 36 35 34 33 32
31 30 29 28 27 26 25 24 23 22 21 20 19 18 17 16 15 14
13 12 11 10 9 8 7 6 5 4 3 2 1
Enter a character:
2
50 49 48 47 46 45 44 43 42 41 40 39 38 37 36 35 34 33
32 31 30 29 28 27 26 25 24 23 22 21 20 19 18 17 16 15
14 13 12 11 10 9 8 7 6 5 4 3 2 1
Enter a character:
3
51 50 49 48 47 46 45 44 43 42 41 40 39 38 37 36 35 34
33 32 31 30 29 28 27 26 25 24 23 22 21 20 19 18 17 16
15 14 13 12 11 10 9 8 7 6 5 4 3 2 1
Enter a character:
q
```

In Java, the **break** command may take a label as a target. When no label is present, it works like its equivalent in C++, by breaking out of the innermost block. However, when a label is present, then execution is transferred out of the specified block. In the preceding program, **break**, by itself, breaks out of the inner **while** loop. **break lab2** breaks out of the outer **while** loop. **break lab1** breaks out of the outer **for** loop, causing program termination when a **q** is entered. As you can guess, the ability to target a specific block greatly expands the uses for **break**. In fact, one of the reasons that Java does not support the **goto** is because of the expanded capabilities of **break**.

The use of a labeled **break** can also be applied to breaking out of a **switch** statement. The **continue** statement may also continue to a labeled block. Remember, the target label of either the **break** or **continue** must be at the start of a block.

11

Before leaving this example, there are a few other points of interest worth mentioning. First, notice that characters are read by calling **System.in. read( )**. This function reads characters from standard input. By default, standard input is line buffered, so you must press ENTER before any characters you type will be sent to your program. This situation is similar to C++, and you are probably already familiar with this style of input. Actually, most real-world applications of Java will be graphical, so it only provides minimal support for console I/O. One other point: Because **System.in.read( )** is being used, the program must specify the **throws java.io.IOException**.

Working with Classes

Java shares many similarities with C++ as it relates to classes, but there are also several differences. While it is well beyond the scope of this overview to discuss all nuances and subtleties, several of the more important aspects of classes in Java will be examined here.

Let's start by stating the similarities between C++ classes and Java classes. Java classes may contain both member variables and member functions (called *methods,* in Java). Java classes may include constructors. Constructors may be overloaded. In fact, any member function may be overloaded. Overloading works in Java more or less the same as it works in C++. Each object that you create will have its own copy of its member variables (again, just like in C++).

Now, let's take a look at the differences between Java and C++. To begin, examine the following program:

```
// Creating Class Objects
class JavaTest {
  private int a;
  JavaTest() { a = 0; } // constructors
  JavaTest(int i) { a = i; }
```

```
int geta() { return a; } // a simple method

public static void main(String strargs[])
{
   // instantiate JavaTest objects
   JavaTest t1 = new JavaTest();
   JavaTest t2 = new JavaTest(100);

   System.out.println("This is t1's a: " + t1.a);
   System.out.println("This is t2's a: " + t2.a);
}
}
```

First, notice that the **private** access specifier precedes the member variable **a**. By default, members of a class are accessible by other members of their class, derived classes, and by other members of their *package*. (Packages will be discussed later.) As such, by default, class members are "more public" than they are in C++, but still not fully public in the proper sense. By specifying **private**, **a** is restricted in scope to its defining class (just as in C++). Unlike C++, however, the **private** access specifier applies only to the variable or method that it immediately precedes. The same is true with the other access specifiers. Java does not use the **private:** (and so on) construct. In this program, **a** is declared as private only for the sake of illustration.

Inside **main( )** pay special attention to how **JavaTest** objects are created. For example, this line:

```
JavaTest t1 = new JavaTest();
```

creates a new object of type **JavaTest** and initializes it using the parameterless **JavaTest( )** constructor. The variable **t1** is *a reference to that object*. It is important to understand that in Java, the following statement does *not* create an object:

```
JavaTest ob;
```

It only creates a reference to a **JavaTest** object. To create an object, you must allocate it using **new**. For example, assuming **ob** as just shown, the following statement links an object to it:

```
ob = JavaTest(99);
```

Remember: all class objects are instantiated in Java using the **new** operator. Thus, all class objects are dynamically allocated. In Java, when there are no

references to an object, then that object is considered inactive and is subject
to garbage collection so that its memory can be recycled.

Finalizers

Although Java has constructors, it does not have destructors. Instead, it
allows you to declare a *finalizer*. A finalizer is called when an object of a class
is about to be recycled via garbage collection. As you can see, a finalizer is
similar in concept to a destructor, but when it executes is fundamentally
different. Further, if the object is never subjected to garbage collection, the
finalizer is never called. Remember, in C++, a destructor is called whenever
an object goes out of scope. In Java, the finalizer is called only when the
object is collected for recycling.

11

Finalizers have this general form:

> protected void finalize( )
> {
>   // *finalization code here*
> }

For example, here is the preceding program with a placeholder **finalize( )**
function:

```
// Creating Class Objects
class JavaTest {
  private int a;
  JavaTest() { a = 0; } // constructors
  JavaTest(int i) { a = i; }

  int geta() { return a; } // a simple method

  /* This is called when an object is about to be
     subject to garbage collection. */
  protected void finalize()
  {
    // shutdown code here
  }

  public static void main(String strargs[])
  {
    JavaTest t1; t1 = new JavaTest();
    JavaTest t2 = new JavaTest(100);

    System.out.println("This is t1's a: " + t1.a);
    System.out.println("This is t2's a: " + t2.a);
```

```
  }
}
```

Java Class Hierarchies

Java, like C++, supports hierarchies of classes. In fact, class hierarchies are a
critical component of Java. However, the way that inheritance is implemented
in Java differs substantially from the way that it is implemented in C++.
First, as mentioned earlier, multiple inheritance is not allowed in Java. This
means that all Java class hierarchies are linear. Second, Java uses the keyword
extends to specify a base class. For example, consider the following
program:

```java
// Inheritance, Java style.

// Here is a base class.
class MyClass {
  int a;
  int geta() { return a; }
  int add(MyClass ob)
  {
     return a + ob.a;
  }
}

// JavaTest inherits MyClass
class JavaTest extends MyClass {
  int b;
  public static void main(String strargs[])
  {
    JavaTest t1 = new JavaTest();
    JavaTest t2 = new JavaTest();
    JavaTest t3 = new JavaTest();

    t1.a = 0;
    t1.b = 100;

    t2.a = 20;
    t2.b = 200;

    t3.a = 30;
    t3.b = 300;

    System.out.print("This is t1's a and b: ");
    System.out.println(t1.a + " " + t1.b);
    System.out.print("This is t2's a and b: ");
    System.out.println(t2.a + " " + t2.b);
```

```
      System.out.print("This is t3's a and b: ");
      System.out.println(t3.a + " " + t3.b);

      // call another member function
      int sum;
      sum = t3.add(t2);
      System.out.println("t2+t3 is " + sum);
   }
}
```

Notice how the keyword **extends** is used to inherit a base class. As mentioned, by default, members of a base class are accessible within a derived class, as this program illustrates.

If the base class contains one or more constructors, then the extending class must provide a mechanism by which the base class constructors are invoked. This is done using the **super** keyword, as shown in this expanded version of the preceding program:

```
// Inheritance, Java style.

// Here is a base class.
class MyClass {
  int a;

  // MyClass Constructors
  MyClass() { a = 0; }
  MyClass(int i) { a = i; }

  int geta() { return a; }

  int add(MyClass ob)
  {
     return a + ob.a;
  }
}

// JavaTest inherits MyClass
class JavaTest extends MyClass {
  int b;

  // these call MyClass Constructors
  JavaTest(int i) { super(i); }
  JavaTest() { super(0); }

  public static void main(String strargs[])
  {
    JavaTest t1 = new JavaTest();
```

```
JavaTest t2 = new JavaTest(20);
JavaTest t3 = new JavaTest(30);

t1.b = 100;
t2.b = 200;
t3.b = 300;

System.out.print("This is t1's a and b: ");
System.out.println(t1.a + " " + t1.b);
System.out.print("This is t2's a and b: ");
System.out.println(t2.a + " " + t2.b);
System.out.print("This is t3's a and b: ");
System.out.println(t3.a + " " + t3.b);

// call another member function
int sum;
sum = t3.add(t2);
System.out.println("t2+t3 is " + sum);
  }
}
```

Since Java does not support multiple inheritance, **super** always refers to the immediately preceding base class. As you can see, it invokes the base class' constructors, passing arguments as needed.

One final point about inheritance: In Java-speak, inheritance is referred to as *subclassing*. Further, what C++ programmers call a base class, Java programmers call a *superclass*. What C++ programmers call a derived class, Java programmers call a *subclass*.

Classes and Files

Although there is nothing wrong with having a base class and derived classes defined within a single Java file, there are times when you won't want this to be the case. For example, if you have a base class that will be extended by various other classes in different files, then you will want to put the base class in its own file, calling the file by the same name as the base class. After you do this, whenever the base class is used, it is automatically retrieved from its file. For example, try this: Break the preceding program into two files. Put **MyClass** into a file called **MyClass.java**. Put **JavaTest** in a file called **JavaTest.java**. Next, compile **MyClass.java**. Then, compile **JavaTest.java**. As you will see, when compiling **JavaTest.java**, the compiler automatically includes **MyClass**.

Packages and Importation

Java includes two class-management features that help make using and organizing classes easier. The first is called a *package*. A package defines a scope. Thus, names declared inside a package are private to that package (unless they are explicitly declared as public). A package is declared using the **package** keyword. Java uses file directories to store packages. For this reason, each package must be stored in a directory that has the same name as the package—including capitalization. For example, here **MyClass** is modified for use in a package called **MyPack**:

```
package MyPack; // this declares a package
public class MyClass {
  public int a;
  public MyClass() { a = 0; } // constructors
  public MyClass(int i) { a = i; }

  public int geta() { return a; }
  public int add(MyClass ob)
  {
    return a + ob.a;
  }
}
```

Remember, this file must now reside in a directory called **MyPack**. The members of **MyClass** have been made public so that they can be accessible beyond the confines of **MyPack**. In a real-world program, most members of a package will remain private to it.

Given the preceding package, the first line of **JavaTest** must now look like this:

```
class JavaTest extends MyPack.MyClass {
```

As you can see, **MyPack** now precedes **MyClass**.

Instead of specifying each class separately, you can include an entire package using the **import** keyword. For example, if you want to import the class **MyClass** from **MyPack**, you would use the following statement:

```
import MyPack.MyClass;
```

Now, you can extend **MyClass** directly without having to specify **MyPack** when **JavaTest** is created.

If a package includes several classes (which it will in most real-world situations), then you can include all of those classes by specifying the ***** for the class name. For example,

```
import MyOtherPack.*; // import all classes
```

imports all public classes contained in **MyOtherPack**.

Interfaces

It is possible to define the shape of a class without defining its behavior using the **interface** keyword. Defining an interface is a little like declaring an abstract class in C++. In an interface no member variables are declared and only the prototypes for the member functions are declared. (Thus, interface function declarations are somewhat like pure virtual functions in C++.) After an interface is designed, a class may implement that interface. To do so, it must create methods that implement all of its parts. While it is beyond the scope of this overview to give an example, it is sufficient to say that interfaces in Java serve (more or less) the same purpose as virtual functions and abstract classes in C++.

The Standard Classes

Java provides several standard packages of classes which provide substantial built-in capabilities for such things as I/O, graphics, and the like. Here are some of the standard Java packages:

Package	Purpose
java.applet	Applet support
java.awt	Abstract window toolkit
java.lang	Support for language elements
java.io	I/O support
java.net	Network support
java.util	Standard classes, such as Stack, Vector, and Date

The abstract window toolkit is used to create applications that work in a windowed environment, such as Windows 95 or Windows NT.

Things to Try

If you are interested in writing programs for the Internet, then you will want to gain a solid knowledge of Java. Because it offers a safe and secure way to transmit applications over the Internet, it will almost certainly be a language with which you will be working. Here is one book that you might want to read: *The Java Handbook* by Patrick Naughton (Osborne/McGraw-Hill, Berkeley, Ca 1996). Patrick has been working with Java since the beginning, and his experience will be valuable to anyone learning Java.

One of the first things that you will want to do once you are familiar with Java programming is to try creating your own applets and sending them across the Web. Remember, applets are the driving force behind the creation of Java.

11

As mentioned at the start of this chapter, Java is still undergoing rapid development. If you enjoy surfing the Net, you will want to watch for information about current developments relating to Java.

Appendix A

C++ Keyword Summary

This appendix contains a brief description of the 62 C++ keywords. These keywords are shown in Table A-1. All C++ keywords use lowercase letters. In C++, uppercase and lowercase are different. For instance, **else** is a keyword, **ELSE** is not. An alphabetical summary of each keyword follows.

asm	auto	bool	break
case	catch	char	class
const	const_cast	continue	default
delete	do	double	dynamic_cast
else	enum	explicit	extern
false	float	for	friend
goto	if	inline	int
long	mutable	namespace	new
operator	private	protected	public
register	reinterpret_cast	return	short
signed	sizeof	static	static_cast
struct	switch	template	this
throw	true	try	typedef
typeid	typename	union	unsigned
using	virtual	void	volatile
wchar_t	while		

The C++
Keywords
Table A-1.

asm

The **asm** keyword is used to embed assembly language commands into your C++ program. It has this general form:

asm *op-code*;

where *op-code* is the instruction being embedded.

auto

auto is used to create local variables. The use of **auto** is completely optional since all local variables are **auto** by default. As such, it is rarely used.

bool

bool specifies the Boolean (that is, true/false) type. Variables of type **bool** only hold the values **true** or **false**.

break

break is used to exit from a **do**, **for**, or **while** loop, bypassing the normal loop condition. It is also used to exit from a **switch** statement. An example of **break**ing out of a loop is shown here:

```
while(x<100) {
  x = get_new_x();
  if(cancel()) break; // exit if canceled
  process(x);
}
```

Here, if **cancel( )** returns true, the loop will terminate no matter what the value of **x** is.

A **break** always terminates the innermost **for**, **do**, **while**, or **switch** statement, regardless of any nesting. In a **switch** statement, **break** effectively keeps program execution from "falling through" to the next **case**. (Refer to **switch** for details.)

case

See **switch**.

catch

The **catch** statement is part of C++'s exception handling mechanism. See **throw** for details.

char

char specifies the 8-bit character type. For example, to declare **ch** to be a character type, you would write

```
char ch;
```

In C++, a character is 1 byte long.

class

The **class** forms the basis for object-oriented programming and is C++'s fundamental unit of encapsulation. **class** is used to define a new data type called a *class*. The syntax of a **class** declaration is similar to that of a structure. Its most common form is shown here:

class *class-name* {
    private functions and variables
public:
    public functions and variables
} *object-list*;

In a **class** declaration, the *object-list* is optional. You can declare class objects later, as needed. While the *class-name* is also technically optional, from a practical point of view it is virtually always needed. The reason is that the *class-name* becomes a new type name that is used to declare objects of the class. Notice that a **class** declaration may include both variables and functions.

Functions and variables declared inside a **class** declaration are said to be *members* of that class. By default, all functions and variables declared inside a class are private to that class. This means that they are accessible only by other members of that class. To declare public class members, the **public** keyword is used, followed by a colon. All functions and variables declared after the **public** specifier are accessible both by other members of the class and by any other part of the program. You may also declare protected members of a class using the **protected** keyword. Protected members may only be accessed by other members of their class or by members of classes derived from their class.

Here is a simple class declaration:

```
class myclass {
  // private to myclass
  int a;
public:
  // public members
  void set_a(int num) { a = num; }
  int get_a() { return a; }
};
```

Members of a class are accessed by use of the dot or arrow operators.

const

The **const** modifier tells the compiler that the variable that follows cannot be modified. It is also used to prevent a function from modifying the object pointed to (or referenced) by one of its arguments. Further, **const** can be used to declare **const** member functions.

const_cast

const_cast performs a cast operation that overrides **const** or **volatile**.

continue

continue is used to bypass the remaining portions of code in a loop, jumping directly to the conditional test. For example, the following loop will not display the number 10.

```
for(x = 0; i<100; x++) {
  if(x==10) continue;
  cout << x << ' ';
}
```

default

default is used within the **switch** to specify default statements. See **switch** for details.

A

delete

The **delete** operator frees memory allocated using **new**. See **new** for details.

do

The **do** loop is one of three loop constructs available in C++. The general form of the **do** loop is

```
do {
  statement block
} while(expression);
```

If only one statement is repeated, the braces are not necessary, but they add clarity to the statement. The loop will iterate as long as the expression is true.

The **do** loop is the only loop in C++ that will always have at least one iteration, because the condition is tested at the bottom of the loop.

A common use of the **do** loop is to read disk files. This code will read a file until an **EOF** is encountered:

```
do {
  myfile.getc(ch);
  cout << ch;
} while(!myfile.eof());
```

double

double specifies the double-precision floating-point type. For example, to declare **d** to be of type **double**, you would write the following statement:

```
double d;
```

dynamic_cast

dynamic_cast performs a run-time polymorphic type conversion that verifies the validity of the cast. If the cast is invalid, the operation fails and the expression evaluates to null. Its main use is for performing casts on polymorphic types. For example, **dynamic_cast** can be used to determine if the object pointed to by a pointer is compatible with the target type of the cast. In this usage, if the object pointed to is not an object of the target type or of a derived class of the target type, then **dynamic_cast** fails and evaluates to null.

else

See **if**.

enum

The **enum** type specifier creates an enumeration type. An enumeration is simply a list of objects. Hence, an enumeration type specifies what that list of objects consists of. For example, the following code declares an enumeration called **color** and a variable of that type called **c**, and performs an assignment and a relational test:

```
#include <iostream.h>

enum color {red, green, yellow};
enum color c;

main()
{
  c = red;
  if(c==red) cout << "color is red\n";

  return 0;
}
```

explicit

The **explicit** keyword is used to declare *nonconverting constructors*. For example, given the following class:

```
class MyClass {
  int i;
public:
  MyClass(int j) {i = j;}
  // ...
};
```

this next statement:

```
MyClass ob2 = 10;
```

is automatically converted into the form:

```
MyClass ob2(10);
```

However, by declaring the **MyClass** constructor as **explicit**, this automatic conversion will not be supplied. Here **MyClass** is shown using an **explicit** constructor:

```
class MyClass {
  int i;
public:
  explicit MyClass(int j) {i = j;}
  // ...
};
```

extern

The **extern** data type modifier is used to tell the compiler that a variable is declared elsewhere in the program. This is often used in conjunction with separately compiled files that share the same global data and are linked together. In essence, it notifies the compiler of a variable without redeclaring it.

As an example, if **first** were declared in another file as an integer, the following declaration would be used in subsequent files:

```
extern int first;
```

A

false

false is one of the two values that a **bool** variable may have.

float

float specifies the single-precision floating-point type. For example, to declare **f** to be of type **float**, you would write

```
float f;
```

for

The **for** loop allows automatic initialization and incrementation of a counter variable. The general form is

```
for(initialization; condition; increment) {
   statements
}
```

If there is only one statement, the braces are not necessary.

Although the **for** allows a number of variations, generally the *initialization* is used to set a counter variable to its starting value. The *condition* is usually a relational expression that checks the counter variable against a termination value, and the *increment* increments (or decrements) the counter value.

The following code will print **hello** ten times:

```
for(t=0; t<10; t++) cout << "hello\n";
```

friend

The **friend** access specifier grants a nonmember function access to the private and protected members of a class. Friend functions do not have **this** pointers, and they are not invoked relative to an object. Instead, they are called like any other normal function.

goto

The **goto** causes program execution to jump to the label specified in the **goto** statement. The general form of the **goto** is

```
goto label;
  .
  .
  .
label:
```

All labels must end in a colon and must not conflict with keywords or function names. Furthermore, a **goto** can only branch within the current function, and not from one function to another.

The following example will print the message **right** but not the message **wrong**:

```
goto lab1;
  cout << "wrong";
lab1:
  cout << "right";
```

A

if

The **if** is C++'s conditional statement. The general form of the **if** statement is

```
if(expression) {
  statement block 1
}
else {
  statement block 2
}
```

If single statements are used, the braces are not needed. Furthermore, the **else** is optional.

The expression controlling the **if** may be of any type other than **void**. If the expression evaluates to any value other than 0, then statement block 1 will be executed; otherwise, if it exists, statement block 2 will be executed.

The following code fragment demonstrates the **if**:

```
if(ch < 10) cout << "Less than 10.\n";
else cout << "Greater than or equal to 10.\n";
```

inline

The **inline** modifier requests that the code to a function be expanded inline rather than called. This eliminates the overhead associated with the normal function call/return mechanism. However, inlining large functions has the side effect of making your programs larger. Class member functions that are defined within the class are automatically inlined.

int

int specifies the integer type. For example, to declare **count** as an integer, you would write

```
int count;
```

long

long specifies the long integer type. For example, to declare **count** as a long integer, you would write

```
long int count;
```

mutable

The **mutable** modifier is used to remove **const**-ness for individual data members of a class when a **const** object of that class is instantiated.

namespace

The **namespace** keyword defines a scope. The general form of **namespace** is shown here:

```
namespace name {
    // object declarations
}
```

For example,

```
namespace MyNameSpace {
  int i, k;
  void myfunc(int j) { cout << j; }
}
```

Here, **i**, **k**, **j**, and **myfunc( )** are part of the scope defined by the **MyNameSpace** namespace.

Since a namespace defines a scope, you need to use the scope resolution operator to refer to objects defined within a namespace. For example, to assign the value 10 to **i**, you must use this statement:

```
MyNameSpace::i = 10;
```

If the members of a namespace will be used frequently, you can use a **using** directive to simplify their access. The **using** statement has these two general forms:

> using namespace *name*;
> using *name*::*member*;

In the first form, *name* specifies the name of the namespace you want to access. All of the members defined within the specified namespace may be used without qualification. In the second form, only a specific member of the namespace is made visible. For example, assuming **MyNameSpace** as just shown, the following **using** statements and assignments are valid.

```
using MyNameSpace::k; // only k is made visible
k = 10; // OK because k is visible

using namespace MyNameSpace; // all members are visible
i = 10; // OK because all members of MyNameSpace are now visible
```

A

new

The **new** operator allocates memory. Its general form is shown here:

> *ptr* = new *type*;

Here, *type* is the name of the type of data being allocated. *ptr* must be a pointer variable compatible with that type. The **new** operator automatically allocates sufficient memory to hold an object of the specified type and returns a pointer to it. If the object cannot be allocated (perhaps because of insufficient memory), then a null pointer is returned. This means that you must always check the value of *ptr* before using it.

To free previously allocated memory, use the **delete** operator. It has this general form:

> delete *ptr*;

where *ptr* is a pointer to memory allocated via a call to **new**.

Here is an example that allocates memory to hold **float** data:

```
float *fptr;

fptr = new float;
if(!fptr) {
  cout << "Allocation error.\n';
  exit(1);
}
// ...
delete fptr;
```

To allocate an array, use this form of **new**:

   ptr = new *type*[*size*];

where *size* specifies the number of elements of type *type* that are in the array.

To free an allocated array, use this form of **delete**:

   delete [ ] *ptr*;

operator

The **operator** keyword is used to create operator functions. Member operator functions have this basic form:

   ret-type class-name::operator#(...) { *body of function* }

where # is a placeholder for the actual operator. Nonmember operator functions have this general form:

   ret-type operator#(...) { *body of function* }

For member binary operator functions, the left operand is passed via **this**, and the right operand is passed explicitly as a parameter. For member unary operators, the operand is passed using **this**.

For nonmember binary operator functions, the left operand is passed in the first parameter, and the right operand is passed in the second parameter. For nonmember unary functions, the operand is passed as the function's only parameter.

private

The **private** access specifier is used to declare private members of a class. Private members may only be accessed by other members of their class.

protected

The **protected** access specifier is used to declare protected members of a class. Protected members may only be accessed by other members of their class or by the members of a derived class.

public

The **public** access specifier is used to declare public members of a class. Public members may be accessed by any other parts of your program.

register

The **register** modifier requests that a variable be stored in the way that allows the fastest possible access. In the case of characters or integers, this usually means a register of the CPU. For other types of objects, it may mean cache memory. To declare **i** to be a register integer, you would write

```
register int i;
```

reinterpret_cast

The **reinterpret_cast** operator changes one type into a fundamentally different type. For example, it can be used to change a pointer into an integer. Thus, **reinterpret_cast** should be used for casting inherently incompatible types.

return

The **return** statement forces a return from a function and can be used to transfer a value back to the calling routine. For example, the following function returns the product of its two integer arguments:

```
mul(int a, int b)
{
  return a*b;
}
```

Keep in mind that as soon as a **return** is encountered, the function will terminate, skipping any other code in the function.

short

short specifies the short integer type. For example, to declare **sh** to be a short integer, you would write

```
short int sh;
```

signed

The **signed** type modifier is most commonly used to specify a signed character data type. It may also be used on any integer type, but would be redundant.

sizeof

The **sizeof** keyword is a compile-time operator that returns the length, in bytes, of the variable or type it precedes. If it precedes a type, the type must be enclosed in parentheses. For example,

```
cout << sizeof(int);
```

will print 2 or 4, depending upon your C++ compiler and environment.

The principal use for **sizeof** is to help generate portable code when that code depends on the size of a C++ built-in data type.

static

The **static** type modifier tells the compiler to create permanent storage for the local variable that it precedes. This enables the specified variable to maintain its value between function calls. For example, to declare **last_time** as a static integer, you would write

```
static int last_time;
```

The **static** modifier may also be applied to class members. When a **static** data member is created, then only one copy of that member is shared by all instances of that class.

static_cast

The **static_cast** operator performs a nonpolymorphic cast. It can be used for any standard conversion.

struct

struct creates an aggregate data type, called a structure, that is made up of one or more members. The simplest form of a structure is

```
struct struct_name {
  type member1;
  type member2;
  .
  .
  .
  type memberN;
} object-list;
```

The individual members of a structure are accessed by use of the dot or arrow operators.

By default, the members of a structure are public. However, you may use the **private** and **protected** access specifiers within a structure declaration, if desired. Formally, a structure creates a class type.

switch

The **switch** statement is C++'s multipath branch statement. The general form of the statement is

```
switch(expression) {
  case constant1:
    statement sequence
    break;
  case constant2:
    statement sequence
    break;
  .
  .
  .
  case constantN:
    statement sequence
```

A

```
      break;
    default:
      default statement sequence
  }
```

Each statement sequence may contain one or more statements. The **default** portion is optional.

The **switch** works by checking its expression against the constants. As soon as a match is found, that set of statements is executed, stopping when the **break** is encountered. If the **break** statement is omitted, execution will continue into the next **case**. You can think of the **case** statements as labels. Execution will continue until a **break** statement is found or the **switch** ends.

The following example can be used to process a menu selection:

```
switch(ch) {
  case 'e':
    enter( );
    break:
  case 'l':
    list( );
    break;
  case 's':
    sort( );
    break;
  case 'q':
    exit(0);
  default:
    cout << "Unknown Command\n";
}
```

template

The **template** keyword is used to create a generic function or class. (These are also referred to as template functions and template classes.) When a template is created, the type of data operated upon by the template is specified by one or more placeholder types. These types are automatically substituted by the actual data types when a specific instance of a template is generated.

The general form of a template function is shown here:

template <class *Ttype*> *ret-type func-name*(*parameter list*)
  {

```
   // body of function
 }
```

Here, *Ttype* is a placeholder name for a data type used by the function. This name may be used within the function definition. However, it is only a placeholder which the compiler will automatically replace with an actual data type when it creates a specific instance of the function. You may define more than one generic data type in the **template** statement, using a comma-separated list.

The general form of a template class is shown here:

```
template <class Ttype> class class-name {
   // body of class
 }
```

Here, *Ttype* is the placeholder type name which will be substituted by the actual data type when a class is instantiated. If necessary, you may define more than one generic data type using a comma-separated list. Function members of a generic class are automatically generic, too.

this

this is a pointer that is automatically passed to member functions when they are invoked. It points to the object that invoked the function.

throw

throw is part of C++'s exception handling, and it is used to throw an exception. C++ exception handling is built upon three keywords: **try**, **catch**, and **throw**. In the most general terms, program statements that you want to monitor for exceptions are contained in a **try** block. If an exception (that is, an error) occurs within the **try** block, it is thrown (using **throw**). The exception is caught, using **catch**, and processed. The following discussion elaborates upon this general description.

As stated, any statement that throws an exception must have been executed from within a **try** block. (Functions called from within a **try** block may also throw an exception.) Any exception must be caught by a **catch** statement that immediately follows the **try** statement. The general forms of **try** and **catch** are shown here:

```
try {
   // try block
```

```
  }
catch (type1 arg) {
  // catch block
}
catch (type2 arg) {
  // catch block
}
catch (type3 arg) {
  // catch block
}
    .
    .
    .
catch (typeN arg) {
  // catch block
}
```

The **try** block must contain that portion of your program that you want to monitor for errors. This can be as short as a few statements within one function or as all-encompassing as enclosing the **main( )** function code within a **try** block (which effectively causes the entire program to be monitored).

When an exception is thrown, it is caught by its corresponding **catch** statement, which processes the exception. There can be more than one **catch** statement associated with a **try**. Which **catch** statement is used is determined by the type of the exception thrown. That is, if the data type specified by a **catch** matches that of the exception, then that **catch** statement is executed (and all others are bypassed). When an exception is caught, *arg* will receive its value. Any type of data may be caught, including classes that you create. If no exception is thrown (that is, no error occurs within the **try** block), then no **catch** statement is executed.

The general form of the **throw** statement is shown here:

throw *exception*;

throw must be executed either from within the **try** block, proper, or from any function called (directly or indirectly) from within the **try** block. *exception* is the value thrown.

If you throw an exception for which there is no applicable **catch** statement, an abnormal program termination may occur.

true

true is one of the two values that a **bool** variable may have.

try

try is part of C++'s exception handling mechanism. See **throw** for details.

typedef

The **typedef** statement allows you to create a new name for an existing data type. The general form of **typedef** is

typedef *type-specifier new-name*;

For example, to use the word **balance** in place of **float**, you would write

```
typedef float balance;
```

typeid

typeid obtains type information about an object. Its general form is shown here:

typeid(*object*)

Here, *object* is the object whose type you will be obtaining. **typeid** returns a reference to an object of type **type_info** that describes the type of object defined by *object*. You must include the header file TYPEINFO.H in order to use **typeid**.

Since **typeid** is evaluated at run time, it can be applied to polymorphic types. This means that it can be used to determine the type of an object that is pointed to by a base class pointer of a polymorphic class.

The **type_info** class defines the following public members:

bool operator==(const type_info &*ob*) const;
bool operator!=(const type_info &*ob*) const;
bool before(const type_info &*ob*) const;
const char *name( ) const;

The overloaded **==** and **!=** provide for the comparison of types. The **before( )** function returns true if the invoking object is before the object used as a parameter in collation order. (This function is mostly for internal use only.

A

Its return value has nothing to do with inheritance or class hierarchies.) The **name( )** function returns a pointer to the name of the type.

typename

typename specifies that a qualified name in a template declaration denotes a type.

union

The **union** keyword is used to assign two or more variables to the same memory location. That is, all members of a **union** share the same location in memory. The general form for a **union** is similar to a structure or class and is shown here:

```
union union-name {
  type member1;
  type member2;
    .
    .
    .
  type memberN;
} object-list;
```

Formally, a union creates a class type. Members are accessed by use of the dot or arrow operators.

unsigned

unsigned specifies the unsigned integer type. For example, to declare **big** to be an unsigned integer, you would write

```
unsigned int big;
```

using

See **namespace**.

virtual

virtual declares virtual functions. Virtual functions are special member functions which are declared in a base class and then overridden by derived classes. When a virtual function is called, which version of the function that is actually executed is determined at run time.

void

The **void** type specifier is used primarily to declare functions that return no value.

volatile

The **volatile** modifier tells the compiler that a variable may have its contents altered in ways not explicitly defined by the program. Variables that are changed by the hardware, such as real-time clocks, interrupts, or other inputs, are examples.

wchar_t

wchar_t specifies the 16-bit character type. 16-bit characters are also known as *wide* characters. Wide characters are capable of holding the character sets of all human languages.

A

while

The **while** loop has the general form:

```
while(expression) {
  statements
}
```

If a single statement is the object of the **while**, the braces may be omitted. A **while** loop iterates as long as the expression is true. Therefore, if the expression is false to begin with, the body of the loop will not execute even once.

The following example displays the numbers 1 to 100.

```
t = 1;

while(t<=100) {
  cout << t << endl;
  t++;
}
```

Index

T

U

V

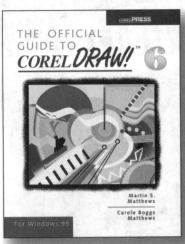

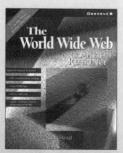

ORDER BOOKS DIRECTLY FROM OSBORNE/McGRAW-HILL

For a complete catalog of Osborne's books, call 510-549-6600 or write to us at 2600 Tenth Street, Berkeley, CA 94710

☎ **Call Toll-Free**, *24 hours a day, 7 days a week, in the U.S.A.*
U.S.A.: 1-800-822-8158   **Canada: 1-800-565-5758**

✉ **Mail** *in the U.S.A. to:*   **Canada**
McGraw-Hill, Inc.   McGraw-Hill Ryerson
Customer Service Dept.   Customer Service
P.O. Box 182607   300 Water Street
Columbus, OH 43218-2607   Whitby, Ontario L1N 9B6

Fax *in the U.S.A. to:*   **Canada**
1-614-759-3644   1-800-463-5885

EMAIL *in the U.S.A. to:*   **Canada**
70007.1531@COMPUSERVE.COM   orders@mcgrawhill.ca
COMPUSERVE GO MH

SHIP TO:

Name _____

Company _____

Address _____

City / State / Zip _____

Daytime Telephone *(We'll contact you if there's a question about your order.)*

ISBN #	BOOK TITLE	Quantity	Price	Total
0-07-88				
0-07-88				
0-07-88				
0-07-88				
0-07-88				
0-07088				
0-07-88				
0-07-88				
0-07-88				
0-07-88				
0-07-88				
0-07-88				
0-07-88				
0-07-88				

Shipping & Handling Charge from Chart Below

Subtotal

Please Add Applicable State & Local Sales Tax

TOTAL

Shipping & Handling Charges

Order Amount	U.S.	Outside U.S.
Less than $15	$3.50	$5.50
$15.00 - $24.99	$4.00	$6.00
$25.00 - $49.99	$5.00	$7.00
$50.00 - $74.99	$6.00	$8.00
$75.00 - and up	$7.00	$9.00

Occasionally we allow other selected companies to use our mailing list. If you would prefer that we not include you in these extra mailings, please check here: ❑

METHOD OF PAYMENT

❑ Check or money order enclosed (payable to Osborne/McGraw-Hill)

❑ AMERICAN EXPRESS   ❑ DISCOVER   ❑ MasterCard   ❑ VISA

Account No. [ ][ ][ ][ ][ ][ ][ ][ ][ ][ ][ ][ ][ ][ ][ ][ ]

Expiration Date _____

Signature _____

In a hurry? Call with your order anytime, day or night, or visit your local bookstore.

Thank you for your order   Code BC640SL